CW01637651

THE ABC OF JAPANESE ART

THE ABC OF JAPANESE ART

Blacker, J. F

General Books

www.General-Books.net

Publication Data:

Title: The Abc of Japanese Art
Author: Blacker, J. F
Publisher: Toronto : Copp, Clark
Publication date: 1911
Subjects: Art – Japan
Art, Japanese – Prices
Collectors and collecting

1

THE ABC OF JAPANESE ART

PREFACE

JAPANESE art, it must be confessed, has not received, as yet, that appreciation which its merits deserve, which its infinite variety warrants, and which its age justifies. Compared with old Chinese porcelain, for instance, its present value is low. That porcelain has advanced so much in price during these last years that fine specimens can be acquired only by the rich, and it still pursues its rising course free from any signs of finality. The Japanese themselves have until recently devoted much of their attention to Chinese art; now they are exerting every effort to restore to the fatherland the works of their old masters and craftsmen. Full well they recognise that such fine antiques are worth buying; full eagerly they seek after them, if peradventure they may secure prizes such as lacquer signed Korin or Kwansai amongst other treasures which will become familiar to you as you read this book.

It seems therefore that the collector should seize present opportunities, before the times of high prices shall come. There can be no doubt in the mind of any one who has considered the subject, that the upward tendency has commenced already. From the ever-growing circle of art-lovers, from the experts and from the beginners, a truer estimation of the arts of Japan is due and can be no longer delayed.

The success which has attended the issue of my books on pottery and porcelainâ English and Chineseâ has induced me to add this as a companion volume in the ABC series. The accumulated material was first considered in connection with two volumes, but in order to maintain uniformity in price and size it was decided to rearrange the matter and to publish it in one volume.

Much valuable assistance has been rendered to me by many, to whom my thanks are sincerely tendered. Especially to Mr. J. S. Happer they are due for his services in connection with colour-prints, on which he is a recognised authority. His researches regarding Hiroshige are embodied in the chapter relating to that artist; his generous gift of rare books upon the subject deserves my warm recognition. The frontispiece and other illustrations came from him; whilst others were kindly lent by Mr. Owen, of Darnell's, Wigmore Street, W.

Some of the illustrations were kindly supplied by Mr. Edgar Gorer, of Bond Street, W.; carved ivory and kimonos, lacquer cabinets, and vases in silver, shakudo, and shibuichi; and amongst the other okimonos, netsukes, and lacquer are some which appeared years ago in the Art Journal, illustrating the articles so ably written by Mr. Marcus Huish, to whom much of my inclination to Oriental art is due, and to whom I owe suitable acknowledgment; which I must also present to Sotheby's for the unlimited use of illustrated catalogues, accompanied by descriptions which have never been surpassed. These can be studied in the Appendixâ Sale Prices.

Lastly, my thanks are due to the Controller of His Majesty's Stationery Office for giving me permission to utilise the marks, signatures, and illustrations in two of the art handbooks of the Victoria and Albert Museum, viz. " Japanese Colour Prints " and " Japanse Pottery," from which I derived much assistance. The specimens of pottery and porcelain illustrated may be seen at the Museum, which is a treasure-house beyond compare.

J. F. BLACKER.

ABC OF JAPANESE ART

CHAPTER I INTRODUCTION

T T 7 HEN each of the arts of Japan richly deserves a volume VV to itself, and when great works have been devoted to some, it will not be altogether out of place to issue this cheap book which deals with these arts, a book which the author believes will be eminently useful to the collector of the treasures of Old Japan. Please think of it like that. It does not profess to be an exhaustive work, too many subjects are considered to make that possible, but in some ways, which will be discovered by the reader, the book is unique, especially in the marks supplied, which have the utmost value. Those who buy solely and rightly for the artistic qualities and merit of every object, and those who buy for profit, again rightly, may receive some guidance from the sale-prices.

I venture to state that the cult of Japanese art is only just at its commencement. Look at the facts. Before Nippon was opened to the worldâ that is, within the lifetime of an ordinary manâ its art was self-contained, except for the few incursions made upon it by the Portuguese, and more effectively and later by the Dutch. During hundreds of years, in the intervals of civil war, the artisan-artists and the aristocratic painters were alike engaged in producing the finest works that human ingenuity could employ as means to express worship and loyalty and a very natural desire to please. To please whom? The gods and the rulers of men.

Looking back in history, we find the feudal system in England and France placing the lives of the serfs at the disposal of the feudal over-lords. Something similar prevailed in Japan, but the similarity was involved. The Emperor, to whom Banzai, and again Banzai, was placed in a peculiar position for long, long centuries. From being " Lord over all " he became " Lord of the Worship "; those to whom he had delegated power usurped the Imperial functions, and by creating a feudal system secured a warlike following, which in the coming years spent its powers in striving for mastery, agreeing only on one common basisâ the seclusion of the Emperor, who, however, now and again visited offenders with all the powers of an avenging monarch.

Still, it was not until 1868 that the real power was once more safely in the hands of the Emperor, wholly and safely. So from the Middle Ages to that time the Shoguns held the reins of military government, and their over-lords, appointed under conditions of military service, became local chieftains and Daimios. All these patronised the arts. Just when Richard I. proceeded on the Third Crusade, Yoritomo became the supreme Shogun, his clan, the Minamotos, succeeding in the struggle, gave peace to the land for a time, and with that peace the arts flourished. But though each Shogun and each Daimio gave to the armourer and the sword-makerâ his vassals, by the wayâ his protection and countenance, there occurred fearful struggles for the Shogunate, in which the professional soldiers, the samurai, were closely concerned. I will show how in a short time. In 1392, just about four years after the border raid we

AN EMPEROR, know as Chevy Chase, the Ashikaga family became supreme, and the country, smiling once more in the sun of peace, put forth fruits which are garnered as belonging to the Ashikaga period (1335-1573). The difference between 1335 and 1392 is accounted for by the reign of the family over the North before acquiring the whole power on the defeat of the Southern dynasty.

From this time onwards, though troubles came and went, the arts, by upward grades, were reaching on to excellence, a career, interrupted by further strife, but settled in 1603, when lyeyasu became the Shogun as the first of the Tokugawa rulers, just in the same year when James VI. of Scotland became King of England as James I. The art of Japan subjected to the influence of China, of the imported religion, Buddhism, and, perhaps, ever so little, to the Dutch, steadily pursued its way towards independence, towards a native art which displayed all the imagination innate in the people. Now and then individual Daimios rebelled or quarrelled, so that the only issue was the harahiri, which left the re-

A DAIMIO ON HORSEBACK. AFTER TOSA MITSUNOBU.

tainers, the fighting samurai, reduced to the condition of ronins, masterless men, who often avenged their chief with all their power and followed him along the course marked by harakiri. This was a favoured subject in art. During the Tokugawa period, that is till 1867, painting and all other arts excelled to such a degree as to astonish us who have no conception of work carried on regardless of the time spent upon it.

For the moment, in England, the collection of various branches of Japanese art is comparatively easy, except with regard to the finest qualities, which are very expensive even in Japan, though examples which have reached this country in various ways may be bought sometimes very cheaply. When demands abound, forgeries abound, and in them is the danger for the collector, for the beginner especially. When I visit some of the shops in London and see colour-prints, I note the reproductions, not where they are honestly sold as such, but where they pretend to be old. They are very modern, but, with the intention to deceive, how closely they resemble the originals!

Hence the beginner must move slowly, until he knows, and knows that he knows. Now where would you like to buy? I know. You would like to stroll round the shops and pick up bargains. Very nice, too. Is it possible?

A SAMURAI BOWMAN.

Yes. Sometimes by luckâ a fickle jadeâ oftener by sound judgment, which has to be striven after. Why not try the sale-rooms? That, too, is a good plan if you restrict yourself. How can you expect to buy against the trade?

"Then," you may reply, "I shall never buy! " Oh, yes you willâ in time. Do you really want to learn something about the art, and the prices paid for examples of it? Go to the sale-rooms when the examples are on view. Study the catalogues, which often abound with expert information furnished by men whose business it is to make catalogues that shall defy the criticism of the expert buyers. Then see what prices are paid at the sales and note them.

This is something like the plan upon which this book is written. Information is spread before you, not enough to satiate, but enough, I hope, to make you wish for more, and sale-prices are given where possible, as in colour-prints and lacquer.

But something will have to be done by you before you make a collection. You must decide which special object or objects shall be your aim.

. In the wide world of Japanese art there is room for a miscellaneous collection, more room than in any other subject which I know, and the sections of this book deal with articles which harmonise with each other, which were intended for that purpose, and which have never been interfered with by foreign influences except in modern times. All, therefore, is quaint, artistic, and harmonious, but none agree with our Western notions, which for this purpose we must be prepared to discard, for the closer we can get into touch with the spirit of that wonderful people, the more will be our advantages and our successes.

In this relation a close study of the religions of the East, their mythology, and their tenets, will be invaluable. In Shinto, or, as it is called, Shintoism, you will find the source of patriotism founded upon great deeds done in the long ago, ever preserved from oblivion as a lasting monument of great traditions, ever treasured as living inspiration from great ancestors. And you must notice that symbols of the

Emperor, the Shogun, and the Daimios show not the individual, but the power which protected the art upon which such signs are displayed amidst the ornament which seems designed to enshrine them.

Even greater power was exerted over art by Buddhism, which, in the early centuries, brought Chinese civilisation

MONJU.

SHOKAKU NO SHAKA. THE BUDDHA TEACHING.

BRONZE STATUES.

in its train, and began the work from which all Japanese art is an evolution. Here again is a religion which, though modified by many sects, in the main covers the same ground as Chinese Buddhism. Gods and goddesses and a multitude of spirits of good and evil, many of them possessing individual symbols, make their appearance in all forms of art; nothing seems exempt from their presence. Painters have drawn them, sword-makers have cut them upon the tsubas or sword-guards, potters have modelled them; they are carved in ivory or in immense pieces of wood, and they are cast into giant figures of bronze. This shows the necessity for knowing all that is possible about the religions of Japan, of which more will be said in the next chapter.

There is much besides. Nowhere do we find such noble expression of dignity; such penetration and force in the expression of feeling; pathos, passion, fun; such extraordinary realism in the representation of animals, birds, and flowers. The Japanese workman, the artisan, the artist, drew and made things as they saw them. We may not easily grasp their mode of painting, but in modelling they make the object like life itself.

I have said nothing in commendation of collecting as a pursuit. Call it the pursuit of pleasure, and you will not be wrong. Call it the pursuit of profit, and again you will be quite right. One thing can be safely promised to those who are worried by too much work, and indeed to all who enter the world of collecting:

"You shall store all your baggage of worries. You shall feel perfect peace in this realm, You shall sail with old friends on fair waters, With joy and delight at the helm."

Though many of the beautiful exhibits of the Japanese Government at the White City in 1910 were magnificent, though they displayed wonderful taste and an astonishing dexterity of execution, they seemed to me to lack that touch of poetic imagination, that play of fancy, which infused the soul of Old Japan. The modern art in its best form is good, nay, it is excellent; but I fear that the art that knew no time is gone for ever. My regret may well take the words of a west-country poet:

"Oh ye have lost,

Mountains, and moors, and meads, the radiant throngs That dwelt in your green solitudes, and filled The air, the fields, with beauty and with joy Intense; with a rich mystery that awed The mind, and flung around a thousand hearths Divinest tales, that through the enchanted year

Found passionate listeners! The very streams
Brightened with visitings of these so sweet
Ethereal creatures! They were seen to rise
From the charmed waters, which still brighter grew
As the pomp passed to land, until the eye
Scarce bore the unearthly glory. Where they trod
Young flowers, but not of this world's growth, arose,
And fragrance as of amaranthine bowers
Floated upon the breeze. And mortal eyes
Looked on then revels all the luscious night;
And, unreproved, upon their ravishing forms
Gazed wistfully, as in the dance they moved,
Voluptuous to the thrilling touch of harp
Elysian 1"

N. T. CARRINGTON.

THE arts of a people are its ideas embodied, its mental conditions expressed, in concrete form. Centuries before the opening of the various ports of Nippon to intercourse and trade with Europe, the Japanese had cultivated their arts to such a position that they fell only slightly below the Chinese in their great Ming period. Both peoples were inspired by Buddhism as a motif, as a means by which larger ideas found expression in beautiful art. The priests were the earliest painters and teachers, and though the religious influence weakened as time went on, it had an enduring effect, and, whether it is called Chinese or Buddhist, it was the ground from which sprang the various schools, eventually to drift very far apart from their original forms. The Yamato, the Tosa, the Sesshu, the Kano, the Popular, the Shijo or realistic, the Ukiyo-ye, and the Gan-Ku schools only marked stages in the journey, new ideas were followed by developments in the mode of expression, and we may hope that the new conditions affecting the great Emperor of Japan and his people may yet bear new and noble fruit.

If the character of the past spirit of Japanese art could be compressed into phrases, those phrases would read something as follows: the spirit to learn and to profit by teaching; the spirit to hold central principles tenaciously, and to develop them along independent and national lines; the spirit of sincerity in expression, of scorn for shams, and of trust in truth.

Whether the coming of the Japanese to conquer and drive back the ancient Ainu people, whose descendants still live, or whether a previous race, the Koro-pok-guru, was the absolute primitive, whether invasions took place from Malay Mongolia, and Korea, are not questions which concern the scope of this book as much as what were the religions which made the art of the people whose position with regard to invasion from the mainland is curiously analogous to that of our own country.

When, in the sixth century, the Mikado appointed Shoguns

THE BEAUTIFUL CARVED-WOOD DOOR KNOWN AS THE YOMEI-MON OR HIGURASHI-

MON OF THE TEMPLE AT NIKKO, SO CALLED BECAUSE A WHOLE DAY COULD BE

SPENT IN EXAMINING IT. THE MODEL WAS SHOWN AT THE JAPAN-BRITISH

EXHIBITION IN IQIO.

to act as military commanders, Buddhism had found its way from Korea across the sea to Nippon. Here are two influences which cannot be disregarded in their relation to the birth and growth of all that made for the advancement of art. Shinto was a naturalist religion with one commandment, a positive assertion, "Thou shalt obey the Mikado '."

Its ceremonials were conducted by the Mikado, or in the provinces by his officials, who were the priests during the usurpation of the Shogunate. Shintoists were no worshippers of images; the sun (Amaterasu) and the Kamis (powerful, invisible, pure spirits) were adored, and the Emperor (Mikado), the direct descendant of Amaterasu, being, therefore, the direct descendant of the gods, held all power, both spiritual and temporal; he governed by divine right, yet his power was usurped.

The introduction of Buddhism effected something of a revolution in the old " Way of the Gods." It revolutionised the forms even of that cult, but it did moreâ it gave to its own ceremonies a pomp which was novel, attractive, and picturesque. Facility of absorption, facility of assimilation, and facility of division gave, at first, quick growth, and later, the last was responsible for the number of Buddhist sectsâ six chief and thirty-six of minor importanceâ all using ceremonial worship, with innumerable idols, amongst which were the Kamis absorbed from Shintoism. The oldest picture existing in Japan represents the first Buddhist missionary to that country, and it dates from the commencement of the eighth century. Further, the priests, trained in the monasteries, devoted themselves to painting as a work of piety, and they devoted themselves also to teaching, not necessarily the art of painting, but all the higher branches of a learned education. In every nation the older professions, except arms and agriculture, were cradled in religion.

Yet there was another power growing up which eventually controlled much of the production of the artist. The feudal system caused a certain emulation between the princes, the rich patrons, and that emulation was all in favour of progress. On the one side may be discerned the authority of the Emperor, who, deprived of his temporal power, confined himself almost entirely to the concerns of religion; on the other, the Shogun, the hereditary head of the governing, fighting class. If one had followers, the priests, the other led the Daimios. Hence the school of Tosa at Kyoto, the ancient Imperial academy, the official school, was destined to meet the rivalry of another official school, the Kano school, the school of the Shoguns, the aristocratic school, always opposed to the realism of popular developments, to the art which is so distinctively

Japanese. Literature had long held sway over art; as a source of inspiration it was second only to religion. Then the arts were the means of expression by which cultivated minds represented thoughts in unmistakable forms, always, however, according to rules, which gradually hardened into mere formulae.

The time came when a counteracting agency asserted itself with a boldness that overcame all opposition; nature-study and its embodiment had been long-suffering, enduring all things, and that which is of all the hardest, slighting neglect. It had expressed nature in her moods, but this did not satisfy the high classical aspirations of the priestly and literary classesâ it now began to Â = appeal to the ordinary

THE PAGODA OF THE TEMPLE AT NIKl to devOte lts tion to the incidents and scenes of the daily life. The history of painting will show with what force, with what success, that appeal was made, and though the Western world can never thoroughly grasp the devotion of the native collector to the works from the old academies, works in all materials as well as paintings, at least it has realised that from the reign of Genroku (1688-1704) onwards, Japanese art is worthy of attention, and the enthusiast will protest that such a weak statement is very far from the markâ he will asseverate that it is worthy of a life-long study, a lifelong devotion.

Of the paintings it may be' said that " if the style be not distinguished by marked originality of inspiration, it is characterised at least by other qualities of the first order: force and neatness of conception, clear definition of forms, sobriety of composition and just sentiment of decorative effect, rare knowledge of design, decision, and suppleness in the stroke of the brush, fine taste in the selection of vivid clear colours, and also in their harmonious combination. It is the style of a healthy and fertile art wnicn also ais- AFTER NISHIMURA SHIGENAGA. SAIGGIO HOSHI tinguishes the bronzes, VIEWING FUJIYAMA; HE WAS A FUJIWARA the carvings in wood NOBLE WHO BECAME A POET AND GAVE UP , HIS RANK.

and ivory, the arms and armour, especially the sword, the other beautiful metal-work, and all the worlds of lacquer, embroidery, and colour-prints, not omitting the porcelain and pottery."

Some subjects are exceedingly popular with artists, out- side the religious and social ones, or even the historical. The landscapes exhibit one of these subjects, the great mountain Fujiyama, or Fujisan, an extinct volcano towering to the height of more than 12,000 feet in the south of the main island, Honshiu. It is said to be sacred to the Japanese. Whether it is sacred or not may be open to doubt, but " viewing " the mountain was a pastimeâ or was it a devotion?â which had great attraction for philosophers as well as for ordinary visitors, and artists revelled in its lofty grandeur, its snow-capped cone and varying aspect, now standing out in a clear sky, now hidden in mist at its base, or with a cloud-mantle covering up its head. Other subjects for the wood-carver and metalworker were furnished by the mythology, the temples of Buddha contained large statues in wood and bronze, the art-craftsmen devoted themselves to classical forms of gods and goddesses, and found ample scope for their labours in their number, and in the varying value attached to them by the different sects. In the East, as in the West, religious worshippers were divided into sects. Buddhism, as I have said, had always displayed a facility for assimilating the native gods existing at its advent, and in Japan its pantheon was increased by the inclusion of idols of the principal Kamis, the gods col-

DJO-ON-QUE-SHA. AMIDA. GILT-WOOD, I5TH CENTURY.

lectively of the first and second dynasties and their reputed descendants, the Mikados, in addition to many deified heroes. Hence the Way of the Kami, the Way of the Gods, the Shinto religion, was grafted on to Buddhism, and images of Shinto gods appeared in Buddhist, but never in Shinto, temples, which were simple buildings constructed of natural wood without paintings or ornaments, in a plain style of architecture. The sanctuary, closed by a white veil which nobody dared to lift, was furnished with a table or altar in white wood upon which were placed a polished metal mirror, symbol of creation; a gohei y consisting of paper streamers on a stick, symbol of purity; and a sword, in memory of the god Susanovo no Mikoto, brother of Amaterasu, the first celestial sovereign of the country, who delivered it from a devouring dragon. Teaching, preaching, singing, and dancing occupied the time and attention of the priests.

Buddhism had, on the contrary, its elaborate ritual, but the idols which were most adored varied according to the sects, of which the six principal were Tendai, Hokke-su, Zen-su, Singon, Sin-su, and Djods-su. The chief gods were Dhyani-Buddha Amida, the Amitabha of Tibet; and the Dhyani-Bodhisattva Kwannon (Avalokitesvara); yet Shaka-muni was scarcely inferior to them, and the two sects of the Singon and Tendai gave the highest rank to Dai Niti Niorai (Vairocana), another Dhyani-Buddha. The images of these and other gods were cast in bronze or carved in wood; sometimes they were of immense size, as will be seen in the bronze Buddha described elsewhere, amongst the bronzes, but most of those which I have seen have been wonderful specimens of wood-carving, varying from giant statues to quite small statuettes, sometimes painted and gilt, sometimes in natural wood. The Japanese ascribe this art to the ancient sculptures of Ganharaâ to the second phase of Buddhist development in Tibetâ for their religion was of the form called Buddhism of the North, and, like that of China, belonged to the school of Mahayana, the outcome of a council held at Djalandhara about the middle of the first century of our era. The books of this school were written in sanserif, those of the earlier Hinayana school were in pali.

Volumes could be written regarding the mythology of this religion, the saints and gods, the genii and demons, and in years to come it may become more familiar to us. Whether we regard the hold it had over millions of people, or merely look upon it as a matter of philosophic study, we cannot help being impressed with the beauty and dignity of the magnificent Buddhas of contemplation, the Dhyani-Buddhas, the types of the faith, and as such they never were human, they, in fact, inspired, protected, and sustained the human Buddhas (Manusi-Buddhas). Of course the purity of every form of religion has been degraded by its followers, yet amongst those who drink from the unpolluted source there remains much of the truth, though the expression of that truth varies with age, changes with environment, and is modified by fluctuating influences.

The six sects of Japan had formerly a rival sect, Rio-bu in which Shinto and Buddhism were mixed, but in 1881 an Imperial decree suppressed this in order to restore to Shinto all its purity. One cannot at the same time drink from two sources. And Buddhism in Japan, with its different sects, now appears to be losing ground. Yet the philosophic doubter must love these old images, the trophies of a glorious past largely free from religious strife, if we except the massacre of the Christians.

How closely some of them resemble others! Here are three of the Niorai, who differ from each other only in the position of the hands, the right hand especially. These gestures, the mudras, have a language, a signification, of their own. The right hand raised implies teaching; extended downwards palm outwards, perfection of conduct; resting palm downwards on the thigh, bearing witness; and clasping the index finger of the left hand is the habitual attitude of the Buddha, supreme and eternal. How each sits or stands upon a pedestal made of the petals of the lotus, Buddha's sacred flower, the nelumbium speciosum! Sometimes the thalamus supporting the divinity is doubled, the second being reversed. It must be noted that there is much of real dignity in these figures, and the classical art in all its forms shares that dignity which is typical of one side of the nation's character.

Another side is revealed when we see the seven gods of good fortune, painted in pictures, carved in wood, or moulded in pottery. Hotei, for example, the merry, fat god, the children's playmate and friend, may be shown pulled along by the children in a game, or with his friends, the other gods, enjoying the pleasures of the table. The humour of a situation strikes the artist, and as these gods do not partake in the sanctity of serious worship they are easily adapted to a funny episode or position, and if smiles mean anything, they enjoy it.

Although these seven, as gods of happiness, have no prominent position in the temples, and although they receive but little adoration, their kindly aspect appeals to the popular imagination, and in nearly every home they are conspicuous on the floor which here raised â of the toko-noma, a recess partly altar, partly picture-

WOODEN STATUE OF

GODDESS OF MERCY AND GRACE.

gallery, at one end of the main room. The position which they hold as the lares, after the manner of the Etruscans and Romans, does not at all interfere with the broad, humorous treatment which they receive at the hands of painters, potters, and carversâ a treatment oftentimes perfectly ludicrous.

Their origin has been traced back to the days of the Shogun Yemitsu, and the story is told that they were the outcome of a dream. Yemitsu, like Pharaoh, awoke one morningâ â to be as accurate as the chronicle, on the first day of the

THE SEVEN GODS OF GOOD FORTUNE. IMARI WARE.

year 1624â and, like Pharaoh, his spirit was troubled. Until Joseph came " there was none that could interpret Pharaoh's dream," and only a famous courtier of the Shogun, the wise Dai Oino Kami could persuade his master that the seven monsters who had frightened him were none other than the disguised gods, the seven gods of happiness or good fortune, paying him a visit at the advent of a New Year. His cleverness convinced Yemitsu, and the more easily because he had his list ready, borrowed from the divinities of the three religions, Shintoism, Buddhism, and Taoism, though, as we know, Shintoism forbade images. Yet a Shinto origin must be assigned to Yebis or Yebisu, god of the fishers and of commerce, and above all, of the daily food. Taoism furnished Jurojin, god of longevity, round-headed, smiling, sometimes accompanied by a deer or stork, and Fukurokuju, god of wisdom, having a remarkable sugar-loaf head. From Buddhism he borrowed Bishamon, god of the North, and made him god of war; Daikoku, god of riches, with money or rice-bag and a miner's hammer; Hotei, the fat-bellied, smiling god of contentment and gaiety, protector of children; and Benten, goddess of beauty. All of these gods except Yebisu were of Chinese derivation, their origin is lost in myths, but many of them may be found in the priceless porcelain statuettes of the Ming period.

But these Chinese statuettes are, above all, dignified, though in the paintings, even of the early centuries, the rishi are often represented as merry boys or youths, by Chinese artists. The rishi, or Taoist sagesâ the eight immortalsâ are represented in Japan by these seven gods of good fortune; and many other fabulous personages, animals, trees, and flowers are common to both countries. The dragon, which in China bears five claws to represent the Imperial family, has in Japan but three. The kirin or kylin y the lion or dog of Buddha, the ho-ho bird or feng huang, may show variations, but the symbolical meaning is the same, just as it is in the trees and flowers, where the pine and plum-blossom speak of immortality and rejuvenescence. The emblems are strongly in evidence in art borrowed from China, whilst in purely native work they are nearly disregarded.

Hence it is that, in painting, the soul of the art of Japan, such subjects as relate to the religions are far more numerous than those which deal with nature. Scenes from the life of Buddha and his followers are more often met with than landscapes, and these in their turn exceed pictures of animals, birds, and flowers in number. For nearly the whole of the first fifteen centuries the natural plant and animal life received but little attention from the Tosa school, but their attraction could not be resisted, and amongst other subjects it, at the last, reigned supreme.

Now painting and colour-prints are so closely allied that for practical purposes they may be taken as one, with a limitation. The other branches of Japanese art are by no means independent of painting, for just as colour-print designs were drawn by the artists and executed by the artificer, so in lacquer, in metal-work, in textiles, and embroideries, and all else, the patterns were furnished by the artists to highly skilled artisans.

Which introduces a speculation. Who were these artisans? At present the artist appears to receive all the credit for the work for which he supplied the designs, for the exquisite gold lacquer designed by Koetsu, Korin, Kwansai, Zeishin, Toyo, and others, leaves no sign of identification from the hand of the craftsman. " Unwept, unhonour'd, and unsung," they have passed away into the silence, and yet they speak to us now, if only to declare how faithfully they strove to interpret the minds of the masters, if only to teach how infinite pains reach onwards to perfection. And the limitation between painting and colour-prints was imposed by the engraver and the printer.

T)AINTING in Japan developed under Chinese inspira-L tion, in which the religions of Buddhism and Taoism were closely involved. During the early centuries of our era Chinese art was closely imitated, but by its side began the evolution of the Yamato style of native painting. From this arose the Tosa school, which for several centuries produced religious works for the temples, and other pictures, such as incidents in the lives of the saints, in the history of the Court and of the country, and in the internecine wars. But after a long interval another school arose, the Kano school, which drew fresh inspiration from the artists of the Chinese paintings of the Sung period, and, though the subjects of the paintings in the two schools were generally of the same class, the treatment by the Kano artists told the tale of the source from which they sprang. The later Ganku, Torii, Shijo, and other schools indicate departures from the traditions of Tosa and Kano which will form part of this section. The most important of the recent developments gave to Japan the art of the Ukiyo-ye school which aimed at depicting life and the world as it was.

In the British Museum there are Japanese paintings of the thirteenth century, and these can be there compared with the earlier works of Chinese painters of the eighth century, of whom Wu Tao Tze was the most famous. In the Japan-British Exhibition native pictures of the ninth century, notably one of a divinity, Kongorikiku, by Kobo Daishi, revealed the Chinese influence which always had a tendency towards the traditional and conventional, so that the other schools, breaking the traditions, set up their own standards, which became so characteristic as to be recognised at a glance by the expert.

The classical schools were largely the academies of the priests, but we shall find that other artists held honourable positions in the Courts of the Shoguns, who chose them because

THE BIRTH OF GAUTAMA BUDDHA IN THE WOODS OF LUMBINI; MAYA, HIS MOTHER, ATTENDED BY INDRA, BRAHMA, AND THE NAGAS.

From an old painting.

the priests were subjected to the authority of the Emperor, the spiritual head of the nation. We shall see that the emulation of the painters in the two schools led to excellence in each, for, the styles being different, it only remained for the artist to display his highest ability in executing his designs. Nevertheless, we must bear in mind that this rivalry had no existence in the early centuries, and that, through the civil wars, painting, and indeed all art, was neglected. During the intervals of peace, the painters pursued their avocation, decorating the temple walls, or drawing on paper such subjects as could be mounted upon a biyobu, a kakemono, a makimono, or a large scroll.

Biyobus were screens, and upon these were displayed the largest pictures on permanent exhibition, though some screens could be folded up and put away. The names kakemonos and makimqnps are used here to indicate the two forms of picturesâ vertical and horizontal. Later, when applied to colour-prints, the kakemono has a regular size. With simple equipment of paper, brush-pencils, Japanese ink, and a limitcd numbcr or colours, thc artists of thc carly ccnturics paintcd picturcs which were usually mounted on paper or brocade furnished with a roller on which they could be rolled up. Very old paintings in water or body colour are exceedingly rare; they are conserved as precious treasures. I have seen examples ascribed to Kose-no-Kanaoka, the painter-poet of the Imperial Court in the ninth century, and by his grandson Rose Hirotaka, but most of the painters before Nobuzane (1177-1265) are unknown, though the paintings are undoubtedly ancient. Difficulties of identification always surround the birth of an art where the work is neither signed nor dated. Even China, which claims for painting an antiquity preceding the Christian era by at least three centuries, can show but few works anterior to Ku K'ai-chih about A. D. 364-405. Little illumination has come from the dark ages, only we can mark the advance of Buddhism, and note the consequent progress in art.

It is said that the Japanese Emperor Kijo, after having travelled all through China, founded, in mo, a school in his own country, whose principles were honoured and accepted as late as the seventeenth century. It was then the Augustan era of the Sung dynasty in China, when, from 960 to 1280, Chinese art gradually developed those characteristics which it still for the most part retains. The only famous painter whom I can trace during the twelfth century is Nobuzane, a member of the great Fujiwara family, whose picture " Sambo Kojin, the Spiritual God of the Three Treasures " is in the British Museum; and that is only attributed to him. Probably owing to the Emperor's visit more attention was paid in the Tosa school to the teachings of her neighbour, though the Yamato school, from which Tosa arose, still existed, and indeed in every age there were independents who attached themselves to no party, but did their work as they pleased, without reference to accepted methods. Some such works have reached our own times, though by far the best of the ancient paintings have been allowed to leave their country only under exceptional conditions for purposes of exhibition, as at the White City, and these have been Buddhist pictures decidedly of the Tosa school.

Further, it is expressly stated that the Tosa school founded in the ninth century owed nothing to the influence of China. Apart from religious subjects, it occupied a special position in art embodying the taste of the Court at Kyoto. Quails and peacocks, cocks and hens, cherry and other branches in flower, were painted as time went on with the extreme care and patience of a miniature, even with an excessive detail. Such pictures found a place in the albums, whilst on the large scrolls historical scenes and Court fetes were depicted, or Daimios with their samurai in gorgeous ceremonial costumes. The Tosa painters afterwards lost much of their prestige to the artists of the later Kano school, whose studies included a wider scope, where landscapes played an important part, and where Chinese subjects were devotedly imitated. Whilst the paintings of the former were distinguished by the elegance and precision of its design, the latter was noted for its breadth, power, and freedom, but many years elapsed before the great Chodensu initiated the reforms which led to the foundation of this school of Kano.

The Shogun Yoritomo, founder of the hereditary Shogunate in 1192, creator of the city of Kamakura, which he made his capital, extended his patronage to the arts, which flourished exceedingly, and became settled in the main principles. A peace followed during the succession of his two sons to that high office, then more civil war. In the Middle Ages the Fujiwara clan usurped Imperial authority, and military affairs were entrusted to the two clans of Minamoto and Taira. These aimed at national power, so, during the struggle which terminated with the victory of Yoritomo, art was neglected. The extinction of the hereditary clan of the Minamotos in 1219 brought further trouble; indeed a family of humble origin â the Hojosâ grasped the supreme power, and ruled with resistless authority. Though many Shoguns succeeded each other, they were either minors connected with the royal family, or rulers easily governed by the Ho jo Regents, until the Emperor Go-Daigo issued from his retirement as Mikado, and not only destroyed the power and arrogant tyranny of the Hojos, but also overthrew their city, the Kamakura, which Yoritomo had made his capital. The two Imperial dynasties of the North and South, after a short peace, came into collision, a fierce contest lasted for fifty-six years, and was only closed in 1392 by the victory of the North, and by the peace which followed the establishment of Yoshimitsu as the Shogun of the Ashikaga family. Peace led to intercommunication with the continent, and to the general promotion of the arts of peace.

Under the Shogun of this family, which marks a period in artâ the Ashikaga periodâ many painters appeared, some of whom have left works which may be seen at the British Museum. When the Shoguns encouraged the artists, the Daimios, who became feudal princes, followed their example. Copying the Chinese models, at the best a delusive habit, gave way to another style in which powers of invention and composition were allied to skilful execution. Chodensu, it is true, presented his conceptions of Kings of Hell, and of Arhats and other Buddhist divinities, but there was a foreshadowing of a representative impressionist manner which, commencing in the silvery tones of ink sketches of landscapes, birds, and flowers, found its interpretation in Sesshu.

Chodensu, or Myocho, known too as Mincho, was an impressionist notwithstanding his subjects. He lived from to 1431, and painted the celebrated " Death of Sakia " for the Tofukuji Temple at Kyoto, a work which has been copied frequently. His new departure included a new method of colouring, as well as a broader style of painting. One of his pictures sent from the same temple was exhibited at the White City. The difference between the old distemper colours mixed with water-glue used by Kanaoka and the Ko-se school, and the thick water-colour body employed by Chodensu, made for the progress culminating in the persons of the Kanosâ Masanobu, and Motonobu.

Josetsu, pupil of Chodensu, a Chinese by birth, worked from 1394 to 1427. His paintings are little known, but Shubun, his distinguished pupil, a landscape from whose brush was exhibited at the White City by the Marquis Kaoru Inoue was the master of Oguri Sotan, who worked about 1450 in landscape and figure painting. These two, Shubun and Oguri Sotan, trained Kano Masanobu, the founder of the Kano school. Saomi, a fellow student with Shubun, became the favourite painter of the Shogun Yoshimasa and he was a celebrated cha-jin y a master of the tea and flower ceremonies, and an author of the standard work on the cha-no-yu, the tea ceremony. The official connection between the Shoguns and the Kano school probably had its origin here. Looking onwards from this period we can associate the Tosa school with the Emperor and his lords, the Kuge. The latter school was on the way to decline, although Tosa Mit-sunobu accomplished great things. But it will be well to consider the artists of this century of the Ashikaga period in greater detail, because in the middle of the next century, the sixteenth, Japan was exposed to further internal turmoil and fierce strife, which again obstructed the progress of the fine arts.

Though the Tosa school had a long and illustrious existence before Chodensu s work laid the foundations of the Kano revival, and though about a hundred years elapsed before Kano Masanobu actually opened the school, comparatively few painters made a reputation in that interval. I have mentioned Shubun, whose best work in landscape was painted about 1400, and his pupil Oguri Sotan, also a landscape painter, who reached his highest level fifty years later. Sesshu, another landscape artist, has been mentioned, and will be noticed later, but I hasten to Kano Masanobu, the contemporary of Tosa Mitsunobu, though he was but one amongst several masters who followed Chodensu's lead. They were mostly Buddhist priests, who often practised mural painting in the temples as well.

Kano Masanobu was not represented in the Japanese paintings shown at the British Museum, but at the White City there were two works by himâ " Angling on the wintry lake " and " Chou Mao-hsu, a Chinese sage " It was in the studios of Shubun and Oguri Sotan that Masanobu improved his talent, which had been fostered in his home, just as he himself encouraged the ability which he saw in his son Motonobu (1476-J 559)- Tne father's works are very rare, even in Japan, where they are valued for their powerful dark colours, firm, strong

SOME LUCKY CHARACTERS AND SYMBOLS.

Kotobaki â Felicity.

Fuku = Happiness.

Swastika = Good fortune.

Tori, or Tori-i Â Â Favour of thÂ gods.

contours, and noble simplicity, which is especially notable in the figures.

Kano Motonobu married the daughter of Tosa Mitsunobu (1434-1525), the chief of the Tosa school, who painted subjects illustrating history and battle scenes, such as those which took place in the early Hogen and Heiji eras. By this marriage the Kanos shared with the Tosas the celebrity attached to this art. The " Sinico-Japanese Encyclopaedia " thus speaks of him: " He was the prince of Chinese and Japanese painters, almost a god in his power. He was often named Kohogen. His works reached China during the Ming dynasty, and his glory spread in all that Empire." We in Europe can scarcely appreciate the full force of his genius; his flowers, birds, and landscapes, as shown at the British Museum and in the Japan-British Exhibition, were altogether admirable, and a painting of Shorikenâ the Chinese rishi Chung-li K'uan, the great leader, crossing the waters on a swordâ was a wonderful work. Monsieur L. Gonse thus criticises four kakemonos: " Japanese art has produced nothing that I know stronger and more delicate than these. One of them represented a landscape with fugitive lines, a Corot bathed in light and transparence. The perspective is admirable, and the most exacting eye would find no fault in it; the succession and gradation of the planes reach an extraordinary delicacy, obtained by means of great simplicity. If Motonobu ignored the scientific laws of perspective, it is well to recognise before such perfect work that his empiricism is worth all our theories." Mr. William Anderson, writing about his manner of painting, said: " Even to unfamiliar eyes, the vigour of the design and the complete mastery of the pencil which he has displayed in the rendering of landscapes and figures produce an impression truly extraordinary."

Without possessing the delightful colour of the Tosa school as developed by Mitsunobu, whose talent he admired, Motonobu showed a harmony and warmth of tone in his paintings which contrast with the monochromes of his own school. In his dull reds, quiet blues, and powerful violets he has never been surpassed, whilst his touch displays the energy and decision of the finest writing, which in Japan was done with the brush-pencil and not with the pen, with the brush held vertically over the surface. This method gave extra-ordinary flexibility to the strokes, which were heavy or thin, flat or wavy or broken, but always clean, strong, denned, admirable, and indeed so distinctive as to furnish the clue to the identification of the work of the master, compared with which the weakness of the copyist cannot deceive the connoisseur who studies the paintings at the British Museum or elsewhere.

Motonobu preferred to paint landscapes, and even more the deities familiar to the Buddhists, such as the seven gods of happiness and prosperity, especially Hotei, the good-tempered, fat, half-naked god of gaiety, the protector of the children. The Kano school it was which made these benevolent protectors so attractive and popular; wisdom and fertility, good luck, beauty and war, were objects worthy of success through the power of such divinities, who in course of time, however, were treated grotesquely as subjects for humour, or even ridicule. From this period this school pursued two styles of painting, oneâ guantai, that is rocky, indicating a powerful, rude method, with angular forms well marked in Chinese fashion; the other, riutai or flowing, in which the soft, flowing lines vanished smoothly in undulations. The latter was the native style in the making.

Some writers emphasise the influence of Persia on the art of Japan, and labour to trace this influence through the medium of the Portuguese, who traded from Macao to the Persian Gulf; and such investigations and speculations are always helpful, often highly interestingâ at present I cannot say they are convincing.

Sesshu (1420-1506) lived in the time of the elder Kano. He was of neither school, and though he, in the second half of the ijfteenth century, attained the front rank as a painter, he was a Buddhist priest, distinguished among the learned men of his day, who retired to end his days in the temple of Unkokuji in the province of Souo. Having learnt the elements of painting in the atelier of Josetsu, he soon became so noted for the vigour and originality of his black-and-white designs, as to attract the attention of the Emperor of China, who invited him to undertake the decoration of a palace. Sesshu went to China, and surprised and delighted the Emperor by an exhibition of his skill. The Emperor wanted to see him sketch, so Sesshu plunged a broom into the ink, and with this curious brush painted such a wonderful dragon that his reputation was at once established. If he became influenced by Chinese principles in painting, in his turn he revealed something of Japan, its scenery and its people, and on his return he left in the palace a wonderful scene representing the loved mountain Fujiyama.

When he died in 1506 his work was carefully preserved; some specimens of it have reached Europe. They show that Sesshu excelled in figure painting, and that his flowers, birds, and landscapes were equal to those of Kano. They too became classical, and the wonderful attitudes of the divinities, their fierce or kindly expressions, the graceful crane flying over the surface of the water, or resting amongst the lotus lilies, all these and more are borrowed by modern painters from the old Sesshu, who, avoiding the reds and greens, with a single stroke, drew his designs, in which the neuter, light and rich brown tones, and a deep black were applied with great rapidity. Amongst his pupils were Sesson, who was noted for his moonlight effects, and Shugetsu, his companion to China, another Buddhist priest, scarcely less famous than his master, with him in the temple, in painting, in foreign travel, and again in the temple. Shugetsu died in 1520. Another pupil of Sesshu founded the school called by his master's name. This was Togan, a landscape painter, who worked about 1600. His full name was Unkoku Togan, and his paintings are even rarer than those of his master, yet they are not so highly appreciated. A landscape by him was on view in the Japanese section of retrospective paintings and drawings at the White City in 1910.

Amongst the celebrated masters of the fifteenth century, Saga Jasoku is given high rank by the historians of Japan, and a Chinese landscape from his brush in the British Museum, a scroll painting with a continuous composition, temporarily re-divided into the original strips of which it was composed, reveals " the freshness, vigour and terseness of the adopted Chinese manner by one of the most powerful and celebrated masters of the revival." The quotation is from the guide to the Exhibition at the Museum, which is well worthy of the serious attention of the student of Japanese painting, especially when the old masters of the Chinese renaissance can be compared with, and their influence traced upon, the development in Japan which ultimately led to the assimilation of the Chinese style with native character, a task performed

A VISIT OF CEREMONY.

From a painting, i6th century.

with more or less distinction by successive masters of the Kano school.

In the sixteenth century the name of Sesson stands out in emulation with Kano Motonobu. Many of his works have been shown in England. He was a disciple of Sesshu. Five pictures by him were shown at the White Cityâ a landscape, roses and herons, Lipo a Chinese poet looking at a waterfall, willow-trees and herons, and a group of monkeys. Others are shown in the British Museum, several landscapes, including "Sunset over a fishing village," which, "with seven others, form a traditional series of landscape subjects, the famous views or scenes originally associated with the scenery of Lake Tung-Ting in China, and afterwards transferred to the scenery of the Japanese Lake Biwa." This note from the guide is noteworthy in view of the prominence given by the painters from this time onwards to scenes from this lake which was situated amongst the mountains not a great distance from Kyoto.

In maintaining the comparison between the Tosa and Kano schools, we note that the former shows decadence in this century, and the latter maintains its advance, borrowing from its rival the glory of colour for which it had been celebrated. Motonobu's son Shoyei, his brother Utanosuke, and his grandson Yeitoku sustained the high reputation of the Kano family, but their work was assisted very materially by other distinguished masters of the Kano schoolâ Sanraku and Takanobu. The fusion to which I referred was completed, and by the advent of the Tokugawa Shogunateâ early in the seventeenth centuryâ an hereditary authority sprang into existence, which lasted till 1867, and exerted a beneficial effect upon art in general, and upon the fortunes of the Kano school in particular.

Between the Ashikaga period and that of Tokugawa the supreme control of affairs rested for a time in the hands of an extraordinary man of obscure origin, who became paramount in Nippon, and even in Korea. This was Hideyoshi, who has been described as viceroy and general. The Ashikaga period lasted from 1335 to 1573, and the next thirty years have been comprised into a period termed the Momoyama period, which was distinguished by the glories of the magnificent castle of Momoyama, where Hideyoshi held his court. The artists who were eminent during these years were Kano Eitoku, who died in 1590, Kaiboka Yusho in 1615, Unkoku Togan, to whom reference has been made, and Hasegawa Tohaku, deceased in 1610. What share these men took in painting the wonderful great screens with decoration upon a gold ground is not clear, but they were the typical productions of the second stage in the Kano art, in which Kano Sanraku displayed his skill as a painter of battle scenes,

A FAMOUS WARRIOR, KAJIWARA GENTA, WIELDING HIS SWORD WITH TWO HANDS.

and Sesson was probably still living, though of this I am not sure.

Still, Sanraku, the son-in-law and pupil of Eitoku, and his master, Eitoku himself, appear to be the most distinguished artists of the Momoyama period, and as they were both Kanos, the official relation between that school and the Shogun was in all probability maintained. Hence there is a reasonable assumption that the gorgeous decorative compositions of this period were the work of these artists. Eitoku died thirteen years before its end, but Sanraku lived until 1635, when the Tokugawa family was firmly established in the Shogunate, through the victories of lyeyasu, who, after the battle of Sekigahara, in 1600, settled the differences between the lords of the east and the west, became Shogun in 1603, and entirely overthrew the adherents of Hideyoshi's infant son Hideyori in 1615, after the siege and fall of the Castle of Osaka. lyeyasu's descendants, the Tokugawas, remained the de facto rulers of Japan for fifteen generations. In 1867 the fifteenth Shogun, Yoshinobu (Keiki) resigned his position to the Emperor, owing to internal troubles, and to his inability to adjust the complications resulting from external relations with other nations. As patrons of art the Tokugawas deserve the highest praise; their fostering care and their splendid example were not lost upon the Daimios, for they, too, learnt to love art and aided its progress.

THE Kano school at Yedo (Tokyo) was distinguished by the advent of three sons of Takanobuâ Tannyu, Naonobu, and Yasunobuâ who not only maintained the prestige of the school, but also won places amongst the great masters. Tannyu, born in 1601, after the early death of his father, became a pupil of Kano Kohi. His home training and his study at the school resulted in great success. When his works, his landscapes, birds, and animals, became known, he grew famous, and the collectors of Japan contend for the slightest productions of his brush. The large paintings in the temples, a panel with four lions in black at Nikko, and the ceiling of the chief gate of the same building, painted with two dragons, also in black, are highly esteemed. His smaller works express his talent no less, a landscape in the moonlight, with two persons dreaming on the terrace of a house; the happy meeting of two friends, a well-known Chinese subject; a man riding on a donkey through the snow,â such as these are much valued. Even slighter subjectsâ a bird sketched in half a dozen strokes, a crane flying over a rice-field, in a few moreâ are appreciated as showing his mastery over form. There are many copies of Tannyu J s works in Europe, which lack the facile touch of the master, and some of them vary the details to give a greater impression of truth.

Tannyu was a picture expert, well versed in old masters, their styles, signatures, and seals, and he was a collector too, whose collection furnished the materials for a book, "The Tannyu Ringwa," which was published in the eighteenth century by a society of amateurs, as a guide to the study of painting before 1600.

Naonobu, also named Kadzuma, was six years younger than Tannyu, from whom he acquired the art, though his style is different, being marked by an absolute freedom and boldness of design combined with charming delicacy. The other brother, Yasunobu, born in 1622, became noted as a landscape painter, whose celebrated pupil Sotatsu left the Kano school, and afterwards excelled in the Tosa style, adopting a new medium for his paintings, a mixture of gold-dust and black ink, which was perfected by the great Korin.

There was one studio, a branch of the Kano school, founded in Kyoto by Sanruku, the Court painter of the Shogun Sama, which preserved and practised Chinese principles. Under the master Sansetsu, who died in 1661, two famous artists were trainedâ Shokwado, also named Shojo, a priest of Nara, and Mitsuoki. Shokwado's impressionist paintings showed an independent style, which received such appreciation that, in 1804, they were reproduced in two volumes with illustrations from his paintings, and published at Tokyo.

The Tosa school in the seventeenth century emerged from its comparative obscurity under Mitsuoki, one of the most illustrious masters of that time, who created a distinctive system, a style at once decorative, refined, and elegant, where the flowers, the birds, and the landscapes assumed soft and delicate forms inspired with grace and beauty. His exquisite designs became the ideals of the lacquerers of Kyoto in the next century. In purity of line, ingenuity of design, and excellence of execution the pencil of the miniaturist combined tones which were bright without hardness, with touches of gold forming a harmony of colour as rare as it was lovely. It was no wonder that the Emperor, the nobles, and the rich families of Kyoto collected and preserved his books. Mitsuoki, who was born in 1616 and lived till 1691, received, as we have seen, his early training in the atelier of Sansetsu, where Shojo was also a pupil.

It was at Tosa that Iwasa Matabel learnt from Mitsuoki the art of painting the subjects which were popular amongst the aristocracy, the designs such as his master excelled in painting, the pictures which were suitable to express the dignity of the princes, to reveal the face of nature in the approved form, and to reproduce mythical god and beast in classic pose. Now under the Tokugawa came the opportunity for what we should term genre painting of scenes from familiar life in town and country, of the manners and costumes of the common peopleâ the vulgar school arose under Matabei. During the period 1624-43 his popularity was at its height as the inventor of the style termed Ukiyo-ye, that is the painting of contemporary life, and therefore he was a realist, whose men in their usual dress, peasants and people of the lower classes, satisfied the instincts of the people, whilst they were decried by the higher classes. In one respect, however, Matabe'i had a lasting influence on Japanese art, an influence which may be traced in almost any of the colour-prints which are at present receiving so much attention, specially perhaps in England, France, and America. Hokusai, Harunobu, Utamaro, and many others show how the paintings by Matabeii of the courtesans, the yoshiwara yukwaku, exerted a power sufficient to affect much of the later art; their luxury, their dress, and their manners played a considerable role in the public life of Japan, and they were educated too. It is not perhaps too much to say that to occidental minds this genre appears to be the expression of the painting and colour-printing of Japan, whilst in reality it only forms a small, very small, section of it. The popular school differedâ it was its office to differâ from the Tosa school, which was of the Court, official.

In that school portraiture was limited to the learned, to the famous, to the dignitaries; other paintings depicted battles or scenes from history or ceremonies of the Court. But the popular school expressed the life of the people, the spirit of Nippon; free from outside and foreign influence, it was Japanese art which developed into Ukiyo-ye art.

Hishikawa Moronobu of Kyoto, who worked from 1659 to the first fourteen years of the eighteenth century, was the real founder of the popular school known as the school of

Utagawa, which practised Ukiyo-ye art. He studied under Matabet, and is considered as the ablest representative of this style of art. Being in his younger days an embroiderer, as a great artist he was distinguished for the sumptuous yet picturesque designs which he furnished to the manufacturers of silk. Many of his works are to be found in the illustrated books which could be bought for a few shillings a few years since. He was the pioneer of the colour-print.

Another artist, Iccho, founder at Yedo (Tokyo) of a school â the school of Hanabusaâ lived from 1651 to 1724, and adopted a realism which gave full play to the native humour and fancy, which is not the least attractive side of the Japanese character. His works are in eager demand. No one has rendered with greater fidelity the unaffected simplicity of the peasants, their good humour, the joyful diversions; no one has jested so freely with the jolly gods of happiness, or poked such gentle fun at the Buddhist divinities. His swift sketches and gay colours have been welcomed by the modern artist, be he worker in wood or metal; painters and decorators have copied his designs, and his influence over Hokusai was considerable, but Hiroshige owed him much more.

There was one artist of the Tosa school who, later than Mitsuokiâ being, in fact, born nine years after that great master diedâ was destined to maintain its reputation; I refer to Mitsuyoshi, who, at the age of seventeen, had obtained an honorific title, and later was appointed keeper of the painting academy of the Emperor. The delicacy of the work of Mitsuoki has been noticed. Mitsuyoshi followed in his footsteps, and produced paintings of extreme fineness with one marked and distinctive design resembling the miniature enamel painting on the Chinese egg-shell porcelain of Yung-ching (1722-35), the subject being quails. In these and kindred subjects this painter acquired nearly perfect execution, and the school afterwards taught by his son devoted itself to birds and flowers, following his designs, and in the mechanical process of mere copying losing that inspiration which had for so many ages influenced and elevated its career.

The Shogun Yemitsu, third ruler of the Tokugawa dynasty, was a magnificent patron of the arts. Whilst he regulated his relations with the European traders, and arranged that the Dutch should trade from the little island of Decima, he built grand temples, and encouraged painting and lacquering amongst all the other arts. The lacquer produced during his reign, especially that having gold in relief, was truly remarkable. Koetsu, the famous lacquerer, was a pupil of the Tosa school, and he himself founded a school from which in due course a distinguished pupil came, the celebrated Korin.

Koetsu was painter, teacher, lacquerer, and more, he was cited as an expert in antique swords, and in calligraphy. I know of no other name which has received the last distinction in a country where calligraphy was one of the elegant accomplishments. His appearance will again be made in the chapter on lacquer, which will emphasise his delicate painting.

If the Tosa school in the first part of the seventeenth century boasted of Koetsu, the Kano school had a pupil, the son of Naonobu, who was nearly as famous,â Tsunenobu, the painter of chrysanthemums, whose chief work in one of the temples of Kyoto was a gallery painted on two sides with giant flowers in relief, and as high as a man. His flowers and birds, peacocks with displayed tails, cranes in wintry snow, and landscapes would favourably compare with any of the other masters, and, further, they were in many respects equal, in some superior, to the landscapes of the Western world. Still in the same family and the same school we find two sons of Tsunenobu who became distinguishedâ Minenobu and Tshikanobu; but biographical details of them are lacking, except that the former died in 1708. During the same century there lived the great potter Ninsei, who, with Korin the lacquerer, Kenzan, another potter, and others, must be classified amongst the painters because they were artists of renown; the mere application of their art to lacquer or to pottery scarcely affects their position as artists in the wider sense. Ninsei of Kyoto was a painter with an original style, a contemporary and friend of Tannyu, ap of his pupil Yeishin.

DOGS. PAINTED BY OKIO.

For the same reason a double reference must be made to the paintersâ not all of them, but the chief â who in the later schools of Torii and Okumura brought to excellence the process of colour-printing, and adapted their Ukiyo-ye designs to block engraving and to the progressive stages which, commencing at first with plain black, hand-tinted with red, added the primary colours one by one and then a whole gamut of secondary tones by superposition rather than previous mixing, until the Japanese colour-print has scored an immense success because of its real merit.

From the middle of the seventeenth century to early in the eighteenth, was a period in many respects remarkable, for lacquer and metal-working as well as for painting; the level of excellence was won and maintained, both under the Emperor Genroku, who governed the country from 1688 to 1704, and onwards, when Nippon and Holland were in full commercial intercourse. The porcelain of Hizen, "the old Japan," was exported in immense quantities, and the wealth that poured into the country excited activity in many directions. Since the Yeyas had been displaced by the Tokugawas in the Shogunate the prosperity of Yedo (Tokyo) had increased, and Kyoto had correspondingly decreased in importance, supplanted by a rival who had perhaps less of attraction, but more of life. Old traditions and refined elegance, severe good taste and aristocratic surroundings, yielded to the actual activity of commercialism.

Korin, born at Kyoto in 1661, entered the Tosa school, and studied also in the atelier for lacquerers founded by Koetsu. He left for Yedo whilst quite young, and though he returned to his native city in 1716, it was only just before his death, which took place in that year. Korin's style of painting was founded upon the sketches of Shokwado and the paintings of Sotatsu rather than any others, but he soon evolved a style of his own which became, during the eighteenth century, the foundation of the school of

Korin. Biyobus and kakemonos and small sketches for albums were painted by him. TSome of the biyobus were large screens with a decoration of chrysanthemums upon a gold ground, the white flowers being

Xln relief. But words fail to describe the beauty of itâ the bending stems with their burden of white flowers, others standing erect, but not less gracefully, upon an opalescent ground of gold which seemed the only fit surface for such flowers. Fit for admiration, worthy of study, possessing a distinction, original, personal, impressionist!

But the impression is confined to the casual glance; examination reveals surprising execution, light and smooth effects from a brush charged with colour in the hands of a master. Then the designs are all his own, a little curious and surprising at first, like all painting outside the conventions, then attracting and holding, finally absorbing the attention and exciting to almost a higher degree than any other painter that interest in and appreciation of Japanese art which are scarcely enjoyed by the most refined collector until some probationary period has been passed in acquiring the powers of analysis and synthesis, the science of form, and the combinations of decoration which Japan, which Korin, reveals. The Western world is quickly learning.

Korin's lacquer attains a high value in his own country. In the proper place it is dealt with more at length. It is only necessary to remark that the same full brush is used on the lacquer designs with equal or higher skill. Kenzan, the most celebrated potter in Japan after Ninsei, was the younger brother of Korin, whose methods he copied. I have read that Korin was the younger brother of Kenzan; the former was born in 1661, the latter in 1663. The lacquer of the former, and the pottery of the latter, both of them painters!-This appears strange to us, because aptitude is usually expressed by our artists in one direction; with the Japanese, painting appears to have been the main stem from which branches spread in other directions, giving to the whole a general unity which I have remarked in no other nation's work.

Ritsuo, also a distinguished painter, was a rival of Korin in that form of decoration in which incrustations were employed on the lacquer, a process of striking ingenuity, strange indeed to Europeans, but of the highest interest and value to his fellow countrymen, amongst whom there is a greater demand for this lacquer than for another unusual product from the same hands, that is, pottery in figures and other pieces, painted and lacquered. Ritsuo died in 1747, with the reputation of one of the great artists of Japan.

It is quite probable that the relation of these artists to lacquer was confined to drawing the designs for it, with possibly some supervision over the work of the craftsmen. So far as I can gatherâ and I make the statement with all submissionâ the artificers were and are uneducated working men possessed of great manual skill. One writer stated that his head workman, a highly skilled artisan over fifty years of age, hardly knew the name of a single article he used.

t(As painters, TCoftt. su. flforin. aad others gave some time aad teaching specially to designs for lacquer, and these designs were executed by men trained to the work of lacquering!" It has, however, become a fashion to ascribe the actual lacquer to the designer, that I noted particularly the lacquer at the White City, where I found in many cases " Design by Korin," " Design by Koetsu," " Design by Kwansai," and other artists, which indicates that the Japanese themselves regard the design by the painter at its proper value. These remarks are interposed in this place because Koetsu and Korin appear amongst the famous masters whose ordinary painting of pictures was accompanied by a special art of design for lacquer and other objects upon which their signatures appear as the designers. Of the actual handicraft they might have been as ignorant as the designers of colour-prints were of engraving. But after this digression we will return to the painters.

The glories of the reign of the great Chinese Emperor Kang-he led a Japanese writer of the eighteenth century to remark: " Our painting is the flower, that of China is the fruit in its maturity." Evidently something of this was in the mind of the governing Shogun, still a Tokugawa, when he invited a Chinese named Namping to reside at Nagasaki in 1720, where his school met with great success. One great writer says that Namping's manner was that of the good painters of the Yung-ching period. This cannot be correct, for Yung-ching began to reign in 1722. However, the new master, whose paintings reached Europe, carried by the Dutch, was regarded there as the representative painter of the Japanese school, whereas he appears to have repeated the usual Chinese landscapes with finely drawn outlines and figures, and the birds and flowers with brilliant colours.

Some of the pupils of Namping have acquired a great nameâ Yushi, who popularised his master's style, and Sho-siseiki of Yedo, the latter being classed amongst the most distinguished men of his time. He lived to 1774. The end of the eighteenth century was signalised by the advent of so many artists that it is impossible to name them all; the chief masters only will be quoted.

The Kano school gave one more master to fame. We have seen the Tosa school lose itself in the painting of mere pretti-ness, in flowers such as the chrysanthemum, peony, camelia, and all the wealth of prunus and cherry blossom which a smiling, fertile land can produce, and now Yosen; and his son Issen appear as representatives of the Kano. Yosen died in 1808, but not before he had placed his name upon the roll of honourâ the last of the great Kano. As a landscape painter working in water-colours, his talent has been duly recognised. Like some of our English water-colourists, he used only a grey ground washed with soft tints, which were almost neutral in those subjects for which he was famous, such as a peasant mounted on an ox returning homewards on a dreary, cold winter's day. The mist which covers the distant plain is creeping over the foreground, over the rice-fields inundated with water, over the hedges of bamboo; the struggling moon-beams scarcely penetrate the watery veil of vapour; the wind scarcely bends the branches of the weeping willow. Yosen was a poet-painter whose dainty drawing showed, if not linear perspective, the greatest ability in rendering distance, which secured very nearly the same results. The Shogun conferred upon him the title of Hohin, and when he passed away, at the age of fifty-six, the Kano school, whose fortunes we have followed, ceased to exercise the power which had so long operated for the promotion of the best success of art. Still, both of these old classical schools have continued their existence to our own times.

Gekkei, better known as Goshin, was a member of the Katsumura family, which we shall meet again in Shunsho. His master was Buson, painter and poet, apparently also " an absent-minded beggar' who one day, wishing to admire the beautiful effect of the moonlight, made a hole in the thatched roof of his house by means of a lighted candle, and started a fire which burnt down a whole district in Kyoto. Buson's works are rare and highly valued because of their poetical sentiment. Goshin, born in 1641, was a deep student of the cider masters of the three preceding centuries, and the results of his studies were seen in the foundation of an independent schoolâ the modern school of Shijoâ which was entirely Japanese, borrowing nothing from China, and distinguished from the Yedo school by its extreme elegance, its harmonious colouring, and artistic composition, as well as its perfect finish. Okio, whose school was of equal importance to that of Goshin, and slightly anterior, had made so great a reputation that Goshin wished to become his pupil. " I can be your friend," responded Okio, " but not your master. Of Okie's teaching more will be said.

Goshin had influenced by his school, and even more by his manner, a number of artists of remarkable talent, whose paintings mark the last of the culminating points of the expansion of art in Nippon, when for half a century its supremacy remained undisputed.

The Torii school was founded by Torii, a pupil of Goshin. He was an eminent artist, in whose works were exhibited all the qualities of powerful expression and exactitude of design combined with wonderful dexterity and sweet harmony of soft colour. For instance, his pictures of deer and of tigers leave one in doubt whether the painting of the skin, the superb movement of the animal, or the finish of such ieatures as the eye, deserves most admiration where all is refined and full of grace. See Kiyonobu, pages 354-5.

There is no doubt that, to the European not fully familiar with native feeling as expressed by the Japanese, the manner of Goshin makes an appeal which, at least at the beginning, is more attractive than that of any other painter, though a host of artists possessed at this period the power of expression by strokes of the brush, instinct with life, charming with colour, breathing with harmony. These masters are worthy of recognitionâ indeed, in their own country the cultured classes collect their works with ardour; but it is to Goshin, whose other name was Yensan, and, also, to Okio, that this progress was made, and also, in some measure, to the further crystallisation which was yet to come.

Okio, born at Kyoto, lived from 1732 to 1795. He was one of the most distinguished exponents of the modern school, by his paintings as well as by his teaching, helping to form the new style which threw aside many of the old formal rules and perfected its methods by direct inspiration from nature-study. The elegance of design in brushwork of exquisite delicacy and power is no less wonderful than the mastery of colour. Okio had two distinct manners. The first was the outcome of his study of the old masters, and upon this much of his reputation was founded. He was an arduous student, who began painting as the decorator of a theatre; the pupil, afterwards, of Nimping, he learnt the traditions of the Chinese academic system and, before settling down, made a journey across Japan, which spread his name to the most distant places. The second manner was that modern one of which we have spoken. He loved to paint the birds, flowers, and fishes. His landscapes were no less delightful, finished with the precision of a miniature; and yet there was another Okio, in a third mannerâ a bold one, large and flexible, but very uncommon. All his pictures are rare and dear, the kakemonos excessively so.

Ippo of Kyoto was a pupil of Okio, who, though showing less charming work and less power of invention, manifested much more energy and freedom in design. He painted in Japanese ink, obtaining the most satisfying effects with a minimum of effort, using the simplest means to depict nature in all her ways, realising sentiment and poetic inspiration as an impressionist. With a few vigorous touches he would paint a stork sleeping amongst the branches of a great old pine, or a house on a mountain side under the snow, with the smoke from the chimney fading away in the winter sky. What does the eye require more than this? Nothingâ the effect is there!

Sosen was a celebrated animal painter, who died in 1821, at the age of seventy-four. Mori was his family name, and by this he was known until Sosen was added, and towards the end of his life Sosen alone was used, though he had other namesâ Morikata and Shikuga. Sosen means the " monkey saint " and indicates the direction of his studies from nature. It is said that he acquired little by little the manners, movements, almost the natural appearance, of the monkeys, which he studied in the forests near Osaka for months at a time, living upon roots and fruits. Never has any artist painted these animals with the spirit and knowledge shown by Sosen, they are vibrating with animationâ not the monkeys only, but the deer and the tigers, and even the rats.

Subjects such as two rats dragging a shell, a deer browsing amongst the flowering plants, a tiger at his toilet or stalking his prey, are rendered with a fidelity which no painter in the world has excelled. But, like all of the artists whose works are renowned, and therefore in demand, monkeys and other animals have in their thousands claimed to be the creatures of Sosen. His works are rare and the qualities of the master so marked in them as to be above imitation. There is always a difference between the work done by the hand with the guidance of the brain, and that done with the guidance only of the eye. " Never take two strokes where one will do," might have been his motto, so certain are his contours, so severe his designs in black as a rule. English, American, and Japanese, these three peoples pay large prices for the genuine paintings by the sennin des singes.

Passing onwards to the end of the eighteenth century, we shall consider the popular school and its exponents; but first a few of the many artists who were not of that school remain to be briefly noted, amongst whom is Tani Buncho of Yedo (Tokyo), whose style was formed on studying the works of Sesshu and Tannyu. He became the painter in ordinary to a Tokugawa prince, Sayasou, the protector of art at this period, and, moreover, he directed the publication of the " History of Art," the immense " Shoko Jisshu." He died in 1841, three years after the celebrated Gan-Ku passed away. Gan-Ku was a noted painter of animals, birds, and flowers, who died in 1838.

The masters of the impressionist schoolâ Shokwado, Sotatsu, and Korinâ left another distinguished painter to follow in their steps, and finally to share their fame. This was Hoitsu, who in his own country is considered as expressing in a supreme degree the conception of art purely Japanese, although nothing is more opposed to European conventional ideas. His original designs in the softest and most delicate water-colours evince certain qualities which, drawn from a close contact with nature, idealise the scenes they depict. They may repel at first, but when knowledge opens the gate of understanding their attraction is irresistible; scoffers have jeered at originality from the beginning, and will continue for all time, but the attitude of the receptive student is that of a seeker after truth. Hoitsu passed away in 1828, but not before he had rendered a great service to the art world by the publication of several volumes of Korin's designs for the decoration of lacquer, the supervision of which he himself undertook. Some of his work at the White City, such as spring and autumn flowers, showed evidences of wonderful skill.

At the end of the eighteenth century the followers of the Ukiyo-ye art, painters of scenes from ordinary common life, became prominent. Iwasa Matabei, the first master of this style from the end of the sixteenth century to the middle of the seventeenth, laid the foundations upon which Hishi-kawa Moronobu (1638-1714) carried on extended operations, aided by the introduction of printing from engraved woodblocks. The early prints were printed in black, afterwards in colour. From this time onwards nearly all of the artists of this school are associated with colour-prints. In some instances the painter's reputation culminates in a mechanical

SAitu HASHI (MONKEY BRIDGE).

Print sold for Â 91 in June 1909. From the collection of Mr. J. S. Happer.

YEISEN.

NI MAI TATE (MOONLIGHT GORGE).

Print sold for Â 84 in April 1909. From the

Happer Collection; now in the possession of

Otto Fehling, Esq.

process in which he had no share, being a designer only, whose signature adorned the print.

Some artists had more than one signature. Hokusai, the marvellous old painter whose history and work are so attractive, had many. " In these pages," said a friend to me the other day, " is nothing but Hokusai, his works, and his signatures." I came to the conclusion that he had sufficient matter for an important monograph, and that it could be treated in no other way.

In this section I shall touch lightly upon a few of the artists of the Ukiyo-ye school, if that expresses its art better than system or style. Really their work was genre painting, with landscape and portrait painting in some instances. Judging, as you will be able to, from the sale-prices, amongst the most popular artists was Suzuki Harunobu (1718-70), whose bold, graceful contours are accompanied by delightful colour schemes. The designs of Kiyonobu are full of energy and nobility of style; those of Chosun distinguished by delicacy and power.

Sukenobu, who was a prolific artist, delighted in the teahouses of Yedo (Tokyo), and painted the courtesans of the Yoshiwara quarter, where those houses were situated. Upon kakemono, album, and screen he depicted beauties viewing chrysanthemums, cherry blossoms and, all those things which the artists of his time vied with each other in painting. But we leave the individual for the moment, and come to the schools, the families, or studios which produced painters.

The school of Katsugawa is credited with a number of print-designers of great ability, and two or three painters of the first rank. It is easy to remember that the pupil whom his master wished to distinguish received a part of his name. Katsugawa Shunsho (1726-92) had many pupils thus favoured; Shun-ko and Shun-ei may be mentioned. The one exception in Shunman of Kubo. A similar method applied to the Torii school gives Kiyo as the prefix, though Kiyochita of Kobayashi and Kondo Kiyoharu are exceptions.

Shunsho though a refined and able painter devoted much lime and attention to designs for coloured prints which were engraved. These prints for a short time were the monopoly of this school; all those selections of scenes from the theatre, or from the sumptuous homes, of magnificent landscapes, of figures of actors and courtesans came from the Katsugawa school. In colouring sober at first, shaded with full dull tones of red and green, brown violet and black, they were, little by little, enriched with all the tints of the palette until they approached excess. Every print had, from the commencement of the process, lines, contours, and colours reproduced from the original work in the school where the latter was drawn. It follows, therefore, that an active establishment would find scope for many artists, and at Katsugawa not a few became famous. Shunsho lived from 1724 to 1792, and upon him rests most of the glory of the great school which, however, was not without rivals, nor was he free from the close emulation of his pupils, Shunjo, Shunzan, Shun-ei, and others, painters and colourists, designers for prints.

Those of his contemporariesâ Toyoharu, Yeishi, Kiyonaga, for instanceâ who equalled or excelled him by the superior charm of colour or of life, by the grace and elegance of their design, failed to compete with his style, which was of extraordinary strength. Toyoharu was particularly appreciated in Japan, where collectors still treasure specimens from his brush, such as pictures on silkâ miniatures painted with numerous small figures grouped with much taste and with technical perfection, coloured, with strong reds, warm greens, and soft violets, producing effects which are most attractive.

The artists of the Ukiyo-ye school were painters, but most of them devoted themselves to the work of designing subjects for colour-prints. That section will contain further information about them, and it will deal with the sale-prices of their works. May I here point out two things which appear to have been overlooked: first, that the artist's work was confined to supplying the design, he had nothing to do with the colour-printingâ I am not sure that he revised the proof prints; second, that the engraver and printer were skilled artisans, whose names are never taken into consideration, although the publishers often affixed their seals to the artist's work. It is

HOKKEI.

HOKUJIU (SHOTEl). 8l true that a few names of engravers come to us from the colour-printers of the Osaka school, together with those of a few printers. Yet, considering that in the West the engraver of a print is all-important, it seems curious that no notice was taken of him in the East, and that his credit is lost in that of the painterâ that is, the print-designer.

This introduces the subject of colour-prints, in which much further information is given about the painters of the Ukiyo-ye school and their designs, which will be considered in a later chapter.

The last hundred years have modified the art of Japan, and though the artist's power of invention compares favourably with that manifested by the Chinese, it is impossible to foresee the direction in which it will trend. The history of the past shows how great has been the nation's individuality both in motives and treatment, and an attempt has been made in this section of painting to show that the relation between it and the kindred arts is largely responsible for the unity displayed.

Generally, we may review Japanese painting under several headings, such as drawing, colouring, composition, light and shade, and perspective, but we must remember that the East is East and that canons of art applicable to the East are not accepted by the West. First then, the drawing, purity of outline, and certainty of touch are indispensable, details purely a matter of taste, but over-crowding is not excusable. In these respects the masters of Japan excel, though we may regard single lines as poor means of expressing so many qualities. The composition concentres the attention upon a few objects, to which the remainder of the picture is purely subordinate, and the colouring is unusually soft and harmonious, though flat. Light and shade are absent; on most paintings where they are used in half-tones the idea is to express the image of some person upon a screen. Perspective is usually absentâ that is, linear perspective, which treats some point in the picture as a converging focus for parallel lines. It is evident that sizes, in a landscape for example, can only be represented by comparisons with some object or objects of known magnitude. Hence distance is rendered by a relative diminution of size, and in this the Japanese excel.

The early and classical schools illustrated the literature of the nation; writing was an elegant accomplishment, and painting was akin to it. The poets of the period wrote their verses and often with the same brush drew the picture of the scene that inspired them, or they drew a picture, and in a poem upon the same sheet they described it. Painting only in the later times became a special profession; constant mention is made of painters who were engaged in other art work in which literature held a pre-eminent position. In Western art the number of cultured artists who have sought inspiration from literature is limited; nature has amongst them its most devoted disciples. I wonder how many eminent painters would endorse Ruskin's opinion:

"The study of Literature, as such, is quite useless to an artist; but the knowledge of history and the affectionate and faithful study of noble books is essentialâ as to greatness of character, so to dignity of Art. But, to goodness of art at all, a sympathy with your fellow creatures and a love of nature, which will often compel you to forgo all other effort, are indispensableâ if you find a joy in the fields which prevents you from reading, it is better than all the books."

THE art which lives is embodied in the old bronzes of Japan. These contrast vividly with those of Occidental lands, but resemble those of China closely, those of India and of Tibet not so closely, except in the images, where the influence of Buddhism affected those countries. Two pro-cesses, the modelling and the casting, each presented their special points of difficulty, but on examining the finished result it is noticeable that if the artist made difficulties by intricate designs, the casting removed them; it is seldom indeed that a fault can be traced, seldom that any after-correction can be seen. The Chinese worked in bronze at a period long anterior to its advent into Japan, for Shintoism had no place in its worship for images; but when Buddhism and Taoism brought gods and goddesses, fabulous animals and demons, in their train, they brought in all probability the artists who could make them in bronze, which, unlike porcelain in China, was free from the restrictions of an exclusive Imperial patronage.

As in the West so in the East, a multitude of objects were made in bronze for the use of the temple and of the home. Amongst them we find vases and koros of all sizes, jardinieres, temple lanterns and candlesticks, animal groups and figures, many of them designed as incense-burners, figures of gods, temple mirrors and bells, tea and water pots, boxes of all sizes, salvers, ornaments of many kinds, chimeras, dragons, beakers, masks, fans, kiseru, midzuire, students' brush-pots, hibachi, door-fastenings (hikite), hand-mirrors, charcoal-braziers, okimonos, and other objects.

The extent to which the Japanese carried the art of working in bronze is not the least remarkable feature of an industry whose products spread to every nook and corner of the Empire. From the list of them just given it will be seen that the temples absorbed large numbers of statues, bells, and other objects used in ceremonial worship, fine examples of which may be seen in the Victoria and Albert Museum. The bells were inscribed with prayers or sayings which, when the bells were sounded, were sent out through the air as the very utterances of the religion itself. The statues, the embodiment of that religion, were often of great size. One at the Museum is a representative of a Boddhisattva, a being whose final reincarnation only was requisite before the attainment of the highest state, the Nirvana. The calm attitude of perfect repose, the inscrutable smile, the traditional position of the hands, are indicative of qualities and powers necessary to that end. It is of great size, 10 feet 8 inches in height and 6 feet 6 inches in width at the base, cast hollow, and having a small door at the back, large enough to admit a man. With the exception of the head and base, which were cast separately, the figure is in one piece, and the metal is never very thick. Indeed, it shows all the signs of age, being a figure of great interest; also it deserves mention for its workmanship.

Compared with the colossal bronze, the largest in the world, in the temple of the great Buddha at Nara, the English bronze is a mere pigmy in size. Its height is 50 feet, circumference 96 feet. The face measures 8 feet 6 inches from top to bottom, the eyes are 4 feet in length, the thumb 3 feet in circumference! It was cast in several pieces. In A. D. 745

PRICKET CANDLESTICK IN BRONZE.

it was brought to Nara, where eight years later a temple, the Temple Daiboutsu (of the great Buddha) was built to receive it.

The pose of the statue is the same as that already spoken of, the habitual attitude of the Buddhas and Boddhisattvas. Seated upon a flower symbolising the lotus, lost in absolute contemplation, they resemble each other so closely that the single name Buddha is often applied to the class, which really consists of three divisions, the Buddha supreme, Dai-Niti-

BRONZE JARDINIERE WITH IMITATION BAMBOO DECORATION.

Niorai being the first. Next to him, and surrounding him in the Mandara or complete assembly of the gods, are eight other Buddhas, human beings deified, personifying the qualities or virtues of Dai-Niti. These won their places by the exercise of constant self-sacrifice and charity, and by the acquisition of knowledge and wisdom. Ever then they stand as emanations of the Buddha eternal, emanations of the first degree, the most powerful and the most perfect.

Four of them take precedence of the others, and these four are Ashikou, the faith; Ho-sho, perfection of conduct; Amida, worshipped in China as Amitabha, teaching and guid-

OLD JAPANESE BRONZEâ GOKEI MONJU BOSATSU (MAJUSRI) SEATED ON A LION, SUPPORTED UPON A LOTUS FLOWER, ON THE BUDS OF WHICH ARE ATTENDANTS.

ing; Foukou-djo-djou, active charity and love to others. Four Boddhisattvasâ Kon-go-s'att'a, Kon-go-go, Kon-go-hon, and Kon-go-hoâ rank next. In Buddhist sectarianism other ranks are given.

Another group contains other Boddhisattvas, whose penultimate existence was devoted to leading men onwards to goodness and virtue by good counsels, good examples, exhortations, science, and eloquence. Among these, Hannia represents the law, Mirokou the future Buddha, Kwannon

INCENSE-BURNER IN RED BRONZE ENCRUSTED WITH GOLD, IN THE FORM OF A MANDARIN DUCK.

charity and divine grace, Mondju knowledge, and Fugen the supreme intelligence.

Amongst the retrospective sculpture brought to the White City for exhibition in 1910 were bronze images of Buddha and Kwannon, some of which were lent by the Imperial Household, but the weight of such large objects prevented a representative display. They represented the benign influence of religion. In fact, neither in wood nor bronze were there any of the fearful representations of the gods. They were not sent. Buddha and Kwannon! Religion and love I

The influence of other agentsâ or should it be other influences of the same agent?â dealt with fear, fear of death and future punishment. Five personages represent the transformation of the Buddhas into demons or genii who had power to inflict severe punishments in this life and after. The chief of these demons or genii, tembou or mio-ho, were Foudo mio-ho, the incarnation of Dai-Niti; Gosanze, representing Foukou-djo-djou; Dai-Itokou, mounted on a bull, the incarnation of Amida; Kon-go-ya-sha of Ashikou; and Goun-dari of Ho-sho. From this conception it will be gathered that the demons were neither the enemies nor the opponents of Buddha, rather were they auxiliaries working through different channels and instruments for the salvation of mankind.

Other statues or statuettes included the four guardians of the cardinal points with their distinctive coloration: Bishamon, the North, in blue; Koo-mokou, the South, in red; Dji-kokou, the West, in green; and Soo-tcho, the East, in flesh-colour.

In all of these figures the position of the hands indicates the work that is being carried on, each gesture showing an act; so meditation is designed by the folded hands in the lap, often wrapped in the robe, the right hand raised indicates teaching, and there are many other " mudras " or mystical positions which, though not familiar, have an attraction for the student.

Shintoism is a naturalist religion addressing itself chiefly to the sun under the name of Amaterasu, the magnificent daughter of Izan-gi and Izanami, from whom the Emperors of Japan claim descent. A world of mythical story revolves around those early beings, stories which the children learn at their mother's knee, inspirations which permeated the old life of Japan, even when the Shoguns usurped the rights of the Emperors, and which are the basis of Japan's power to-day; butâ and this must be insisted uponâ Shintoism had no place for idols: the only bronzes used in the ceremonial worship appear to have been a polished mirror, symbol of the creation; the sun rising over the waves; torii, models of the temple-gates, furnished with lanterns; incense-burners; and bells.

Having indicated that Buddhism and its worship, its deities and demons, its temple utensils of all kinds, from lanterns in the gardens to the koros or incense-burners, exerted great influence on the bronze-work of Japan, it is only necessary to state that in the early ages the examples of such work executed for the laity are rare. Even the pots and pans appear to have gravitated towards the temples, to be preserved amongst the treasures, to be used in the ceremonies, to be admired and kept with the same care which was bestowed upon those collected into the treasure-house of the Mikado at Nara. The Mikado was the Emperor in forced retirement. He was the head of the religious life, nayâ he was a religion!

The most famous names of the eighteenth century, Seimin, Toun, Teijio, Keisai, Jiouguiokou, Somin, Seifou, Tokousai, and Nakoushi, have received better appreciation in the market than the classical productions of earlier times, probably because collectors have not yet realised their qualitiesâ the excellence of the designing and the casting, the skill of hammer, burin, and chisel, the beautiful patina, so varied with the alloys. Natural chemical processes or long burial in the ground affect these patinse forming the crust of decomposing metal, a rust which may be veined with tints of red, malachite green, and turquoise, a crystalline coating which, though a valuable test of age and authenticity, may be counterfeited. But by scraping the surface with a knife, or by boiling the object in water, the fraud may easily be discovered, being generally only wax artificially coloured, varying, it may be, in hardness. Probably the chemist could secure a rust by chemical action, but the process does not appear successful at present. The artist whose name stands first is Seimin, who excelled

BRONZE PRICKET CANDLESTICK.

in modelling the tortoise, and who has long received the devoted attention of the fraudulent copyist. Yet the fraud is less than nothing to the work of the master, whose reptiles are so life-like that it has been said that such perfection could only be obtained by moulding from the living animal; but the Japanese, until recently, practised moulding but little, and, moreover, Seimin has fixed in wax with thumb, burin, and chisel, so many groupings and attitudes, such movements and such life that moulding could never secure; only the skill and sureness of hand and eye, only the genius of a master had the power to embody in bronze such faithful imitations, of course

GROUP OF TORTOISES IN BRONZE, BY SEIMIN.

with nature as a guide, as the original pattern. The vases and the koros by this artist are highly valued, but his tortoises have earned him the curious title, "the Michael-Angelo of tortoises."

Another artist, Toun, a celebrated painter of the Kano school who lived from 1625 to 1694, has received the name of " the creator of soft bronze," which was capable of decoration in open-work. Thus, in decorating such an object as an incense-burner or koro it would be exceedingly difficult, though not impossible, to leave such narrow spaces as would convert high relief into open-work, and at the same time it would be comparatively easy to carve in soft bronze the requisite openwork. For the incense-burner enfolded in the contortions of a dragon as decoration, the head with open jaws, the three-clawed feet, and the adherent folds of the body, the cire perdue process of casting would suffice, and for the open-work folds the carving would be just the same as if the material were wood. The soft bronze would facilitate the process, nothing more; the Japanese carved and pierced the hard stones! Soft bronze was carved!

The patina, the curious and interesting green rust adhering to old bronzes, the cerugo nobilihs, is no less distinctive in the

INCENSE-BURNER IN BRONZE IN THE FORM OF A GOOSE. I7TH CENTURY.

early work of Japan than in that of Europe. The connoisseur revels in the patine, which, like the slow change of tone in china and pictures, can only be copied with the poorest results. The old bronzes of Japan of archaic form have a patina which may be easily distinguished from that of the seventeenth-century work, but such fine distinctions are difficult of explanation in the absence of the object-lesson. It may, however, be noted that the bronzes of the latter period have three qualities which may be applied as tests: first, there is the severe style; second, the strong, sober, and restrained execution; and lastly, the patina which is a dull blackâ patine noire un peu mate.

Although the eighteenth-century and later bronzes have a merit which cannot be denied, the seventeenth century was

BRONZE INCENSE-BURNER IN THE FORM OF A QUAIL. I8TH CENTURY.

the golden age of bronze, when, under the third feudal prince of Tokugawa, the great renaissance furnished Buddhism with sacred utensils of all kinds, of the purest designs, in sober harmony, executed with a decision and elegance without equal. The bronze-workers did more, for, although it is said that in the modelling of the feet and hands the artists of Nippon failed somewhat in their treatment of the human figure, this fault cannot be ascribed to the representations of animals, which may be placed in a class alone, above that of any other people, a class which in Japan includes all living animals, and many mythical ones, covered with the black patina, and sometimes, too, decorated with gold in delicate and effective touches.

During the eighteenth century the forms of the bronzes

JAPANESE BLACKSMITHS, AFTER HOKUSAI.

acquired new expression, in fact the effort to secure lifelike expression was responsible for the breaking down of the classical, severe style which had preceded the epoque in which wax-modellingâ the ceroplastic artâ and the process of casting, cire perdue, alike testified to the absolute skill and control of the metal-worker, whose alloys of copper and tin varied according to the use for which the article was designed. The style now became more florid, though at first this quality was restrained, and the interpretation of animals especially aimed only to give the illusion of life. Examples of this period, when Japan reached its maximum of production, are far more numerous than those of the earlier centuries, and indeed after the revolution of 1868, when commerce became free with Europe, the demand was equal to the supply, and prices accordingly were good; though again I must note that the Japanese art in bronze shares the temporary neglect, for the moment, which has been exhibited in its other branches.

"There is no worker in metal comparable to the Japanese," is an opinion we may not entirely accept; but when the varieties in size, from the largest giant figure to the smallest netsuke", are considered in connection with the varieties in form, when the certainty of the processes of modelling in wax and casting in clay are compared with the slight necessity for engraving and carving to complete those processes, and when we remember that the processes employed are and were similar to those used elsewhere, the conclusion is clear that the conscientious artistic Japanese of the old times suffer nothing by comparisons. So much cannot be said for the work of modern times.

The simplest old bronzes are the torii, small models of temple-gates which are placed at some distance from the temple itself. The sun was compared to a flying bird, and the torii formed a perch on which he could rest. This was a Shinto ornament. Buddhism had an elaborate ritual, and the temple vessels were numerousâ sacrificial wine vases and wine jars of large size, libation cups and wine vessels, some of which were on wheels so as to move easily over the altar, sacrificial crocks with covers for meat offerings, some of which had three legs resembling those of an ox, koros or incense-burners in many forms. Every temple had a bronze gong, which was struck with a wooden mallet to call the shippers to the frequent services.

The finest bronzes and the most beautiful carvings are in the temples, as well as the most extraordinary masks, which were used in the religious ceremonies, and these were not only in metal, but in wood and lacquer. I do not propose to devote much space to masks, although they have for the Japanese great interest and attraction owing to another use, not religious but theatrical, to which they were put in the roles of men or of women. Whereas the masks of the divinities, of the genii and the devils, were conventionally coloured with black, red, green, or gold, the actors' masks were imita-

MASK IN WOOD, BY D ME-JIOMAN.

tions of the human face, sometimes ornamented with eyebrows and beard in real hair. The eyes, mouth, and nostrils were pierced. The robes of the actor hid the cords by which the mask was attached. You will have noted the use of the word actor. All of the performers in the theatre were men who played women's partsâ a curious custom which prevailed in Europe for a long period. Exceptions were only occasionally permitted to the regular practice of men as actors, but in these later times the custom had fallen into desuetude; and such, too, has been the fate of the masks, only the use of these ceased at the end of the seventeenth century, when the models served as copies for the carver of netsukes.

The majority of the old masks were made of wood lacquered or painted, and the process reached its climax at the beginning of the same century when Dne'-Jioman demonstrated his power as a master of expression, giving to the mask wonderful force in revelations of hatred and amusement, in grimaces the most horrible, in faces the most charming. Here the Daimio shows a pale and languid countenance; there the young girl smiles sweetlyâ happy analogy, the flower of the prunus smiles; or the old poetess Komati, who died in misery and starvation in the midst of a swamp after having enjoyed a career as the most beautiful, most envied woman of Japan, displays to our eyes her hideous mummified skeleton face.

One can easily imagine how suitable and how striking these masks were, when an actor in costume, aided by distance and the illusion of the scene, by gesture and the movement of the players, personified some well-known celebrity, whose face was familiar to the people as a national inheritance. It is scarcely a wonder that these masks were prized by their owners, were wrapped in fukusas or squares of rich stuffs similar to those which enveloped the present which was sent to a friend, or the letter enclosed in a small lacquer box. The fukusa, however, was returned to the sender. Here, again, may be noted how the refinement of the Japanese extended to the smallest details; the fukusa around the mask was in harmony with it and with the lacquer box in which it was placed, even with the silk bag which contained the box. In fact, the most precious specimens of old silk are to be found in these envelopes, which were used for all treasures. They were not exposed in the rooms, in the Western style, but kept wrapped up and stowed away in the many drawers of the main room, or in a special go-down built for the purpose, to be produced at ceremonial functions or exhibited one at a time to favoured guests. Other pieces of these valuable old silks were used in the scabbards of swords, and in the frames of the kakemonos, which again were stored in a special cupboard, and shown two or three at a time, when occasion required, or changed when necessary, to suit season or ceremony.

The chapter on bronze would be incomplete without some mention of the elegant vases, etc., which were made of gold bronze or shakudo, and silver bronze or shibuichi. Decorated with gold lac, with mother-of-pearl, etc., inlaid with finely wrought silver and enamel, these vases are lovely, though they cannot claim great antiquity. They deserve the appreciation which is lavished upon them.

Shakudo is an alloy of bronze and gold, and shibuichi an alloy of bronze and silver; in both the proportion of the precious metal varies according to the effect which the metalworker wishes to produce. The shakudo has a peculiar qualityâ by pickling and boiling, it acquires a rich coat or patina of beautiful deep bluish violet, which takes an exquisite polish. The shibuichi assumes a remarkable silver grey tone. The gold alloy consists of about 95 per cent copper, i J to 4 of gold, i to ij of silver, and traces of lead, iron, and arsenic. It possesses the curious quality of recovering its patina when worn out; if it is handled, the moisture of the hands and the atmospheric oxidation bring the colour back. The silver alloy contains from 50 to 70 per cent of copper, from 30 to 50 of silver, with traces of other metals. Shibuichi means one-fourth, so the amount of silver may be set down as a quarter of the whole alloy.

These two metals were essentially adapted for incrustation or for inlaying. Nothing looks richer than shakudo associated with relief designs in gold, silver, mother-of-pearl, or with enamels. Some of this decoration was applied by firing in the enamel-kiln, some was soldered, but the main part of the decoration was performed without the aid of fire by means of the burin and hammer. The incrustation was set in reserves cut out, having the edges slightly re-entering, so that no THE ABC OF JAPANESE ART it could be fixed and held by hammering, just as the panes are held in leaded windows; the other effects were produced by the graving-tool, and by the polisher.

The workmanship is usually so fine that the joinings cannot be seen, even with the aid of a magnifying-glass.

From the variation in the alloys various tones of colour were derived. The shakudo has a range of golden greens,

STAND, IN CARVED SILVER.

yellows, and reds of which the Japanese made wonderful use; no nation has ever treated the patina so effectively. The pickling process was either hot or cold, and the pickle itself consisted largely of verdigris and copper in water or in vinegar, to which, for some patina, nitre, common salt, and sulphur were added. Mokume, or wood grain, was also produced by an ingenious process. Thin sheets of metal were soldered together in layers of different colour, and conical holes or trenchlike cuts were made to remove some portions of the mass, which was then hammered until the holes disappeared, and were replaced by irregular bands or veins producing the effect of wood-graining.

THE policy which Japan followed for so many centuries of closing her ports to intruders and, in later years, to all but the Dutch, would have been fatal to her art industries if her supplies of minerals at home had been less than sufficient. Fortunately, they were so abundant as to meet all needs: gold was plentiful as silver, and no more valuable; lead, tin, antimony, abounded; alloys were common. The value of the precious metals had one effect upon the metal-work which had anciently been applied, even to articles of daily use, an effect which has led to their destructionâ they have been melted down.

Fortunately, carved work in wood and ivory has escaped this evil fate, and in this branch of art the Japanese sculptor â or, is he a carver?â was superior to the Chinese, though in hard stones jade, agate, etc., he remained inferior. The dignity and the grace of the Chinese have an added quality in Nippon; it has vitality. That is its great charm to-day. The expressionâ dignity and reserve where necessary; terror, even horror, in evil genii; beauty in Kwannon and Benten, divinities and types, fun in gods, men, and animalsâ is beyond any art of any other people. All this applies to the class we shall now considerâ the netsukes.

If you ever visit the Musee Guimet at Paris, you will be vividly impressed with the pervading influence of religion over art, especially in the early ages. This is true of all art everywhere. And it applies with great force to Japan, where, in 1614, a law was made by Hidetada that every house should set up the image of some deity. The idol-makers were kept busy, and the quality of their work reached a high level.

When the demand naturally ceased, and when every house had its miniature god, most of the craftsmen who had revelled in unwonted activity found themselves out of occupation. It was then that they turned their attention to the piece of wood or ivory which, slipped through the belt, held the tobacco case and pouch or the medicine case safely suspended. Tobacco was at that time a new luxury, but one destined to fold in its embrace the nation, men and women. So from the simple lump of wood or ivory grew the netsuke", which was an ornament through which the cords or chains of the pouches, etc., were fastened for the purpose of suspension at the belt. It is perhaps just necessary to put stress on this, because some people persist in giving the name netsuke" to any small carved figure. If the attachment can be tied through pierced work in such small figures, they may be, but if there are two special holes for the purpose, they are,

WOODEN STATUE OF BISHAMON, THE GOD OF RICHES.

netsuke"s. Then in a moment it will be noticed that, as an article of adornment of daily use, the netsuke" or toggle, made to keep the ends of the suspensory cords from slipping through the belt, would naturally be free from awkward corners or points which would catch in the dress or break off.

Scarcely any single Japanese object has excited keener interest amongst collectors of Oriental curios than these precious net-suk6s, which are getting very scarce, especially the old ones which can be identified by the marks of rubbing, not only where the cord has passed through the holes, but the results of the friction caused by constant use. The oldest are the wood ones, and these are most valued, as the wood, generally the core of the cherry-tree, acquires a rich, warm brown tone, which is one of its chief charms. I have three before me of wonderful workmanship and expression. One is an old monkey, whose four paws hold a flattened fruit, whilst he bends forward in the attitude of sleep. Another shows a small monkey mounted on its mother's back, with paw outstretched for the nut which she holds tightly in her two fore-paws. The expectant expression of the open-mouthed little one is in marked contrast to the indifference of its mother. In both, the hair on the skin and all the other details are remarkable. The third is a curious man who has just taken a rat from a trap, and its execution is no less extraordinaryâ the animal, though tiny, is life-like.

CARVED FIGURE IN WOODâ THE DEVIL AS A BUDDHIST MONK. I7TH CENTURY.

The artists have made netsukes of all materials and of all forms. I have two others in white porcelain of " Daruma in contemplation' but they are much more valuable when carved in jade, onyx, or crystal. Ivory was one of those

OKIMONO IN IRON, INLAID.

substances which were imported; walrus tusks, and those of the boar, and smaller teeth of animals were used, but it was not before the eighteenth century that elephants' tusks in any quantity were imported, and these were used chiefly for okimonos â alcove ornamentsâ 'figures which, being small, evi- dently are not netsukes, or, large, come in a different class. It may be well to warn young collectors, those who are beginning to take an interest in ivory carvings, that both netsukes and okimonos are produced even now in immense numbers; that they are rubbed and coloured to give an appearance of

VASE CARVED IN WOOD, BY MINKOKU.

age; that they imitate the old forms, which were seldom or never duplicated by the old carvers, whose designs were original, and as varied as are the figures in the old gargoyles and hinged misereres in our cathedrals.

In the old ivory carvings the Japanese employed the very best ivory, having that rich milky tone which time gives as a kind of patina, a soft yellow which the eye easily learns to distinguish from the coffee-stained reproduction which a rub will often remove. At the same time it is not well to assume that all ivory figures up to the height of six inches are netsuke"s. The evidences will be found wrought in the material by use. If some of the quaint unsigned figures show that they have been used by suspended cords, the

THE BEARERS OF THE BELL IN CARVED WOOD. I7TH CENTURY.

corresponding parts on the opposite side must show evidences of rubbing, unless, as rarely happened, they were unused. The pipe was a necessary adjunct of the daily life; a small bowl, a long stem, meant a short smoke, but put no limit to its frequencyâ in fact I have seen a Japanese picture of a woman smoking in bed! The collector will perforce be compelled to rely upon his own judgment in the collection of netsukes, and again the watchword, caution, must be linked with anotherâ handle all you can. In no branch of curios is the necessity for handling more obvious than in this, where the best book cannot indicate the points which demonstrate age as effectively as can the careful inspection of genuine old pieces and comparison between them and others. Look for colour, look for signs of wear, look for careful yet bold design and execution, and at the beginning limit yourself to the price you are prepared to pay for the lessons which experience only can teach. But do not expect to enter this arena in the hope of beating the skilled practitioner, unless by a careful preparation you are fully equipped for the contest. After a certain point you will rely upon your own judgment.

Turning to the history of netsuk6s and their makers, Mr. Anderson's remarks form a fitting introduction: " The designs of the netsuke-carvers embrace the whole range of Japanese motives, and the artist tells his story with the utmost lucidity. Nothing is safe from his humour, except, perhaps, the official powers that be, of whom the Japanese citizen has a salutary dread. Religion, history, folk-lore, novels, incidents of daily life, all provide material for his tools, and his subjects are mostly treated in a comic or even flippant vein. The pious Dharma, aroused from his nine

CARVED WOOD STATUE OF BUDDHA.

years motionless contemplation by the attentions of an obtrusive rat who ventures to nibble the saintly ear, is made to assume an expression suggestive of the strongest equivalent for swearing, of which we may suppose a good Buddhist to be capable. The Thunder God is seen extracting the storm-cloud from the basket that gives it stowage-room in idle days of sunshine. An inquisitive bird has unwarily inserted his long beak between the valves of a giant clam whose gaping shell had invited the incautious search after the unknown, and now, with straining thighs and flapping wings, struggles vainly to regain his liberty. An expectant domestic party surround a fish-kettle, while the head of the family triumphantly extracts a carp of tempting proportions, but the averted heads, disgusted faces, and finger-tweaked noses of the hungry group eloquently proclaim the central idea of Buddhismâ the impermanency of all things and the vanity of human wishes. Such examples might be multiplied without end." Netsukes, okimonos, and masks!

The use of masks was largely discontinued at the end of the seventeenth century, and the image-making consequent upon the enforcement of the law of 1614 had run its course. Mask-makers and image-makers found a new outlet for their industry in the netsuk6, which furnished full scope for their talents and developed into a special and separate craft in the eighteenth century. D6me-Jioman and the other mask-makers appear to have had some success in this new branch of art, though he excelled, as we have seen, in his representations of the human face, and indeed he has furnished examples for the artists of the present day. " Masks for ' No ' dance " were on view at the Japan-British Exhibition in lacquer-work. But the Japanese were catholic in their tastes regarding the precious netsukes, and made them in many forms from various materials, so that they may be found signed by Korin the painter-lacquerer, by Ritsuo, another celebrated painter, and by others. So, should you find a signed netsuke, it will be well, if the signature does not appear in the list given, to turn to the other lists of painters, lacquerers, and even potters.

Shunzan, at Nara, the city of temples, was one of the most famous of the netsuke-carvers about 1800. He worked in wood, for this material preceded and excelled the carvings in ivory. Towards the middle of the eighteenth century Miwa I., also at Nara, executed the most original designs of

SAKE BOTTLE CARVED FROM A BAMBOO ROOT. I7TH CENTURY.

figures and animals in miniature, endowing them with dramatic expression, influencing his contemporaries to an extraordinary degree by his masterly skill. Netsukes in wood by his hand are valuable, more so than those by his successors Miwa II. and Miwa III., whom we must regard as the makers of some of the earliest netsuke"s in ivory, and though there were other schools at Yedo and Kyoto, scarcely less successful, the pupils of the Miwas, such as Gamboun and Ikko, acquired

great reputations for the extraordinary fineness and quality of their handiwork, which forms such a contrast to the modern productions made for the outside market. The fine carving is of itself a test, because the old master, with loving touch, spent days and weeks in perfecting the design which was the creature of his brain. We are indeed far from knowing much abcut these older artists, but the signatures of many of them have been traced, and in time these will be a sure basis of classification.

The netsuk6 was created from almost any object upon which the eye of the artist dwelt; the gods and the philosophers, scenes of history and of the comical side of life, were present to the imagination, and therefore treated more in accord with acknowledged conventions; but in the flower and the plant, the bird, insect, and reptile, what the eye saw, the willing, skilful fingers translated and glorified with a patience passing belief, with no regard for time or money, with a success which astonishes us still. Six months, a year, what did that matter? the work would be finished in due time, for there was no shirking, only a devoted perseverance!

Many of the difficulties in securing satisfactory lists of these men come from their position and environment. Sheltered under the protection of some feudal prince, having no personal needs, no ambitions, the craftsman won his way steadily through life, content with little if only his master were pleased. Other arts such as embroidery, sword-making, and decoration, and lacquering, tell nothing about the men who did the work, from the same reasonâ they were merged in their clan. Throughout whichever side we examine, we find the number of independent artists, men who lifted themselves out of their class, who travelled and founded schools, who made themselves famous, is only a vcry small minority.

We may go further and say that the greatest part of our information has been obtained regarding those men who almost always signed their names upon their work, and sometimes dated it by marking the nengo in which it was completed.

Then comparison is unnecessary. When an occasional signature occurs, comparison becomes essential.

Hence has been determined the speciality of a few artists. Itshimin was noted for his ruminants, Tadatoshi for snails, Ikkuan for mice, Masanao for fowls, Masatami for rabbits, and so on. The later netsuke-makers adopted another principle. They copied one celebrated work all the time and did nothing else, or they borrowed designs from the prints of Hokusai and others. Now the Japanese have no use for such articles, yet still the manufacture goes merrily on; mechanical methods, added to ready sales at market prices, have reduced yet another art of Old Japan to a state which is worse than

POUCH ORNAMENT.

extinction, because it is a flaunting degradation of work which embodied much of that culture and spirit which, in time of sore need, stood the nation's test and triumphed.

On the opposite page are the signatures of the chief sculptors and carvers, commencing with the mask-maker whose works have been noticed: (i) Deme'-Jioman, (2) Shunzan, (3) Miwa, (4) Bokusai, (5) Gamboun, (6) Hidemasa, (7) Iccho, (8) Jugioku, (9) Kwaigioku, (10) Masafusa, (n) Masanao, (12) Masatoshi, (13) Minkoku, (14) Riomin, (15) Riukei, (16) Tadatoshi, (17) Tomiharu, (18) Tomotada. These were of the early period before 1810. Then follow (19) Homin, (20) Ikkuan, (21) Itshimin, (22) Ittan, (23) Masahiro, (24) Masatami, (25) Noboyuki, (26) Norisane", and (27) Shibayama, the founder of the school bearing his name.

SIGNATURES ON CARVINGS.

THE almost universal favour with which collectors regard old Japanese lacquer is a testimony to its singular beauty, its never-ending individuality, and the genius of the artist-craftsman superior to all others. In the specimens which I have examined, no two have been alike in design, and the variety in decoration is accompanied by variety in form; there are many classes of wares decorated with lacquer, so that no collection can be completeâ it can only be representative. Every piece is singular in some respectâ in the decoration it may be, or in the workmanship.

The mere enumeration of the classes of articles enforces the fact that the ingenious Japanese loved his work, and employed it on the decoration of everything possible. Lacquer was a passion; and though the native collector of pottery and porcelain is satisfied with rough, sketchy, but effective design, in lacquer he demands elegant forms and rich decoration, though some collectors still prefer the older, simpler forms and styles. Each taste can be satisfied; choice ranges over a wide field.

The most famous lacquer made included inros (pill-boxes) of various shapes; sudzuri-bako (paint-boxes); large oblong. and round clothes presses and chests many bearing crests (mon) and covered with antique brocade; other chests and boxes of all imaginable shapes; small tables for incense-burners, dinner-tables (zen), sake-tables; travelling-trunks (hasamibako); book-coffers (oi); dinner-sets, sake-sets, smoking-sets; tobacco-boxes, (tobakobon); palanquins (norimonos); clothes-horses (iko); writing and toilet sets; dinner and sake dishes; sake-bottles; sake dish-stands; water-pots; incense-boxes, round and go games; pictures, easels; hair combs and pins; neck-rests; boxes to hold tea-services (chadansu), tea trays, chests, and urns; fans; footbaths; hats;

braziers (hibachi); kogai; letter-boxes; bowls with covers (hira), sugar-bowls, little boxes for fumigating (ko-bako), rouge-boxes, kake-boxes; mirror-stands, sword-racks

JAPANESE SWEETMEAT-BOX ON WHEELS, IN RED LACQUER.

(katanakake); horses' saddles, stirrups, etc.; brush jars and cases; water-bottles, tea-pots, cabinets, 6tageres, vases, koros, figures, tobacco-cases (tabakoire), tea-caddies (chaire), tea-bowls (chawan), charcoal-boxes, cake-boxes, pipe-cases (kiseruire), boxes for writings and papers, dinner-chests (bentobako), book-chests (bunko), fruit-dishes (takatsuki), screens, sliding doors, and a multitude of other objects which furnish and decorate the home, of which this list is an in- ventory which simply, had to appear somewhere; and many of the objects can be easily identified in the pictures which deal with the social life of the country.

The viscid sap of the lacquer-tree of Japan, a slender branched member of the cashew family, botanically named rhus vernicifera, is known as kiurushi or crude lacquer. Later a full account of the varieties of mixtures into which this

LACQUER BOX. QTH CENTURY.

crude sap enters is followed by the various modes of lacquering. But first we will go into the forest, and see the tappers at work with knives, making horizontal incisions upon selected trees, from which the sap exudes so slowly that they can pass from tree to tree collecting it into wooden dishes by the aid of shells or small scoops. Then, after the day's work is finished, the day's tribute paid by the trees is poured into a larger vessel, and stirred with a spoon to aid the evaporation of superfluous water. Day by day the work goes on, but the busiest time, when the best quality of lacquer is gathered, lasts from the end of July to the middle of September. Not an inspiring occupation at the best, and rendered less pleasant by the blistering power of the raw sap, which makes it necessary for the tapper to wear a long glove to protect hand and arm.

Then to the merchant the harvest is garnered, and he supplies the artist who, with this natural varnish as a basis, proceeds to perform miracles, by processes of almost endless variety, supplying sumptuous robes to plain articles and converting them thereby into objects of the greatest beauty. I should imagine that the preliminary processes before the application of the decoration would have the same relation to the decorator as the preparation of a canvas would to the painter. Yet I do not know. In those olden days, if there was a watchword, it was, "Thorough," and just as the old painters prepared their own canvases very often, so too the old lacquerers may have made the skeleton of the work, covered it with its preparatory coatings, smoothing each perfectly, and finally bestowed upon it the marvellous decoration which seems to defy the action of time, which, indeed, under the influence of the atmosphere, attains a softer beauty, just as a bronze gets a patina. The artists of Europe, especially Huygens in Holland and Martin in France, met with some success as imitators of the Oriental processes, or rather results, and to the latter was granted a monopoly for twenty years from 1744 to make lacquered work, which was known as Vernis-Martin as, in fact, a varnish which he discovered. In our illustrations are some magnificent examples of furniture where slabs of black and gold lacquer were effectively employed in the Louis XVI. period. But we must return to Japanese art, where time brought changes, especially after 1868.

The hasty later work from the time which followed, when Japan opened her ports to western trade, was the natural reply to European and American demand. Forcing the pace spoiled the ware; quicker methods, the result of commercialism, destroyed the old manufacture by robbing it of its solidity, its coalescence. It was therefore not surprising that when, after a year's submersion in the wreck of the " Nile " near Yokohama, in 1874, the cases containing lacquer sent by the Japanese Government to the Vienna Exhibition were opened, the old lacquer was perfect, the modern completely destroyed. The test applied was a searching one, the severest possible, and nobly did the old masters meet it, whilst the modern artists of Kyoto and Tokyo failed utterly.

MIRROR-BOX IN GOLD LACQUER, INCRUSTED WITH MOTHER-OF-PEARL. I3TH CENTURY.

Lacquer dating back to the middle of the seventeenth century is as sound to-day as it was then; modern lacquer cannot stand the damp.

Amongst collectors in the East, black lacquer is most highly appreciated, but outside China and Japan this fine mirror black is only now receiving some measure of attention; the plain gold and decorated gold grounds have been far more favoured. As, later, the processes will be described, I need only note a few points to be recapitulated after the mysteries of Nashiji, Togi-dashi, Hira-makiye, and Taka-makiye have been exposed. Gold applied to lacquer may be in powder, in foil, or grain, all of which vary in size and qualityâ fine powder, coarse powder, pure gold, alloyed gold, and so on. About twenty-two operations are necessary to prepare the ground for the gold ornament, and also for making the best red and other coloured lacquers. These generally follow what is called the Honji (real basis) method for the best ware, and consist of a series of smoothing processes, preceding the first application of the lacquer, and following each application when the coating has become perfectly dry. The kind of lacquer for each coat varies, but their order follows a fixed rule, in which hardening the wooden basis stands first in order. Hardening in the muro (damp press), smoothing with whetstones or with charcoal, covering with silk or cotton-cloth, painting with lacquer, and upon the lacquer ground building up the design in gold raised work, or bringing it out by polishingâ such, in short, are the stages which mark the progress of a piece of fine ware onwards to completion. And, last of all, the final gloss, an exceedingly brilliant polish, given to the last coating by the fingers with the aid of deer's horn ashes and a little oil, accomplishes the task; the artist can now regard the perfection of his painstaking labour, a labour of love.

Nothing limited the early lacquerer. Beside the use of gold in its various forms, incrustations of mother-of-pearl (laque burgautee), of ivory, and the metals, demanded skill in designing, harmonising, and, above all, affixing these materials in their couch of lacquer, forming a mosaic where each morsel of ornament in nice adjustment, polished or dull, was, in the hands of the master, an integral part of the design. And the difficulty was great, the process was long, I will not say tedious, but the result more than justified the means. This kind of work is sometimes termed inlaid lacquer, and there is another kind which requires a few wordsâ that is, aventurine lacquer.

If you look into a box or inro, you will find that the inside is lacquered as well as the outside. Generally the decoration appears like particles of gold in a transparent bed of reddish-brown hue, resembling the hard semi-precious gold-stone variety of quartzâ aventurine. This is only a special method (Nashiji) of using tiny particles of gold-foil, but I mention it here to emphasise the careful finish which marks all of the old work, in which interior decoration was added wherever possible.

After the black and gold come the iron-red and vermilion lacquers. They are preferred by some collectors to all others

LACQUER BOX WITH BLAZON OF THE MIKADO, BY SHUNSHO. DAIMIO LACQUER.

because they are so brilliant. It is said that no vegetable colours can be used, and that this accounts for the few colours in lacquer-ware; the artists never appear to be able to produce white, purple, or any of the more delicate shades. In the iron-red, the colouring matter is ochre or red peroxide of iron, which differs from the colour in the vermilion, where cinnabar is applied in the coating. Shu (vermilion) is used alone, or with gold-dust for shading. As a ground the red may be treated by methods similar to those adopted upon black in the schemes of decoration.

One name occurs frequently amongst collectors, that is Daimio lacquer, indicating a class in which the blazon of the Emperor, or the Shogun, or of the feudal princes, is a feature of the decoration. The kiku-mon, the sixteen-petalled chrysanthemum, was the Imperial badge, and the kiri-mon, the three leaves and spikes of the paulownia, the family badge. The Tokugawa Shoguns adopted a design of three flowers in a. trefoil. Many others may be seen in the marks of pottery, but in lacquer-work they formed a part of the actual decoration, and probably indicated the prince for whom the article was made. In the Muse"e Guimet at Paris is a treasure-chest in brown lacquer, decorated with the blazons of the 269 great Daimios who were in the service of the Shogun Yeyoshi, 1838-53.

Do you desire more information on the preparation and application of Japanese lacquer? And do you wish to see for yourself the tools which were used by the artists in their work? You should visit the Museum in the Royal Botanic Gardens at Kew, where there is a very complete and unique exhibit illustrating the whole process. From the stems of the lacquer-tree (rhus vernicifera), with incisions made by the knife, which is also shown, you can trace the gum until it reposes in its setting, a dead gold ground with raised gold ornament, showing the application of kuma, that is, shading lacquer. Tokyo and Kyoto lacquer-ware! Naga, Wajima and Nambu, Aidzu and Tsugaru, all partaking in an art in which their craftsmen excelled. The tools, the spatulae, the brushes, are only ordinary; the results from them are marvellous.

Here are liquid lacs, Yoshino urushi, Jo-tane urushi, Jo-chiu urushi, and the colours used in and with them, benigara, red oxide of iron, sei-shitsu, green, shu, vermilion, and others. There is a fine, but incomplete, panel, left unfinished in order to show how the process was carried out: the branch of a fir-tree and a creeper, one part in raised lacquer, with or without gold, the other a dull outline on the polished black ground. Gold, veined, burnished, and shaded, may excite admiration for its brilliancy when in company with black, and red, and green, no less remarkable; gold in clouded grounds, in waves, and trees, upon black as its only decoration, or upon red, even upon plain wood or metal; gold particles or flakes in many of the grounds, which are shown together in a frame.

Togi-dashi work, hira-makiye, and taka-makiye, in elaborate designs, stand side by side with guri and tsiu shu in carved red lac, or tsiu koku, carved black. In one case are specimen boards showing designs on red lac, of gold, and the so-called " rose," which should be ro-se decoration under a transparent glaze, and boxes illustrating various modes of applying kiri-kane, awo-gai, and hirame ornament, in various stages of progress. In another are the burnt clay, the camellia charcoal, the cloths in hemp and silk, and all the materials necessary to give form and strength to the object, to provide for its decoration, and to ensure its perfection. The drying-press, a small cupboard with sliding doors in front, faces a case containing about fifty different examples of methods of lacquering a single object, a scabbard.

At Kew you can realise something of the lacquerer's task in copying a master's design. The article must be perfectly shaped and seasoned, the design must be traced and built up, and clearness must ever be maintained, so that a magnifying-glass will reveal the smallest details, as if they were cut in a block of metal, and in the gold lacquerâ in addition, the deep, warm, melting tones of gold, free from coppery and false reflection, must be developed.

JAPANESE PIPE-CASE AND TOBACCO-BOX IN LACQUER.

The processes, in any one method, in the fabrication of a single object seem nearly endless. What must be the skill of the artist who, without repeating a design, brings his individuality, his taste, and his invention, to such a list of articles as I have given early in the chapter? The old lacquerers are gone; all the mixtures which they tried, all the substances which they employed, all the colouring which gave such wonderful effects, are nearly gone too. Their works vanishing, some into the destruction which never restores

BOWL-BOX IN GREEN LACQUER, TNCRUSTED AND DECORATED WITH SILVER ON A BLACK LACQUER GROUND, AND WITH CHRYSANTHEMUMS IN GOLD LACQUER.

some into private collections to be no more seen, the time has come when the gold lacquers in green and red and yellow, separate or merging into one another, the lacquers of bronze, of tin, lead, iron, and silver, the green and red lacquers, and, above all, as some think, the beautiful red lacquer, with its powerful and yet delicate harmonies, must be gathered into the museums before the hand of the millionaire closes over them.

Another class of lacquer deserves attentionâ the lacquer incrusted with mother-of-pearl, ivory, plaques of metal, nuggets, etc., or with grains or spangles of gold in mosaic, stippled or seeded, either regularly or as if by chance. When the grains of gold are very numerous, when they crowd together in forms resembling the crystallisation of sugar-candy, or when they appear like rock-crystal charged with particles of mica, the lacquer takes the name of the hard semi-precious gold-stone or aventurine. This quality of lacquer plays an important part in the process, being used to decorate the bottom and the interior of boxes; yet when employed in the design itself, as a ground for gold lacquer in relief, the whole piece gains in distinction and in value. Amongst the incrusted lacquer, the first place would be given to the inlaying of nuggets in a regular pattern, such as a mosaic, because such work presented the greatest difficulty, and was only undertaken by notable craftsmen who had to fit each morsel of gold into its resting-place, to polish, and to match it with all the others, and at the same time to maintain the beauty of the lacquer. No work required more time, more patience, and more skill, but the result justified the labour. Lacquer in such a mosaic was the supreme work of the master! The black mirror lacquer and the gold lacquers were wonderful, but this was almost sensational.

After the black and the gold come the iron-red and the vermilion lacquers, which were shortly noted above. They are more sumptuous, more brilliant.

THE art of lacquering is one of the oldest industries of Japanâ its origin is lost with other arts in the early centuries of our era; but there is no doubt that, like them, it came across the seas from China and Korea, findeed, the technique of the two countries differs but little. though the Japanese have mt stripped all competitors, their superiority is incontestable.) Two boxes preserved in the treasury of the great temple of Nara date back to the seventh century, and form the earliest known examples. In the year 880 red and gold lacquer were referred to by the philosopher Shihei; in the tenth century praises are bestowed upon them by Minamoto No louin, who, however, gives no names; and late in the same century a celebrated woman-writer, Mura-saki Shikibu, describes a new kind of lacquer incrusted with mother-of-pearlâ the inner layer of the haliotis shell. This last kindâ the lacquer with mother-of-pearl incrustationsâ is known to us under its French name as laque bur-gautte. Other early specimens in the same temple of Todaiji in Nara, and many which were shown at the Japan-British Exhibition, reveal the wonderful qualities of old lacquer which has been in existence more than a thousand years. All of these were in one colour, or in gold, but we scarcely need to dwell upon them, even to praise their form and colour, because they are of the greatest rarity.

After the tenth century, for a long period only one school maintained a high reputa-tionâ the Kamakura school, which produced excellent work during the fourteenth and fifteenth centuries. Then came a renaissance at Kyoto corresponding to that which took'place in China. Yoshimasa, a Shogun of the house of Ashikaga, took a personal interest in lacquer, which, under his protection, became equal to all except the very best of the earlier products, and in some respects even excelled them by the adoption of original methods in which the inlaying of gold and silver nuggets in mosaics, the incrustations of metal, the application of decora-

ETUIS IN LACQUER.

tion in relief, and the introduction of grounds of silver and of vermilion played important parts. The fifteenth century was distinguished by the overpowering influence of China, which brought increased freshness and vigour to the Kano school, whilst at the same time depressing the opposing school of Tosa. So the lacquer of the Yoshimasa period bears the impress of the Kano painters, and it is highly valued for its ornament and for its solidity, although the mosaics of gold are not perfectly smooth, nor has the polish- ing by the whetstone entirely removed the roughness of the wrinkled grounds on which the grains of gold project. These points are important in determining the age of lacquer in the absence of signatures, which appear with Koetsu in the sixteenth century. The insetting of the gold grains, polished as each was, proved to be a task requiring the utmost skill of the artist, who had not alone to set them in their bed of lacquer, but to build it up around them by successive layers which fixed them there in the requisite design, so that they were immovable without breaking up the body of the lacquer. The tiniest pliers or pincers were the tools used for the in-

LACQUER INRO, BY KOETSU.

setting. Then, again, it was not until the seventeenth century that the ground of gold in spangles of foil, diapered in various patterns, reached its full perfection, giving complete smoothness to the touch, and to the eye an indescribable beauty. In the next century this process, magnificent though it was and costly, was almost entirely abandoned.

No artist's name reaches us before the sixteenth century, when, near its close, Koetsu, a famous painter, devoted himself to the art of lacquering with signal success. We shall notice that many painters adopted a similar course, which was not surprising when we consider that the ability to design was as necessary in lacquering as it was in painting.

In the latter the facility of the artist, the boldness and strength of each stroke of the brush, was in vivid contrast to the eminent capacity for taking pains, the slow and careful elaboration in the former. Koetsu, the painter, became one of the first of the artists in lacquer, embodying in that work some of the qualitiesâ the style and the graceâ of his painting, excelling in those pieces, especially, which had designs in relief in gold, the taka-makiye, a process which is described later in this section on lacquer. Not only so, but his influence, his methods, in fact his school, became the inspiration of many of the fine artists who succeeded him.

Shunsho, another celebrated painter, founded the Yedo school in the eighteenth centuryâ a school of painters and designers for colour-prints, which had great success. Yet the master gave to lacquer his personal preference, relinquishing altogether the colour-print designing to competitors, who were numerous and eminent. In the sections on painting and colour-prints, further notice is given to this artist. Here we may note that, having been summoned from Kyoto by the Shogun, he soon rivalled, in his lacquer-work, the efforts of the Koetsu school by his bolder decoration and his greater freedom in method, and attained such success that the higher prices were paid for specimens from his hand; the Japanese valued them highly for their refinement and elegance, and successive Shoguns afforded to the school such effective protection and support that lacquer was extended to the decoration, not only of the utensils of the temple and home, but to the columns and doors of those buildings, and to every object suitable for such decoration.

In considering the friendly rivalry between these two schools, we have been carried further forward than was necessary from the chronological development, so we will go back to Yosai or Yose"i, who imported from China the carved red lacquer which can scarcely be differentiated into old and new, but is judged, like the Chinese, according to the depth of the cinnabar coating, the bright tone of the red, the fine polish and solidity of the piece itself, and, therefore, by its weight, the heaviest being the best. Yosai of Naga-8 saki has so identified himself with the fine, red lacquer that, in Japan, he is regarded as its inventor, his full, fatty work being distinguished by much originality, although it differs considerably from the so-called red Pekin lacquer, famous under the Yuan dynasty of the Chinese.

It is usual in reference to Japanese art to quote the various periods, which I have given elsewhere, which correspond somewhat to the Chinese dynasties, especially under the

LACQUER BOX, DESIGNED BY KORIN.

later Shogun families. The Nara period, from A. D. 709 to 784, and the Heian, from 794 to noo, may be disregarded for all practical purposes as far as lacquer is concerned. The third period was named the Kamakura, from the first capital of the Shoguns in the province of Sagami. The period extended from the date last given, noo, to 1335, when the Ashikagas became the Shoguns; and the Ashikaga period extended to 1573, when the Momoyana period, for thirty years, marked the rule of the Shogun Hideyoshi. Lastly, from 1603 to 1868, the Tokugawa family ruled at Yedo, and the period bore their name. The Emperor always resided at Kyoto.

Daring the Shogunate of Genroku, some years on either side of 1700â to be exact, 1688 to 1704â appear two great masters in lacquer who rank amongst the most original and eminent designers of that country.

Korin, the great painter, was one of these who revolutionised the art of lacquering, which had hitherto submitted to the influence of the Tosa school of Kyoto. He studied this school at first with the lacquerers of the master, Koetsu, but when he came to Yedo he extended his studies to other artists' works, with the result that he, as a noted master, set up his own school, which excelled in its lac quer-work, so that the Japanese collector of the present day sets great store by the precious specimens from Korin, especially when signed by him; they bear evidence to his independent style, and to the vigour of an active imagination. His brother, the potter, Kenzan, also a painter, acted with success in the same direction, against the conventional Tosa decoration, a style which was adopted from the Chinese. Kenzan and Korin broke down this foreign influence, substituting original and purely Japanese designs."" 1 Korin, as a painter f scarcely apppated to k p people of this country–thejruejqyÂ rs of art were his devoted followers. But in lacquer he fore ed admiration from all. Even to-day " Korin's gold " is a standard, a little dull, but so even, so warm and pulsating, so like solid gold, with a peculiar distinction of its own. Working with a full brush, he secured fine, broad effects, whilst his incrustations of mother-of-pearlâ laque burgautee â silver, lead, and tin, yielded effects which he brought to perfection; he made them notes in a delightful harmony.

The scope of the lacquerer was so great, his operations

INRO IN SILVER LACQUER, BY RITSUO.

covered so many articles, that Korin's work may be found upon various objects, such as a netsuke of shakudo in gold with incrustation, having a circular veined frame, and a central panel with birds perched upon a branch; an encrier decorated with gold lacquer in relief; a cabinet with gold lacquer trees and flowers on one part, and quaint, but beautifully executed, figures on others; and so on. L Indeed, there appear to be no limits to the exercise of his talent, and I can only advise those collectors who have already been attracted by the beauty of this particular ware to give special attention to the ac-, quisition of examples of the art of this master, as well as of the others whose signatures or names appear in the list. And will you please note that the signature may, and often does, contain words other than the name, which is, however, its essential part, and further, the same want of care is often evidenced by the Japanese artists in their signatures upon their works, as is shown by some distinguished men of our own times. The name Korin, given amongst the lacquerers, is followed by his signature upon the list. By examining both you will see my point.

The art of Korin cannot be called a renaissanceâ it was an emancipation from the Tosa traditions. As I have remarked in the section on painting, all of the great decorators were painters. The nengo of the celebrated Genroku marked an epoch in Japanese art which, in metal working and carving, was no less distinguished than in lacquer. Greater activity

INRO IN GOLD LACQUER, INCRUSTED WITH MOTHER-OF-PEARL, BY HANZAN.

in intercourse with China and Holland gave an impetus to this art amongst others. As early as 1630, dated examples or pieces with inscriptions by which the date may be fixed were made by the Japanese for the Dutch.

Ritsuo was the second of these masters. He lived for a long time at Yedo, where he excelled in the art of incrustation; lacquering, with him, was a means to an end. His works are so completely Japanese, so original in execution, and yet so perfect, that they may be soon recognised, even by the uninitiated. His ingenuity was displayed over a

RED LACQUER DECORATED WITH GOLD, BY KWANSAI.

multitude of forms, ranging from magnificent panels to objects of slight importance, and he beautified everything he touched. One method of incrustation he made peculiarly his own, creating wonders by working with lacquer and ceramics, pottery and lacquerâ porcelain, too. We have noted, not only the individuality of the worker, the individuality of the work is not less striking, never repeated, always interesting, compelling admiration by conquering difficulties, and by a colour scheme which leaves nothing to be desired. His favoured pupil, Hanzan, to whom he accorded the second right to use his seal, was skilful in incrustation, emulating his master, and he also had a reputation for gold lacquer.

Koma Kwansai of Yedoâ school of Komaâ was an artist celebrated at the end of the seventeenth century and the beginning of the eighteenth for the perfection of his aventurines, in which he stands unrivalled, though also excellent in laque frottee, and in relief upon a vermilion ground. Master in the front rank, teacher of the first order, he taught his pupils so well that, through the eighteenth century, they too, in many cases, became famous.

Kadjikava, also of Yedo, had an atelier whose origin dated back to the end of the seventeenth century, and whose reputation was equal to that of Koma. The speciality of this school was its inros, which, like all of the works produced, were irreproachable in execution. We have said something of aventurine; and the aventurine interiors of Kadjikava, with great stars, rich and vibrating, were very much appreciated by connoisseurs. The schools of the families of Kiyo-kava and of Shiomi have acquired an equal reputation.

We give the names of other noted lacquerers, Toyo, Kwan-shio, Toshihide, Yoyusai, and Ze'ishin, amongst many masters who worked before or about the beginning of the nineteenth century; the last, Zeishin, appears also to have been the last of those who thought, and embodied their thoughts in original work; later artists have been content to copy the old masters. Each period of lacquer-work has some special quality, and, as in all art, the passage of ages, the ripening of opinions, the truer judgments which are formed with increased knowledge, these all have been applied to the ancient lacquer, which issues from these severe tests with such eclat that no collector need fear depreciation of valueâ and more, Japan will soon desire to buy it back.

THERE are several modes of making gold lacquer, of which the chief are given. Togi-dashi (bringing out by polishing).â The article having been subjected to the twenty-two first processes is then treated as follows: The picture to be transferred to the article is drawn on thin paper, to which a coating of size, made of glue and alum, has been appliedâ that known as Mino-gami is best. The reverse is rubbed smooth with a polished shell or pebble, and the outline very lightly traced in lacquerâ previously roasted over live charcoal to prevent its dryingâ with a fine brush made of rat's hair. The paper is then laid, with the lacquer side downwards, on the article to be decorated, and is gently rubbed with a whalebone spatula wherever there is any tracing, and on removing the paper the impress may very faintly be perceived. To bring it out plainly it is rubbed over very lightly with a piece of cotton-wool charged with powdered white whetstone or tin, which adheres to the lacquer. Japanese paper being peculiarly tough, upwards of twenty impressions can be taken off from one tracing, and when that is no longer possible, from the lacquer having become used up, it only requires a fresh tracing over the same paper to reproduce the design ad infinitum. This tracing does not dry owing to the lacquer used for the purpose having been partially roasted, as previously mentioned, and it can be wiped off at any time.

The next process is to trace out the veinings of the leaves, or such lines to which, in the finished picture, it is desired to give the most prominence, and these lines are powdered over with gold-dust through a quill. The qualities called Mijin, Koma-kame-mijin, and Aragoku, are generally used; either finer or coarser qualities cannot be used. The article is then set to dry for twenty-four hours in the damp press. The outline is now drawn carefully with a rat's-hair brush over the original tracing-line with a mixture of black and branch lacquer called Rd-se. The whole is then filled in

LACQUER BOX, BY NAGAHIDE, SHUNSHO SCHOOL.

with Rd-se, applied with a grounding brush of hare's hair. Gold dust of a slightly coarser quality than Mijin is scattered over the lacquered portion, and the article is set to dry for twenty-four hours. Another thin coating of Rd-se lacquer is again given to the gold-powder portions, and the article is set to dry for twelve hours. Next, a coat of Ro (black varnish) is applied over the whole surface of the article, which is set to dry for at least three days. It is then roughly ground down with Magnolia charcoal, the surface dust being constantly wiped off with a damp cloth, till the pattern begins to appear faintly. Another coating of Ro lacquer is then given, and the article set to dry for thirty-six hours. It is again ground down with Magnolia charcoal, as beforeâ this time till the pattern comes out well. The ensuing processes are the same as for black lacquer. In making Togi-dashi on hard woods, transparent lacquer is used instead of Ro.

Hira-makiye (flat gold lacquer).â A tracing is applied to the surface of the thoroughly finished article, as in Togi-dashi; the outline is carefully painted over with a fine brush

BOX FOR FANS, DECORATED IN GOLD LACQUER.

of rat's hair, and then filled in with a grounding brush of hare's hair, using Shitamaki lacquer (branch lacquer and red oxide of iron). Over this surface gold-dust, of the quality called Aragoku being generally used, is scattered with a horse-hair brush (Kebo) till the lacquer will not absorb any more. The article is then set to dry for twenty-four hours. A thin coating is next applied over the gold, of transparent or Yoshino lacquer, and set to dry for twenty-four hours at least. It is then most carefully smoothed with Camellia charcoal, and finally polished off with Tono-ko, and a little oil on the point of the finger, till the ornamental portion attains a fine polish. The veining of the leaves, and the painting of stamens, etc., of flowers, or such other is now done with a fine rat's-hair brush charged with Ke-uchi lacquer, over which fine gold-dust (Goku-mijiri) is scattered from a horse-hair brush, as before, and the article set to dry for twelve hours. Some Yoshino lacquer is then applied to a piece of cotton-wool, and rubbed over the whole surface of the box or other article, and wiped off again with soft paper.

GOLD LACQUER ON BLACK. A ROUND BOX WITH FOUR COMPARTMENTS AND COVER

It is set to dry for twelve hours, after which it is polished off with deer's-horn ashes and a trifle of oil. When very high-class work is desired, Yoshino lacquer, to which a little water has been added, is applied, and polished off a second time, and a very brilliant surface is attained.

More ordinary " flat gold lacquer " differs in the manufacture as follows: The tracing is accomplished in the same manner, but Shitamaki-nobe lacquer (branch lacquer, red oxide of iron and camphor) is used for filling in the ground of the pattern with a brush of hare's hair. The article is then set out to dry in the press for ten to twenty minutes, during which time the lacquer has begun to harden, and less gold will adhere. Then gold-dust (Goku-mijiri) is applied with cotton-wool, thinly, and the article is set to dry for twenty-four hours. The whole surface is then smeared over with Yoshino-nobe lacquer (Yoshino lacquer and camphor) on a piece of cotton-wool, and wiped off again with soft paper. The reason is that it is less trouble to smear over the whole surface thinly, and it is, moreover, not necessary to give a thick coat of lacquer to the decorated part, as the gold-dust has been very thinly applied. It is set to dry for twelve hours, and ground smooth with Camellia charcoal, and polished with powdered whetstone and oil on the point of the finger. The fine lines are then drawn with a rat's-hair brush charged with Shitamaki lacquer, and sprinkled with gold-dust (Goku-mtjin) from a brush (Kebo), and the article set to dry for twelve hours. The whole is again smeared with Yoshino-nobe lacquer, and carefully wiped off again with paper, and set to dry for twelve hours. It is then polished with powdered whetstone and oil on the point of the finger, and a second application of Yoshino-nobe lacquer with a little water, wiped off with soft paper, set to dry for twelve hours, and finally polished off with deer's-horn ashes and oil on the finger, which finishes the operation. This quality is far inferior to that which was first described under this heading.

Should any dark spots or lines be required, such as birds' eyes, human hair, etc., or other shading, this is done last of all with Kuma "bear" lacquer, Jo-hana, and lampblack. The more common kinds of flat gold lacquer are treated by other less intricate processes, which here I need not describe, as such articles have but little interest or value to the collector.

Amongst the most valuable products of this art is the interesting Taka-makiye (raised gold lacquer). In this process the ground may be either black or coloured lacquer, Nashiji (pear basis of gold-dust), or the plain wood. The outlines of the pattern are transferred upon the article as described in Togi-dashi. These are then painted over with Shitamaki lacquer, and this is covered with powdered Camellia charcoal. If the outside is to be higher than the inside, a broad margin is painted, and covered with the charcoal-dust, leaving the centre untouched, and vice versa; if the centre is to be higher, a faint line only is painted outside, and the inside is given a thickish coating, which is sprinkled with the charcoal-dust, and the article set to dry for twelve hours. When taken out of the press, it is well brushed, to get rid of any loose charcoal-powder, and it is also washed, using a brush made of human hair (Hake), to clean out all the crevices, and bring out all the lines, etc. Some Yoshino-nobe (branch lacquer with camphor) is now rubbed on with a piece of cotton-wool, and carefully wiped off with soft paper, and the article set to dry for twelve hours. The raised parts are next carefully ground smooth with a piece of Magnolia charcoal, and a second coat of Yoshino-nobe, or of branch lacquer, is applied as before, and

LACQUER BOX IN THE FORM OF A dried. A thorough drying is BIlirat OR LUTE, RAISED GOLD. indispensable after each painting.

If a well-raised pattern is required, one, two, or even three coats of Sabi (branch lacquer and Tono-ko) are applied, the outside edges being painted with a brush of deer's hair (Menso), and the inside lacquer applied with a small Sabi spatula, the article being set to dry between each application, for twelve hours. For coarser work it is then ground smooth with a white whetstone, and for finer work with a yellow whetstone. Over this some " branch " lacquer mixed with camphor, is rubbed with cotton-wool, and wiped off with soft paper, and the article set to dry for twelve hours.

If the pattern is not to be very high, the operations described in the last paragraph are omitted. A coating of Taka-maki lacquer is next applied, the outside edges being carefully drawn with a rat's-hair brush, and the article set to dry for thirty-six to forty-eight hours. When taken out of the

LACQUER BENTO-BAKO. 18xh CENTURY.

press, the surface is ground smooth with Magnolia charcoal, and then partly polished with powdered Camellia charcoal, on a cotton cloth. A little oil is now rubbed on, and a further polishing takes place with powdered whetstone on a cloth. Next, "branch" lacquer is rubbed over the raised parts with cotton-wool, and wiped off with soft paper, and the article set to dry for twelve hours. It is next polished with deer's-horn ashes, and a little rape-seed, or sesamum oil applied on the point of the finger. Up to this point the formation of the raised pattern, whether mountains, waves, trees, men, birds, or animals, has been gradually completed.

If small squares of gold-foil (Kiri kane), or of coloured shell, etc., are used in producing the pattern, they are now applied, one by one, on the point of a bamboo stick (Hirame fude) â the spot where they are to be affixed having been smeared with a little Ro-se lacquer, to make them adhere. When all that is required has been affixed, a piece of soft absorbent, or blotting-paper, is spread over the freshly done parts, and pressed very carefully with the finger to get rid of as much Ro-se lacquer as possible. The article is set to dry for twelve hours, and then the portion covered by the gold-foil is gently polished with a little Camellia charcoal, on the point of the finger, to get rid of the remaining Ro-se lacquer. Shell patterns and the coarser kinds of gold-dust are applied in the same manner. The finer kinds of gold-dust are applied next, over a coat of Shitamaki lacquer, and the article set to dry for twelve hours. The remaining processesâ polishing, drying, etc.â are the same as in the best " flat gold " lacquer.

For making raised lacquer patterns on plain wood, the whole surface is covered with tin-foil, stuck on with rice-paste, to keep the wood quite clean, and then the part where the pattern is to come is cut out. In making all high-class lacquer, the edges of every article are pasted over with tin-foil, to prevent rubbing or injury by the workman, and each portion as it is finished is similarly treated.

There are innumerable modifications of the processes sketched above, yet nearly every piece of good lacquer exhibits either Nashiji, Togi-dashi, Hira-makiye, or Taka-makiye processes, generally in combination.

In making raised lacquer on inferior articles, the methods are nearly the same, but the work is less carefully executed; the gold is poor in quality and quantity, or it is displaced by silver or tin. In the cheapest kinds, burnt tin-dust is used, instead of charcoal, over the first coat of Shitamaki. This is burnished bright, and over it a thin coat of lacquer and gold-dust is applied. At first it looks well, but loses its colour in a year or two. By using tin-powder the same height is acquired in one coat that would necessitate at least three coats of lacquer and charcoal-dust. This kind of tin-powder work is only used for cheap articles for foreign export, and is of quite modern origin.

One of the most interesting processesâ and one of the most artisticâ is lacquering on metal. Iron, copper, brass, or silver may receive lacquer decoration. The metal is smoothed and polished, and then given a coating of " crude lacquer " or " black lacquer." This is burnt on the metal, over a charcoal fire, till all smoke has escaped. The fire requires careful regulation, it must not be fierce, and the metal must not be allowed to get red-hot, or the lacquer burns to ashes. When the lacquer has been burnt quite hard, it is rubbed smooth with Lagerstrcemia charcoal, and these operations are repeated three or four times till a good foundation of lacquer has been obtained. Then the processes follow exactly the order of the other lacquers, which have been described, except that the lacquer is burnt dry over the fire instead of drying in the press, though, after the first three or four coats have been burnt on, the press may be used for the remainder. Burnt lacquer is quite hard and very durable.

In winter, or when any article is required in a hurry, a charcoal fire is put into the press, with a pan of hot water on the fire. The steam helps to dry the lacquer in an hour or two, instead of the ordinary twenty-four hours; but the pieces so treated are never very hard, never very strong, and the " black lacquer " soon turns a rusty brown. Therefore this method is only used for poor work.

Nashiji (pear basis).â This process is intermediate between plain and ornamented lacquer. Till the opening of Japan to foreign trade, this style of decoration was in the hands of the workers in gold lacquer, but now all Nashiji on articles intended for exportation is applied by workers in plain lacquer. The best Nashiji, the best Togi-dashi, the best Honji, have the first twenty-two processes alike. Then in the Nashiji a coating of Ro-se is applied, and the gold-dust is sprinkled over this surface by means of bamboo tubes, according to the fineness required. The drying follows for forty-eight hours in the press, and next a coat of pure transparent lacquer is applied. This visits the press for three or four days, when the article is roughly ground with Magnolia charcoal, and then coated with the same transparent lacquer. Forty-eight hours' drying follows, and more grinding with Magnolia charcoal, till a perfectly smooth surface is obtained. Transparent lacquer is then applied with a piece of cottonwool, and wiped off again with soft paper. After twenty-four hours' drying the article is polished with a mixture of Tono-ko and Camellia charcoal and a little oil. Next a coating of Yoshino lacquer is given, and wiped off with paper. Twelve hours' drying is followed by polishing with deer's-horn ashes and oil, repeated three times to finish the process. Silver is treated similarly. Again, for cheap qualities, tin-dust is used, and a coating of Kanoji (whiting and glue) forms the ground.

Of necessity the information given in this chapter is highly technical, and perhaps not of the greatest interest to the ordinary reader; but I believe the collector of lacquer will value it, because it is uncommon, and because it deals with gold lacquer, etc., in such detail as to enable us to realise that the finished product, which may lie before us, actually passed through the processes here described.

In the Aidzu district the light coloursâ yellow, green, etc.â are produced in the greatest perfection. In Tokyo the colours are inferior and darker. In Aidzu no after-polishing takes place with coloured lacquers. The lacquer is applied like paint. Tokyo is best for black lacquer, and high-class red, etc., such as receive the after-polishing. Kyoto black lacquer shows a reddish-brown tinge. These two cities, with Osaka, Kaga, Tsugani, Wakasa, Nagova, Suruga, Shidzuoka, and a very few isolated places, practise the processes of smoothing with charcoal, and afterwards polishing by hand. These processes require infinite care; a constant devotion is accepted as a matter of course.

The tools and materials used in the manufacture of gold lacquer include a number of rat's-hair brushes, others made of hare's-hair, deer's-hair, human hair, and horse-hair, in various sizes, brush-cleaners, brush-rests, spatulae for mixing the materials, etc., in addition to the general outfit of the ordinary craftsman. The Tsutsu (a quill from the wing of a swan or crane), over one end of which is stretched a piece of silk gauze, is filled with gold-dust by a Saji (spoon), and the dust is dusted and scattered upon the prepared surface. The gold and silver dust varies in the size of its particles and in its purity. There are twelve qualities of each, differing in fineness. In addition there is an extra large kind used for ground-work, called Hira-me (flat-eye). The coarsest filings

SIGNATURES ON LACQUER.

(i)Koetsu. (2) Shunsho. (3) Yosei. (4) Korin. (5) Ritsuo.

(6) Kwansai. (7) Kadjikava. (8) Koma Kyuhaku. (9) Kiyokawa.

do) Toyo. (ii) Kwanshio. (12) Toshihide. (13) Yoyusai.

(14) Zeishin. (15) Ritsuo's seal mark.

of pure gold or silver are rolled out flat on an iron plate, and there are eight kinds of Hira-me. Next comes the Nashiji, resembling the skin of a pear. This, in pure gold-Koban or Koban-kin; Jiki-ban, and Nam-ban, alloys, each containing ten parts of gold, and from two-and six-tenths to three-and-six-tenths of silver, as well as in pure silver (Gin), has seven qualities of fineness.

In describing so minutely the work of lacquering, it is necessary to insist on the facts that the actual lacquerer was a skilled artisan, and that the design for the piece, whatever it might be, was furnished by an artist, sometimes a famous painter. The signatures that appear are often those of the designers whose names are attached to paintings of recognised merit. So that in lacquer, as in other branches of Japanese art, the actual executant is unknown, though scarcely less than the designer does he deserve a niche in the temple of fame.

The signatures of the chief designers whose names appear on lacquer are given in the list on page 181. Other names, beside these, will be found amongst the painters.

THE glorious panoply of war contributes a world of articles connected with the life of the soldierâ with the Samurai, whose prominent position in the Japanese world led them to devote extreme attention to personal adornment, for even when not fighting, they were fighters, with as much pride in their equipment as we should expect in a superior caste, the military who did no work. Really the history of arms and armour only commences with Yori-tomo, the founder of the hereditary Shogunate, and an illustration shows what a formidable person the fully armed soldier appeared. The wearing of the sword, "The soul of the Samurai' was a privilege, and when under the Ashikagas, in the sixteenth century, two swords became obligatory, Daimios and Samurai alike strove after the best work of the best makers; yet swords, with their accessories, were but a part of the necessary outfit of certain ranks corresponding to our ancient knights armed cap-a-pie.

There were suits of armour comprising helmets, headpieces, breastplates, arm and leg coverings, epaulettes, masks, and gauntlets, in addition to the mail. Lances of different kinds, pikes, halberds, swords, and their accessories, which I shall describe presently; daggers, bows, arrows, and quivers; masks, saddles, bridles, and stirrups; battle-fans, standards, flags, drums, shell trumpets (horageii), sword-rests,â all these, and more, formed the equipment of the warriors of old, in addition to the later guns, pistols, powder-flasks, etc. Evidently such a list could receive no adequate treatment in a book like this; even the ever-ready sword would require a volume, for Japan suffered from internal troubles, personal quarrels grew into family feuds, differences were settled by death, where honour or even etiquette was concerned; personal disgrace, whether due to loss of favour

A SAMURAI STANDARD-BEARER IN COMPLETE ARMOUR. BADGE ON STANDARD AND ARMOUR OF THE FEUDAL PRINCE OF SEN-DAI.

or to a sin of commission, was expiated by the harakiri, and, above all, personal ornament illustrated better than anything else the rank and the individuality of the bearer.

Upon a single sword large sums were expended, to show the taste of the soldier, who would suffer hunger rather than forego an emblem worthy of his rank on a scabbard, which varied with the occasion, so for full-dress it was lacquered in black with a tinge of red and green. Generally, fine swords have a scabbard covered, not with shark's skin, but with the

HEAD-PIECE IN IRON. 16TH CENTURY.

palate of the shark's mouth. The scabbard was only one item in the sword's furniture. Upon the minor adornments, the collector has already cast covetous eyes, relegating' to one side the bladeâ I think, only for the moment, for the Japanese sword-blade has no rival. In view of the fact that few come to Europe we will pass pn. to consider what pieces, beside the blade, make the sword, and here we have a ground fertile in interest, with examples which are both numerous and striking, some of them valuable, many designed by famous artists.

The sword-guard (tsuba) is a flat, round, or oval piece of metal pierced with an aperture for the blade, and with others

SWORD-GUARD IN IRON, PIERCED. I5TH CENTURY.

for the heads of two implementsâ the kodzuka and the kogai. We shall see what magnificent decoration was applied to them; but first it will be best to take these and the other parts and explain them. The illustrations will help the explanation.

The kodzuka was a knife, or small dagger, whose sheath was placed on one side of the sword; whilst the kogai was a kind of skewer, on the other, the use of which is not clearly defined, though it is said that it was thrust into the dead

KODZUKA.

body of a slain opponent as a mark of personal prowess. Both kodzuka and kogai were ornamented, generally quite as elaborately as the tsuba, which alone left the scabbard when the sword was drawn.

The small ornaments placed on either side of the hilt were the menukis (tiny plaques of metal), which helped to give a iirmer grip. The wakizashi, or short sword, which was about

SWORD-GUARD IN IRON, WITH DRAGON-FLIES IN INTAGLIO, BY UMETADA.

a foot and a half long, had menukis for the same reason, as well as for decoration. It was expedient to get a strong gn. sp on the scabbard when the sword was drawn for hara-kiri. Then quite at the top of the hilt was an oval metal cap, the kachira, and at the bottom of it, resting on the tsuba t a flat oval ring also of metal, the fuchi. A cord passing through two eyes at the sides secures the kachira and the blade fixed in the hilt passes through both fuchi and tsuba. The combination fuchikachira is frequently used, because both pieces were usually made and decorated by the same artist, whose name may frequently be found on the kachira.

The art of Japan, in all its branches, appears to move along parallel lines of progress. When in the early centuries painting advanced in style and execution, metal chasing advanced too. From the period anterior to the end of the fourteenth century, strength rather than ornament met the needs of a people who were always fighting. The blacksmith made the tsuba, and hammered out its ornament in the forge with such designs as skill and opportunity permitted, and probably every feudal prince maintained his own staff of armourers, sword-cutlers, with other artists, for damascening and chasing, and yet others to make and decorate the auxiliary parts, the tsubas, etc. Huish's classification appears to be the best of those that I have seen, as it takes into consideration that constant element, the schools, though, in early days, these metal-workers were, no doubt, soldiers, and not of the Samurai classâ just the ordinary fighters, who, in their times of peace, prepared for war, who developed certain skill which brought them into notice, who attained promotion to the service of the Shogun, and who eventually founded their schools. The difficulty is to trace the pupils of these masters, which is shown by the adoption of one of the masters' names. Possibly, later investigators will trace the historical connections, as in the case of the schools of print-designing.

And here may I interpolate one remark bearing upon the relation between the artists who worked in bronze and iron figures, and those who made armour and weapons. It will be found that many of these masters worked in both branches. Proof of this will be found in the Myochin bronzes.

The Myochin family were armourers dating back to the twelfth century in a continuous record, which reached onwards to the eighteenth. Even now sword-guards made by them in earlier centuries may be found, and all are of iron, which was the only metal they used. M. Gonse remarks: " L'ceuvre la plus remarquable a tous egards qui soit venue en Europe et Tune des plus importantes qu'ait produites cette famille d'artistes est l'aigle en fer martele, de grandeur naturelle, qui se trouve an Kensington Museum de Londres. II est pose sur un rocher, les ailes deployees, les plumes herissees, et comme pret a s'elancer sur proie. Toutes les plumes sont separ es et articulees les unes sur les autres. Cette oeuvre de fer est pleine de fierte et de caractere. Comme dimculte vaincue on n'en "pourrait citer une plus surprenante." It is signed with the Myochin signature. You should see this eagle.

Passing onwards through the fifteenth century, we note that

SWORD-GUARD, CRAY-FISH, IN IRON DECORATED WITH GOLD BY KI-NAI.

succeeding Shoguns were protectors of the sword-makers, of whom one name is prominent, the Goto family, founded by Goto Yujo, who received the latter name from the Shogun Yoshimasa Yujo, in recognition of the excellence of his work. He lived from 1440 to 1512, and in 1603 the family removed to Yedo with the Shogun Iy6yasu, Viceroy and General, where their descendants worked up to the last century. Again, the early products were iron, hard-tempered iron, but such as permitted but little ornament. The later work was far more delicate, especially the nanakoji on shakudo. The gold ground was punched with tiny dots, forming a surface resembling a fish-roe, hence its name.

I am inclined to the opinion that the artist named Shinkodo should be Shingoto, but I am not sure, though Shinkodo was one of the great masters of note in the sixteenth century, Kinai and Nobuiye shared with Um6tada the premier position, and all of them signed their works. The process of inlaying, which had been in operation for some time, now reached a

SWORD-GUARD WITH DRAGONS AFFRONTJzs IN SHIBUICH1, BY high level. Red and yellow bronze were employed with fine effect, and the solidity of the tsubas became varied by pierced work, which resembled casting in bronze; really it was fretwork in metal. This style of sword-guard was more for ornament than use, but the troublous times had passed, and with the close of this century opened a long era of peace, which lasted for some two hundred and fifty years. That guard, which had to resist a blow from a two-handed sword, 2 feet long, wielded by a strong man, now advanced into the dignity of a cherished ornament, which in common with the other ornaments received the lavish care of the worker, the artist in metal. Nobuiye excelled in inlaying, Kinai in piercing, Ume tada in chasing and engraving; his signature is easy to remember as the first, that is the top, character is a flower, the prunus.

One test can be applied to the old iron tsubas, a test of sonority. The name of Ume'tada is associated with this,

SWORD-GUARD, SERPENTS INTERLACED, IN SHAKUDO, BY NAGAYUKI.

because his guards, made of iron, ring with the sound of a crystal bell when struck, owing to the density and homogeneity of the metal acquired under the hammer before being chased. It certainly was not an easy task to cut in a metal, often harder than steel, such wonderful engravings and reliefs, especially as we know that no other tools were used than the point, burin, graver, and mallet. The quality of the sound then, clear and high, is, as a general rule, the test of age, though the necessity for a good eye and some experience must be modifying factors, for the deliberate, scru- pulous devotion of the artist of the seventeenth century yielded to the more hasty processes of the eighteenth, in the early part of which the iron sword still held sway. No sound-test can be applied where the iron is inlaid, or in any way soldered with cloisons, and these became much more frequent.

The Chinese, who were the great artists in cloisons â their cloisonne enamel to witâ rarely tried cloisons for such enamel upon iron, a process in which the Japanese were masters, inserting the delicate walls of gold with such skill that the enamels appear like precious stones set in the dull metal. Amongst many artists whose names appear in the list of signatures, mention must be made of Somin, not in the hope that you may acquire a sword-guard by this master, but because of his reputed skill in chasing silver in the manner of Umetada, the iron-worker. Somin's works are very rare. Huish gives him as the founder of the school of Yokoya, but in the absence of information this must be taken with reserve.

From the beginning of the eighteenth century sword-mountings in shakudo and shibuichi and other soft alloys give further evidence that, as a weapon, the sword was for parade, a thing of beauty. Freed from the hammered iron, as a necessary working base, the metal-workers ran riotâ not that they transgressed the limits of simplicity and good taste, for the brilliant metals were used sparingly to heighten the general effect in definite relation to the design as a whole. It was a century later, when sword-furniture was made for sale as such, rather than for adjustment to the sword blade and sheath, that the work lost its dignity and acquired an elaborate over-decorated style, which was still worse as we come nearer to our own times. The hammered iron gave place to cast-iron, though it was still used sometimes as the ground for the ornament. The variety of combinations towards the end of the eighteenth century and at the beginning of the nineteenth was astonishing, and this was not confined to sword-furniture, but extended to a variety of other articles.

Three able artists at Kyoto at this period obtained great success by their work in yellow bronze. The guards were decorated with flowers or with animals in high relief, or carved in the metal. One of them, Toshinaga, delighted in bird-subjects, especially the crane; another, Mitsuoki, was an incomparable engraver; the third, Mitsuhiro, chose the scenes of evening, the moon shining, rabbits playing on the grass, or cranes sleeping amongst the reeds. But where so many masters were employing their talents in the decoration of

SWORD-GUARD IN HAMMERED IRON INLAID WITH SILVER, BY YUSAN.

accessories of the sword, it appears useless to individualise thorn, except by a list which is only imperfect because of the lack of agreement amongst the English and French authorities.

What has been hitherto written regarding the tsuba applies with equal force to the kodzuka and kdgai. The handle of the kodzuka is never a bit inferior to the other parts of the mountingâ sometimes it is superior, often the whole of the mounts are done by the same hand, and the same signature is engraved upon them as upon the highly decorated face of the tsuba, that is the face towards the hilt. The fuchikachira and the menukis are equally worthy of notice. The latter, which are metal ornaments applied to the hilt or scabbard, have been treated by the Japanese somewhat differently, for some artists, whose names appear on the netsuke"s, did not disdain to carve these tiny objects in solid gold or silver. All through the various branches of the metal-worker's art there is a close connection which was noted when the Myochin family was under consideration. The carver of netsukÂ s made and engraved the fuchikachira and the menukis, and so on, as, too, they made the okimono, the statuettes for alcove ornament, though these in metal have not the usual grace of those carved in wood or ivory. Other articles in metal were used upon the same alcove, or platform, as objects necessary for the family worshipâ rishi or Taoist immortals, dragons, shishi (lions), candlesticks, koros, vases for flowers, gongs, and bells. If in the home the Japanese collector had artistic treasures, they were not exposed about the house for ornament, but kept in a separate store or godownâ that is, when they exceeded the accommodation furnished by the cupboard. There might be an incense-burner and a vase or two in metal, a fire-stand or holder (hibachi), kettles, and a few other domestic utensils, and such objects for personal use as pipes (kiseru), inkstands (yatate), etc., also in metal.

The class which includes masks, spears, swords, and helmetsâ the metal-work of Japanâ yielded to none in its decoration, in the beauty and delicacy of its engraving and chasing; in the fineness and fixity of its damascening; in the projection of the designs sculptured or worked in relief, giving the light and shade which were required; and in that form of ornamental incrustation of gold and silver upon the steel or iron ground, in which damascening was a necessary preliminary, so that the ornament might be fixed rigidly in the narrow, long, line-like channels, before undergoing further processes of decoration-chasing, engraving, or carving.

There are many methods of ornamenting metal. I cannot do better than adopt with due acknowledgment Mr. Audsley's classification, as set out in his fine book, "The Arts of Japan ":

"Kebori, or fine hair-line chasing, where lines are chiselled out of varying depth and thickness, and effect is produced by the light and shade on their sides, any burr being cut off.

HEAD-PIECE BY NAGATSANE MASANORI. I7TH CENTURY.

â It is this style which is the most affected by the Japanese, especially when the engraver succeeds in imitating successfully the strokes of the painter's brush in the design which lie is copying.

"In hira-zogan (hira, flat; zogan, inlaying), or damascening, all lines are equal in depth, but their bottoms are widened, so as to receive and retain the gold or silver wire which is beaten into them. This and kebori are often used together.

"Kata-kiri-bori is where designs are cut in relief from portions of the metal raised for the purpose; this ' is unmatched in the entire range of ornamental metal-work in Art." Here no advantage is obtained by other coloured metals, but light and shade only have to be relied upon. This literally sculptured work is almost entirely produced by a cold chisel and hammer, and in old work it is usually left untouched and unpolished.

"Lastly, there is the mixture of many processes, called kata-kiri-bori-zogan y or figured, sculptured, and encrusted metal chasing, or painting on metal, an achievement peculiarly Japanese. An alloy capable of taking a dark patina is used as the basis; much of the design consists of pierced work, and the remainder is in relief, encrusted and damascened.

"The background of Japanese metal-work is often as remarkable as any part of it. The artist seldom omits to treat it in a way which adds to the decoration, and to his labour. He does not hesitate to attempt a misty twilight or night effect, an imitation of wood or leather, and it is needless to say he succeeds. One thing only he usually avoids, and that is the bright polish which Western nations esteem so highly. Glitter and garishness are not in his line."

It will be evident that the kata-kiri-bori-zogan processes, excessively difficult upon a ground of tough iron or hard steel, would be much easier upon a soft alloy, such as shakudo, which is composed of base metal and gold, or shibuichi, composed of a similar metal and silver; hence these are often used for purely ornamental incrustation or inlaying, and I have seen some vases which have been marvels of the art of incrustation, where mother-of-pearl and various stonesâ jade, malachite, coloured rock-crystal, lapis lazuli, etc.â with fine ivory, have been combined in a bouquet of flowers eminently pleasing and astonishing. Was the metal-worker also a glyptic artist, or did he call to his aid some lapidary? We do not know, but the production is so admirable that only master-hands could have accomplished the work. Shakudo and shibuichi need further description, which will be found in the chapter on bronze.

Amongst the interesting exhibits of the Japanese Government at the White City, the retrospective section of works in metal was as attractive as it was uncommon. There were several suits of armour, including one of hammered iron by Myochin Munesuke. Several helmets with their haramaki or horns were included in these. Myochin Sosatsu was represented by a muneate, a defensive breastplate in

A SAMURAI WAITING FOR NEWS, WITH HIS SWORD EVER READY.

hammered iron, and by a fragment of kote armour for the arms. Face-guards, worked by Horai Munenaga and Myochin Yoshimichi, were as interesting as the suneate, armour for the legs. Several pairs of iron stirrups, with gold and silver inlaid, displayed the skill of the metal-worker in artistic work, whilst the simpler iron arrow-heads told of the village blacksmith. The beautiful decorative or dress swords, ornamented in various styles, were lent by princes and nobles. I said various styles, because each would require a long description â shio-no-yama-no-tachi, for instance. These swords differed from those of the samurai. They were magnificent examples of art reserved for the Daimios, though the long and short swords, the well-known samurai swords, were scarcely less excellent. One of them was embellished with an engraving on iron of a thousand monkeys. Few of these appeared to have any signature. In fact, I only found one set signed. That was a long and short sword by Toshikage.

Then as to accessories, " the swords' belongings," there were hundreds. One exhibitor sent a collection of four hundred and fifty. Tsubas were shown in nearly endless variety, some of them ornamented with cloisonne. Two pieces of historical interest attracted my attention. One was a short sword, said to have been used by the Taiko, that is the Shogun, Hideyoshi, who sprang from humble birth to the rank of Viceroy and General, and became paramount in Japan and Korea in the sixteenth century. The other was a nail-cover, decorated with cloisonne, used in Hideysohi's splendid and luxurious castle of Momoyama, which gave its name to the Momoyama period of Japanese painting, 1573-1603, when the Kano school flourished.

Amongst other objects were a few dirks, which I mention because some dirk ornaments were signed by Hirata Hiko-shiro, who died in 1646â exquisite metal-work, to which scant justice has been done, brilliant art from the hands of eminent masters, with whom must be ever associated the name of Myochin.

The chief metal-workers' signatures here given are: (i) Myochin, (2) Sanemori, (3) Kinai, (4) Shinkodo, (5) NobuiyÂ, (6) Um6tada, (7) Somin, (8) Toshinaga, (9) Mitsu-hiro, (10) Konkuan, (n) Yeijiu, (12) Shindzui, (13) Riuo, (14) Mitsuoki, (15) Kadzunori, (16) Takuti, (17) Harunari, (18) Kuniharo, (19) Masanori, (20) Nagatsune, (21) Tomoyo-shi, (22) Fussamasa, (23) Yoshitsugu, (24) Teikan, (25) Seidzui, (26) Johi, (27) Haruakira, (28) Noboyoshi, (29) Yatsushika, (30) Natsuo.

SIGNATURES ON METAL-WORK, ARMS, AND ARMOUR.

WEAVING is the process by which fibres are converted into fabrics by means of the loom, and in Japan the textile art has been, for centuries, one of its glorious industries, which is just what would be expected in a land where the people always had a passion for sumptuous robes, and where the material, the raw sijk, was abundant and excellent. The records show that both silk and the art of weaving came from China, but, again, the date of its first importation is uncertain, just as in the other arts introduced either directly from China, or indirectly through Korea. In the year A. D. 238, the Chinese Emperor Ming Ti, of the Wei dynasty, presented five rolls of brocade, with dragons woven upon a crimson ground, to the reigning Empress of Japan, who sent an embassy to the Chinese Court in that year. In the mediaeval age, when the Fujiwara, a sept or clan, usurped the Imperial authority, and the military affairs of the country were entrusted to the two septs of Minamoto and Taira, when the local chieftains gradually assumed the title of Daimios, it was the fashion to wear Chinese brocades and embroideries. During the fierce struggles in which the Minamotos and Tairas, having secured a firm hold upon the soldiery, fought one against the other for the mastery, all art suffered; but when Yoritomo, chief of the Minamotos, grasped the supreme authority, and became the Shogun in 1192, peace came, and with it the new birth of the arts; the development of the textiles led to the establishment of many looms at Kyoto, which in the thirteenth century had a flourish- ing industry, renowned for silks, fragments of which are preserved with the most religious care.

The loom consisted essentially of two rollers, between which was stretched the warp, consisting of a large number of vertical threads. Suspended from the top of the loom

ROBE OF A DAIMIO IN FLAME-COLOUR BROCADE.

were two frames or headles, which could be raised by means of a treadle. One of these headles, connected with the alternate threads of the warp, raised them, whilst the other headle raised all the other threads. By means of a shuttle, containing a bobbin of thread, one thread was thrown through the warp when all the odd-numbered threads were raised, and this was thrown back again when all the even-numbered threads were raised. By thread after thread the weft grew, that is, as each cross-thread fastened together the vertical threads of the warp, passing under one and over the next, returning with similar effect. The threads of the weft were driven together by a batten, shuttle and batten being worked by hand, the headles by a foot-treadle. Thus the simple web grew. But in weaving brocades the process was complicated, and the number of headles increased according to the design which had to be reproduced. The skill of the painter-designer had to be invoked for the designs, which included an immense number of patterns upon grounds of cloth of gold or colour, of damask or gauze.

The most complicated loom, that used for weaving flowered brocades, was worked by two persons, the weaver seated below, and his assistant above. He threw the shuttles and changed the threads; sheâ for the assistant was generally a womanâ worked the headles, and helped where necessary in changing or knotting the threads.

The silk-worm, a native of China, comes from the eggs produced by a moth (bombyx mori), and it looks like a caterpillar, which it is, yet a caterpillar of marvellous capacity, changing, in a process of digestion, the leaves of the white mulberry into a gelatinous thread, which becomes silk by exposure to the air. From the spinneret, projection of the silk continues until the caterpillar assumes its pupa state as a chrysalis, quiescent in its shroud, the cocoon, a silken web which nature intended for its protection. Then, in the East, in due season the first step of the manufacture of the silk fabric was taken, in securing the raw material.

"The scent of cocoons boiling fills the street, The women in each house, in busy bands, With smiling faces gather round the stove. And rub together their steam-scalded hands; They throw the bright cocoons into the basin, And wind out silk in long unbroken skein; When evening comes they've earned a moment's rest, To chat with friends outside in the walled lane."

Afterwards came the spinning, whereby the raw silk acquired the substance of a thread, fine or coarse, according to its intended use. I imagine that the first efforts to secure a thread were confined to simple twisting by the fingers, but the first weaver must have had great difficulties with thread made in this way. The distaff and spindle must have been contemporary with the earliest attempts to make textures for dress, simple coverings for the body. Solomon, the great proverbialist, wrote in praise of the good wife: " She layeth her hands to the spindle, and her hands hold the distaff." " She maketh herself coverings of tapestry; her clothing is silk and purple." " She maketh fine linen, and selleth it; and delivereth girdles unto the merchant." The process of making the silk-thread might have been this, yet, considering that the silk was wound off in a fine thread, it appears more probable that the necessary thickness and strength were obtained by a simple spinning-wheel which could twist any numbers of threads of raw silk into one. The old Grecian myth of the Three Fates represented them as spinning the thread of human destiny, and, indeed, the whole subject of spinning possesses much interest, from the old spindle, a wooden pin a few inches in length having a neck or hook at the small upper end, by which to fasten the thread, and a weight of some sort at the lower end to make it hang properly, to the elaborate satinwood spinning-wheel of the eighteenth century. Then the machinery for spinning, too! But the Orientals, Chinese and Japanese alike, used only the hand-loom for weaving.

The embroidered robes worn by the aristocracy of Japan were magnificent. The Emperor, the Empress, the Shogun, the royal Princes, the Daimios, the Court ladies, and society, right down to the Geisha girls, the Yoshiwara beauties, and even the degraded joro class, all had stated costumes. Sumptuary laws and restrictions bound all classes, and though under the feudal system the robes of the men were more splendid than those of the women, in the seventeenth century, and later, the women's dress increased in brilliancy, but always robes were distinctive of rank. They were woven, for the highest classes, entirely of silk, diapered, interwoven, and perhaps embroidered in gold or silver. The word diaper came from Constantinople, and the word damask from Damascus, but both are applied to certain classes of Japanese fabrics. I said that gold and silver were interwoven in the loom, and the early process consisted in covering the threads

COURT ROBE OF THE HOGO. I4TH CENTURY.

of silk with long narrow strips of foil; later, fine gold and silver wire were used in the same way. The kimonos were decorated with woven designs, sometimes regular, even geometric in pattern, sometimes with the blazons of the feudal princes, with palmettes or sprays of flowers upon a plain or ornamented and coloured ground.

During the fourteenth century the decoration was severe to simplicity, but from the fifteenth century onwards, the style became more florid, arabesques and branches of large flowers were in favour, but all of these bore evidences of the influence of Chinese art. However, in the sixteenth century, the freedom from foreign influence became as marked in the textile art as it was in all of the others; beautiful coloured and ornamented grounds carried decoration which was purely Japaneseâ arms of the Emperor, of the Shogun, and of the feudal Princes, for the nobles; flowers and diapers of all kinds, for their ladies. Yet the seventeenth century was noted for greater display. All the arts, under the protection of the Tokugawa Shoguns, enjoyed the blessings of peace. Kano Tannyu and his brother Naonobu, Kano Tsunenobu and Sotatsu, Kano Toun and Kano Yasunobu, revelled in the painting after their own styleâ the Kano schoolâ and they were designers, too; but the Tosa school, with Tosa Mitsunari and Tosa Mitsuoki, rivalled its great opponent. The action of the patrons, the elevation of the art of these schools reacted upon the textile art, though Ogata Korin confined his attention to lacquer, and the pioneers of the Ukiyo-ye school, Matabei and Hishikawa Moronobu, were more concerned in developing the principles and unfolding the beauties of scenes from daily life, as their exclusive province.

The next, the eighteenth, century gave full play to the genius of the popular school, except that they had no influence at the Court of the Emperor or of the Shogun, both of whom were devoted to their own schools, the classic Tosa and Kano. Kano Yousen, amongst others, furnished designs for robes, as did Sukenobu, Goshin, Toyokuni, and Hokusai, inside the limit stated. In studying the contemporary pictures of this age it is impossible to overestimate the fancy, the richness, and even the elegance shown in the costumes of the women, in which the kimonos and the obis vie each with the other in the display of elaborate design and brilliant colouring.

It should be recorded that silk was the stuff most used in

China for ages, when the Western world used wool and flax and cotton, though these were mixed with gold and silver thread, and all of them were dyed so that coloured cotton, linen, and wool were embroidered and ornamented with other designs. It was during the dark ages that the Emperor Justinian, 485-565, by a successful stratagem, and by the aid of two pilgrim monks, secured silk-worms from China, which they had hidden in their bamboo staffs, and brought

A FUKUSA WITH A DESIGN OF CARP IN THE WAVES.

to Byzantium. From that event dated the silk manufacture of Europe, before which time silk had been imported from China, at the current rate of exchange, " a pound of gold for a pound of silk."

Both China and Japan exported silks to Europe by the Company ships of Portugal, Holland, and England, and amongst them were costumes of all kinds such as are dear to the heart of the collector, though fine antique robes, etc., are rare. Costumes of extraordinary beauty were worn by the Kuge, Daimios, actors, and No dancers, and by the courtiers. Magnificent kimonos, obis, priests' cloaks (koroma), kamishimo, hirao, etc., were made in silk, satin, and brocade. Embroidered silk covers included a whole series of those fukusas, or covers wrapped around offerings, in gold brocade, tapestry, and embroidery of unique and beautiful designs; then there were velvet and silk pictures in embroidered panels, kakemonos of stamped velvet, and even silk, embroidery, and gold and silver brocade, made in rolls measuring about 20 yards long. The Kuge was a Court noble, a lord having high rank, but no land or power, a follower of the Emperor, and therefore opposed to, and by, the Daimio, who served the Shogun.

The actor's robes were ornamented with pictures, and just now I noted the influence of the artists of the Ukiyo-ye school, which was displayed, in a striking, but somewhat coarser form, upon the designs for the theatre, which had to be seen from a distance by the audience. Landscapes and rivers, animals of all sorts, fishes and shell-fish, gigantic spiders, ducks swimming in a stream, flights of birds, and clouds of insects, sunsets, ice and snow scenes, and all the flowers of Nippon, were displayed in fantastic, capricious, but impressive colouring, which was designed for effect. These garments were often made in cotton or other cheap material, covered with a figured pattern, and similar cheap kimonos and obis, designed by artists such as Kunisada were worn by the women of the Yoshiwara. Cotton robes were, of course, worn by the working people, and these were generally of a neuter tone, having none of the character which the later artists gave to the garments of the tall, graceful figures so constantly represented in the Ukiyo-ye paintings and colour-prints. On the one side are these cheap, but striking dresses; on the other are those which are more elegant, more rare, and very costlyâ the ancient Court dresses, the hiraos, hanging belts, the famous No drama robes, the long-sleeved, fine old kimonos, and the fukusas.

In no single object is the art of the weaver and embroiderer more delightfully shown than in the fukusas, the squares of brocade, more or less richly ornamented according to the rank of the owner, which have a special use already indicated by the words " covers wrapped around offerings." When a man wished to make a present it was carefully enveloped in a fukusa, and forwarded by a messenger, who carried also

A FUKUSA WITH A DESIGN SHOWING THE SUN SETTING BEHIND A PINE FOREST.

a letter in a small lacquer box. The fukusa was returned to the sender as an acknowledgment of the receipt of the present. This has been said elsewhere, but the repetition will do no harm. In the old Chinese pictures the present wrapped in its fukusa may be often noticed, and in the hands of many of the old porcelain figures they form a problem unless you know that the present is enclosed in the fukusa. Really, this fukusa is a silk picture, with wonderful gradations of colour embroidered upon a gold ground, it may be, or a coloured one. But, although I can give some specimens of the designs, these do not even suggest the colouring, the realism of the birds and the flowers, the reflections of light upon their surfaces, the shining of the scales of the carp in

ENGLISH TEXTILE DESIGN FROM THE JAPANESE. LATE IQTH CENTURY.

the water, work of the weaverâ a textile fabric with all the detail of an embroidery done by an artist upon a frame or a tambour. Some day these fukusas will be justly esteemed, not only for the essentially Japanese design so delicately, so skilfully, executed, but for their charming coloured grounds, which display the rarest tints, for which I have no names. Rose and shades of green, yellow, dead-leaf, cream-white, silver-grey, are only indications of a list that could be copied from an encyclopaedia; but I must leave them to the imagination.

The finest of these works date from the eighteenth century, but the later nineteenth-century examples are often admirable. They resemble the Chinese K'o ssu pictures made of woven silk. Some say they are intended for the decoration of the reception-room, but no provision is made for hanging

EMBROIDERED FUKUSA, A CRANE FLYING ABOVE A PINE UPON WHICH MANY BIRDS ARE PERCHING.

them, and in Japan the furniture was scantyâ the general attitude of kneeling or sitting upon the floor made large tables unnecessary. They were not hung upon the walls, nor laid upon the tables, but they might have been shown in the biyobus, the screens having two, three, or more folds. But why speculate? They are fttkusas which deserve to rank with the Gobelins tapestry. Under the guidance of

Louis XIII., the Royal factory commenced its career at La Savonnerie; under Louis XIV. it was removed to the place consecrated by time, where the famous dyers named Gobelins had exercised their profession.

Japanese tapestry must be added to brocade and embroidery, and this, in its method of careful and artistic treatment, approaches the very stitch, le veritable point, of Gobelins. Tapestry is a sort of link between weaving and embroidery; though wrought in a loom, and upon a warp stretched out along its frame, it has no woof thrown across those vertical threads by a shuttle or any such thing, but the weft is done with many short threads, all variously coloured, and put in by a needle or knotted with the fingers. It is not embroidery, though so very like it; embroidery is worked in a frame, upon a web, having both warp and woof; tapestry is worked upon a series of closely set fine strings. When did the Japanese begin to make tapestry? This is a question which is the more difficult to answer because the Japanese say that their tapestry had a Chinese origin. We know that the Chinese borrowed the art from Western Asia, where the designs, even now, show no Chinese influence. Tapestry in Japan made at Kyoto, towards the end of the sixteenth century, was exceedingly restricted in its output, but the pieces that are known are marked with the native decoration, with no sign of outside influence. It is possible II

TAPESTRY PANEL WITH A GOLD GROUND.

that the Portuguese merchants, about 1540, may have brought some specimens of European tapestry, or the Dutch later. In any case, whilst the Japanese specimens are entirely delicate and charming in their colouring, they are almost as uncommon as carpets, and these can scarcely vie with the famous silk carpets of Persia, India, and Turkey, or even with those of Yarkand and Manchuria, which produced the best Chinese carpets.

I may note that amongst the fabrics in the retrospective section of the Japan-British Exhibition there was not one piece of tapestry, which shows how rare it was.

All of these wonderful textile fabrics must be prized for their intrinsic beauty. They owe much to the designer, whose signature only rarely appears upon this kind of work. The craftsmen belonged to the artisan class, and just as their brothers in the other arts displayed the highest skill, so these, working on a pittance, wrought marvels in weaving, embroidery, and tapestry, which will endure as silent memorials of manual dexterity beyond compare, of patience beyond belief, and of devotion as singular as it was altogether admirable. A purely utilitarian age offers small compensation for the lost arts which reached perfection when men hastened slowly.

IF you have opportunities to handle and study colour-prints, to compare one artist's work with another's, you will provide most interesting object-lessons for yourself. Let us take one by comparing the prints of Harunobu (1703-1770) and Toyonobu (1710-1785) on the one hand, with those of Utamaro (1754-1806) and Toyokuni (1774-1835) on the other. We will confine our attention to one subject, the lady in the picture. The four artists resembled each other, and all figure painters resembled them in some respects. Their celebrated beauties are seemingly alike in the face; the later artists gave no added charm by putting what we should call expressions of love, hate, or fear upon the universally oval faces, which show two slits, wide apart, for eyes, " the almond eyes," two black curves high up on the forehead, not eyebrows reallyâ they had been shaved offâ but imitation eyebrows, a long nose, which, however, is slightly more aquiline in the early pictures, and tiny lips, again with a slight difference in form; but, as I said, apparently alike, even to the form of the face. In their robes some differences appear, which should be studied; they cannot be explained except by saying that the set or fit at the neck is different, early robes being closer.

Now we find differences much more marked if we compare the arrangement of the hair. The early coiffure shows a frame which curves from the ears backwards in CO form, and the front is arranged in three ondules on each side of the brow. The later arrangement has a frame with two wings, between which the hair pulled from the forehead passes in a flat band under a comb or fillet, and the back hair appears like a chignon on a pad or frame. Such a difference might have marked a change of fashion, as it does a period of time. Something more is said about the hair a little later in this chapter. A glance at this difference will distinguish between Harunobu and his contemporaries, and Utamaro and those who lived about when he did. Again, Harunobu approached the classic Chinese styleâ his women, full of charm, have somewhat short, rounded figures; Utamaro, Toyokuni, and others reveal a different type tall women, full of grace and abandon; less severity, less purity, but more delicacy in design, exquisite lines, and skilful composition. Harunobu's colour-prints are highly appreciated by collectors, and the best of Utamaro's are almost as costly. But we will now leave comparisons, and the suggestions they offer, to consider more closely the woman and her adornment, and the man and his work, the woman at home, the soldier and his Daimio.

Before describing the actual dress of the women, I am using two opinions to correct some errors which have accompanied the adoption of the kimono as a woman's gown in England, and France especially.

Mr. Ponting, in his book, has criticised the western Woman's use of the kimono, as follows:

"No class of Japanese womanhood is more misunderstood, by foreigners, than the geisha. The geisha has no prototype in Europe; she is uniqueâ a purely Japanese creation. To mention the name geisha amongst English people unversed in matters Japanese is to cause uneasy looks and suggestive smiles. Why the geisha should be so misapprehended is difficult to tell. I have often wondered, too, why it is that when European ladies wear Japanese clothes, or array themselves as ' Japanese geishas," they invariably make the most glaring errorsâ wear elaborately embroidered kimonos, stick many long pins in their hair, tie their sashes in front, and, in short, make themselves resemble neither geishas nor ladies, but public women of the yoshiwara. Neither Japanese ladies nor geisha wear embroidered kimonos; they never wear a halo of long pins in their hair, nor do they tie their sashes in front. These things are the badges of prostitution."

A clever Japanese actress visiting England in 1910, Mrs. Hanako, has also criticised the Englishwoman's use of the same garment.

"In a strange country, or a country new to me," she said, "I should not, perhaps, be surprised at surprises. But there is one thing in particular that I cannot help expressing my astonishment with. In my Continental travels, and in my stay in England, I have observed that ladies have a fancy for wearing our kimono as a dressing-gown! I wonder what they would say if they went over to Japan and found some of my countrywomen leaving their morning bath, or taking their first meal of the day, in English ball-dresses or afternoon gowns! I think they would say, or at least get the impression, that the Japanese ladies were quite mad!

"And if English and French ladies must wear the kimono for a dressing-gown," continued the Japanese actress, " why don't they have it made to fasten as we fasten it? It should lap over from left to right, not, as is the case with your womenfolk, from right to left. When a Japanese lady walks, her draperies must fall from left to right. The ladies of Europe do not know this. If they delight to wear the dress of Japan they should delight to wear it properly, or there is neither sense nor compliment in the fashion. If they do not know how the kimono ought to be made, surely your manufacturers might be expected to have some knowledge of the dress.

"In Japan, the older a woman gets, the smaller are made the sleeves of her kimono. I have not noticed any small sleeves on the kimonos worn by English ladies, however old they have been! But Japanese ladies are proud of their age; they never want to shorten it by a single month."

The fact is that English admiration of Japanese fashions is not accompanied by such knowledge as would make those fashions properly applicable. A lady in Japan had her stipulated dress which no other class could use. But in copying the kimonos and the obis, which are pictured upon a colour-print, the easiest mistake in the world is to believe that fine feathers make fine birds. The gorgeous robes of Yoshiwara beauties, as they are called, simply advertise their connection with institutions under state control and medical supervision which were frequented by many painters of the Ukiyo-ye school, whose standard of morals cannot be properly judged by outsiders holding divergent views of morality.

In dress, variations of material and fashion marked rank and wealth for men and women, but in these modern days such distinctions are passing, if they have not all gone. The chief, sometimes the only, robe is the kimono, so well-known in the West, resembling our dressing-gown in opening down the front and leaving the neck exposed. Around the waist a sash (obi) is worn, which may be elaborate in a certain class of ladies' dresses, of which it forms the chief ornament, being wound round the body and tied behind, or in front, in a large butterfly bow with long streamers. The wide sleeves of the kimono form the receptacles for paper-handkerchiefs and trifles of all kinds, and the train of the ceremonial dress of the ladies may be some feet in length. The material varies with the season, in those classes which can afford heavy silk for winter instead of the usual cotton; but all classes in the cold season wear pantaloons and stockings.

The head-dress of the women is an elaborate coiffure which necessitates the hard pillow to avoid disorder; if it is a work of art to dress the hair in the modern fashion in the West, the Yoshiwara beauty must devote a large part of each day to secure the perfect shape, which is maintained by a large rounded comb in front, and by a number of long pins, all serving to secure the hair on the frame which forms the foundation for its conventional shape. Indoors the comb and some of the pins can be removed, and the hair tied with a ribbon fillet. It may be mentioned that these combs and pins have often a high value because of the fine workmanship which distinguishes the lacquer, the ivory, etc., of which they are made.

Head-coverings are not usually wornâ a kind of paper square cap is used to prevent the wind from interfering with locks that might stray if exposed to its force, and the mushroom rice-straw hat for rainy weather, in which case a hood or handkerchiefâ

Western shapeâ may be wrapped round the head under the umbrella. Clogs, or pattens, of Kiri wood, held fast by a strap over the foot round the big toe, are frequently shown in scenes of storm and rain, but the common footwear is a waraji or sandal of rice-straw which must be removed on entering a house, though it may be only a shop. Rice for food, rice-straw for hats, rain-coats, and sandals, rice in sake for strong drinkâ so much does the ordinary peasant in his blue cotton kimono, and his wife in a similar dress, with a red obi, owe the rice-plant. The tilling of the rice occupies a considerable share in the world of Japanese art, and though the aroma arising in the processes is disagreeable, the farmer takes no small pleasure in viewing the rice-fields, and still more in a plentiful harvest.

Fans played an important part in the daily life of the Japanese, serving a multiplicity of purposes. The farmer winnowed his corn with a fan, and the smith blew his fire. The general directed his soldiers with a fan, and they used them sometimes as weapons, or shields, which bore the blazon of the feudal prince, which was repeated on the mushroom-shaped helmets and upon the backs of the armour. The standard of lyeyasu at the siege of Osaka in 1615 was a fan.

Emperor and Empress, Shogun and Daimio, Kuge, Samurai, all classes carried fansâ not always in evidence, sometimes reposing in the pocket-sleeve of the kimono or robe. Great painters decorated them for their patrons. Before me lies a print, by Kiyomitsu and Kiyosune, of a painter painting a fan, a folding paper-fan, which in its inception was Japanese; the round-leaf and fiddle-shape fans came from China through Korea.

How vast was the difference between the common fans used in hot weather, or in cold when the fire in the hibachi needed attention, and the fans of ceremony! Upon the ivory-tinted paper surface of these were displayed the paintings of artists such as Korin, Kenzan, Kano Masanobu, Motonobu, and others, in scenes historical or poetical, perhaps with portraits of the heroes of the past. Fans were regulated by laws; they differed according to social position. The philosopher carried a sober fan of plain material, mounted on delicate ribs of cedar or pine, uncoloured. The geisha in her graceful rhythmic posturing, made full play with a showy fan with rich gold or vermilion ground decorated with a bold design of flowers or birds, a profuse fluttering, like a butterfly settling upon a flower. Then she presented the fan to the friend she most admired. What a contrast to its ceremonial use by the priests and the No dancers!

The use of the fan in every-day life was peculiarly charming. When a gentleman visited another, he made his first salutation on his knees, with his fan on the floor in front of him. Then he placed his present upon the half-opened fan, having first ceremoniously wrapped it up and tied it with emblematical threads. Holding the fan forward, he presented it to his host or hostess, who took the offering.

In the illustration, fans of various forms are shown, and a girl with a box containing fans which could be attached to the mounts. Many of the folding-fans could in this way be utilised upon the same mount, and varied according to the season or the ceremony, and so on, through numerous pretty but declining customs, which were singularly appropriate to the genius of the Japanese.

The display of dress by the womankind of Japan, with kimonos and obis of brilliant pattern, or in softer tones of embroidered silk, paled before the war panoply of the

Samurai headed by the Daimios, the feudal princes whose large revenues supported palaces and armies, whose ceremonies, so often depicted, whose almost royal progresses and reciprocal visits, and whose patronage of the arts, alike caused them to be regarded by their followers with a loyalty that death itself could not conquer, by their artists with a devotion which found constant outlet in works worthy of high praise. The artist was often a noble, but a poor one, and the patronage of a prince was to him very good, for it meant life and some honour, congenial work that might, perhaps, attract the great Shogun himself. When the Shogun, after the civil wars of the tenth and eleventh centuries, practically became the supreme ruler, many noble families lost their possessions with their power, and the ruling class, the military, attached to itself the civil power from 1192 to 1868.

From this aggrandisement sprang the soldiers, the fighting men, the Samurai who did no other work. They were ready to fight and ready to die, but they could not engage in business; they gloried in their armour, helmet, and coat of mail, they gloried in the privilege of wearing two swords, they were, in fact, magnificent fellows, but very idle. During long centuries taxation supported them and their mastersâ the Daimiosâ and if the latter sustained large companies of bow-men and spear-men, banner-bearers, and a few horsemen, they also did what was better, they encouraged the literature and art of the country and spurred them on. The great art progress under the Ashikagas and under the Toku-gawas showed the effect of the protection of the Shoguns, whilst, if we except the period covered by the nengo of the Emperor Genroku (1688-1704), there appear but few of the Emperors whose influence was distinctly exerted in favour of that progress. Yet all the time the active principle in the Mikado was only dormantâ the awakening came in 1867; henceforth the Shogun disappeared, though the Princes of the Tokugawa family became leaders of the Peers.

For the swords and helmets of the soldiers how many devoted craftsmen hammered at the forge until the bright blade, the splendid helmet, and the curious armour grew under their hands? how many more damascened the blade and its accessories, incrusted and inlaid the helmet, and produced an accoutrement which, though cumbrous, was in active service at a period much later than our Middle Ages, as late, in fact, as about 1853, when foreigners were allowed to trade with Japan? Even in 1860 the Japanese percussion light muskets were so badly made that, on trying the locks, Sir Hope Grant found that " many of them would scarcely go off. 1 '

THE houses built by the Japanese appear to be more or less flimsy structures, and quite unsubstantial from our point of view, but the earthquakes which trouble them are responsible for this. Built of wood and resting upon foundations of unhewn stone, they are particularly liable to destruction by fire; and the use of oil-lamps for candles has considerably increased this danger. The worst side faces the street; the other opens upon a garden whose size is largely dependent upon its position. The walls, usually untouched, as they came from the hands of the carpenter, are permanent on two sides; the others are formed of shutters, or movable partitions, which, facing the outside (shoji), are covered with white paper. Two or more stories may be built, and a balcony or engawa may give a wider outlook upon the world around. No chimney deforms the roof, which is either tiled, shingled, or thatched.

Inside, the rooms are divided by movable partitions, so as to accommodate a certain number of regulation mats, 6 feet by 3 feet, which cover the floor. The rooms are oblong in shape, and have no recesses, except the chief room, which has twoâ the toko-noma, where the kakemonos are displayed, just two or three at a time, being removed to a cupboard at the side, from which others are taken in turn, according to the season or the ceremony. The other recess, raised, like the first above the floor-level, is the chigai-dana, in the top of which are numerous drawers and shelves, having below a cupboard for the bedding. Upon the platform of the toko- noma is the altar, upon which are vases with flowers, incense-burner, a figure of the household god, etc. These are clearly shown in the illustration of a Japanese marriage.

Access is given to the rooms above by means of steps which can be scarcely dignified by the name of a staircase. The upper rooms have movable partitions, too, so that when they are removed they form a kind of gallery to the main room. These inner screens are of thicker paper, often decorated with paintings, but on the verandah (engawa), wooden screens called amado are placed at night and in the rainy season. Beside the main, or guest-room, a special and separated chamber is usually set aside for the tea ceremony, and this, like the go-down, which is a storehouse for valuables, may be a pavilion in the garden. In this matter and in the general equipment of the house and its contents, of the garden and its floral decoration, much depends upon the wealth and inclination of the householder, though in these latter days the ceremonies have Jost much of their eclat, and they will soon be altogether discontinued.

Tea came from China early in the ninth century, and six centuries later, under the influence of the Shogun Yosimasa, rules were adopted to regulate the observance of the cha-no-yu, or tea ceremony, which had a great influence on Japanese art, because the members who formed the highest circles, the chajins, were the cognoscenti who criticised both artist and author, judging them according to certain standards which were fixed and only liable to slow change as time went on. We find that the Tosa school, the great Imperial academy, from the severity of the religious and classical style, only degenerated to the painting of flowers and birds about the beginning of the eighteenth century, and that the great Shogunal school of Kano always maintained its military and historical classica 1 style, notwithstanding the popularity of the more modern and independent painters. It was the authority of the cha-no-yu circle, or club or association, which maintained such standards over so long a period, not alone over painting, but the other fine arts.

A description of this ancient ceremonial will introduce many articles which were of the rarest and most valuable kind. Their owners delighted to trace the origin, age, and history of these utensilsâ a single tea-bowl, old, and from a noted pottery, would be worth hundreds of pounds, and

CARVED FIGURE OF A CHAJIN, IN WOOD.

before the last act in the ceremony, when the host washed the utensils, the bowl, from which all drank in rotation, made a special journey round the circle, so that each one could admire it. The guests forming the circle, an exclusive one, assembled either in the morning early, at four to six, or in the evening at six o'clock; if in summer, in the garden strewn with fir-branches, and retained their shoes: if in winter, in the house, and discarded them. The strictest rules of etiquette marked every stage in the proceedings, from the entrance, where the host knelt to receive the guests, who crawled into the room before him, to the conclusion.

After seeing them seated in a semi-circle he gave the formal salutation, and brought in a basket (sumi-tori) containing the prescribed pieces of charcoal, a brush (mitsu-ba) made of three feathers, a pair of tongs (hibashi), the stand for the kettle (kama-shiki), iron handles for it, too, a lacquer box containing incense (kobako), and some paper; following these, a vessel with ashes (hai-ki), and its spoon. Then he made up the fire and burned incense to overcome the fumes of the charcoalâ pastilles in winter, chips from the santalum album or sandal-wood-tree in summer. Meanwhile the incense-box was, by permission, passed from hand to hand for examination. The tea-bowl, we have noticed, was a rare one; the kobako, beyond price, disputed with it the place of honour. After it had been returned by the last guest to his host, the first act closed, everybody withdrew.

The second part commenced with eating, and, as it was a rule that nothing should be left, the guests carried off, wrapped up in paper, any fragments that remained. The utensils used in this part of the ceremony were as follows: 1. An iron kettle (kama) with a copper or iron lid, resting on a stand (kama-shiki).

2. A table or stand (daisu), of mulberry wood, two feet high.

3. Two tea-jars (chaire) containing the fine powdered tea, and enclosed in bags of brocade.

4. A vessel containing fresh water (mizu-sachi), which is placed under the daisu.

5. A tea-bowl of porcelain or earthenware (chawan, or, when of large size, temmoku), simple in form, but remarkable for its antiquity or historical associations.

Besides these, there are a bamboo whisk (chaseu); a silk cloth (fukusa), usually purple, for wiping the utensils; a spoon (chashaka), to take the tea out of the chaire; and a water ladle (shaku). All these objects were brought in singly by the host in their prescribed order.

After solemn salutations and obeisances the utensils were wiped and some of the powdered tea was placed in the tea-bowl, hot water poured on it, and the whole vigorously stirred with the whisk until it looked like thin spinach; a boy then carried the bowl to the chief guest, from whom it passed round the party to the last, who returned it empty to the boy.

Amongst those treasures connected with this tea ceremony, the chawan and chaire supply some of the masterpieces of the potters of Japan, the gifts of princes, not purchasable in the market. These pieces have received but little appreciation from the Western world, but at home they have always been highly treasured and carefully preserved by their proud possessors in brocade bags of extreme antiquity and beauty. Clothed in this tunic, the tea-bowl, or jar, was securely enclosed in a separate box, only to be produced on special feasts, always to be handled with reverent care.

The burning of incense, whether in connection with the tea ceremony, the incense gameâ a popular amusement in polite circlesâ or for other purposes, also brought into use certain utensils often fashioned in pottery by the best makers. Scent-boxes (kogo), in which little tablets of incense were kept, braziers (koro), in which they were burned, and clove boilers (choji-buro), vessels in which cloves were boiled to give an aromatic odour to a room, are the forms usually met with; and these often present such ingenuity of idea in their construction and decoration as to render them scarcely, if at all, inferior in interest to the tea-jars and tea-bowls. And it must be remembered that very few treasures were exposed to view in the home, two or three kakemonos, a hachirakaki or two, gave all the pictorial embellishment, the other articles, vases, makemonos, kakemonos, lacquer and bronze, were carefully packed away in the chigai-dana, a cupboard under which the bedding was stowed.

The celebrated Hideyoshi, viceroy and general, whose magnificent castle of Momoyama gave its name to a period in the history of the Kano school of painting, before he died at the age of over three-score years, had appointed an officer named Kikiu to revise the regulations of the tea ceremony, and, subject to what I have said earlier in this chapter, the revised code still applies to the different methods of carrying out the ceremony, which, like religion, had its sects, of whom the chief were the Senke", Enshu, Matsu-o, Yabu-no-uchi, and Orib6. These used powdered tea stirred with a whisk in boiling water, and drank it strong and thick from one bowl;

VIEWING THE CHERRY-BLOSSOM. A PICNIC PARTY.

but the less ceremonious drinkers of weak tea, Usa-cha y had each for himself a separate brew in a common bowl which was washed before use.

The same vice-regal commander-in-chief, or Sei Tai Shogun, Hideyoshi, greatly encouraged the manufacture of tea-bowls (chawan), especially those made by a Korean named Chojiro, at Juraku in Kyoto, about A. D. 1566. Ameya, Chojiro's father, a potter, settled there, and to his son the Shogun gave a gold seal having the engraved character Raku, meaning " enjoyment," which was impressed upon the coarse yellow ware covered with a gritty glaze and made entirely by hand. Raku tea-bowls were held in high favour by the cha-jin. Further reference will be found to this family in its relation to pottery, but there were other reasons for the popularity of such tea-bowls in addition to their artistic appearance. The tea-drinkers had to hold and pass the bowl, the irregularities of its surface were helpful in obtaining a firm grasp; they liked their tea hot, the thickness of the clay kept it hot without hurting their fingers, and so on. The Victoria and Albert Museum possesses a number of tea-bowls, some of them by great potters, but the special point to which I wish to draw attention is that the tea ceremony was apparently the great social function, which influenced the art of the country for good, as, indeed, it affected the moral, for three subjects were banned, three subjects, indeed, that could be often with advantage spared from our own social circlesâ politics, scandal, and flattery!

Like Tennyson's " Lotus-eaters," one thinks of the guests of the cha-no-yu:

"They saw the gleaming river seaward flow
From the inner land; far off a mountain-top, A silent pinnacle of aged snow,
Stood sunset-flush'd and dew'd with showery drop."

Though this social life was a ceremonial, more or less solemn, the religious ceremonies of the Buddhist temples were grander. I must say something about the temples.

The architecture of Japan, one of its most distinctive and important arts, deserves much fuller treatment than can be given here. Those who studied the models of the old buildings exhibited at the White City must have admired the triumphs of the carpenter, for wood is almost exclusively used for all buildings, ranging from the humblest to the grandest; temples and houses, theatres and palaces, have no other support than pillars of wood, wonderfully decorated in the temples and palaces. The beams supported by the pillars are in those buildings carved with marvellous skill after designs furnished by the great artists. This you have already seen.

YEISHI. A TRIPTYCH.

Some of the temples form an immense assemblage of pavilions and pagodas accessory to the main temple, and in the courts, where many stone or even bronze lanterns are found, there are cisterns or wells covered with elaborate roofs supported on pillars, whilst outside, at the entrance of the avenues leading to the temple, are the tori, or gateways, composed of two beams inclining upwards, and supporting a transverse horizontal beam curved upwards at the ends.

Upon the temple doors carved panels and friezes of extraordinary beauty display the richest fancy; the roofs, ornamented with ridge-tiles and with borders of wood covered with tiles in pottery or bronze, rest upon beams where the projecting timber-work is a veritable maze of joints and mouldings; whilst inside the building the ceiling is as remarkable as an evidence of the carpenters' skill. The fir-trees which covered the mountains of Japan furnished the material for the building; upon their colossal forms the old artisans worked their will, and from the far-off ages their masterpieces have lasted to the present day. The models referred to above represented temples, pavilions, and pagodas, dating from the seventh century onwards.

Elsewhere a distinction is drawn between the Shinto and Buddhist worship. In the temple-construction the difference between the two religions is evident at a glance, for the Buddhist temple is as elaborate as its ritual, and the Shinto temple as simple as its worship. The miya indicates the precincts enclosing the plain, straight-roofed, wood-tiled Shinto temple, and the word tera is applied to what we might term the enclosure, occupied by gardens and numerous buildings allied to the chief temple though not necessarily joined to it. I read the other day that the pupils of a Japanese school thought nothing of going a hundred or a hundred and fifty miles to see the famous mountain, Fujiyama, and that they slept at night in the Buddhist temples, which seemed rather an unusual use for a temple.

It was at Nara, the old capital of Nippon, that the temple of Horuji was built in the seventh century, and in that city remain many temples of more recent times, such as the Toshodai-ji of the twelfth century, and the Todai-ji of the same period. Then come some of the temples of Kyoto, where amongst the temple buildings may be found the Kinkaku, or Golden Pavilion, built for a Shogun's villa; the Hiunkaku, one of the buildings of the Taiko's palace at Momoyama; and the gateway of Daitoku-ji temple, which was brought from the same palace. The temples and palaces were elaborate.

The graceful pagodas, several stages high, are amongst the most distinctive of the Buddhist buildings. Though they resemble the Chinese pagodas in form, some of them are in red lacquer, and when seen on a background of emerald green foliage softened by the mist, they form very striking and beautiful elements in the landscape.

Other buildings are much more simple, even the theatres resemble the ordinary houses, always in natural wood of a neuter tone, in contrast to the Buddhist temples painted in vermilion and ornamented with carvings which are often coloured. The homes of the rich and poor are built on the same plan, the roof being the chief part. This in the country may be of straw or bamboo; in the town it is of tiles.

Square joists are set up in the earth at a certain distance from each other, and about three feet inside these a second rank of joists. The space between forms the verandah, or engawa, which usually surrounds the house. Between the joists in the second rank the sashes are fitted and covered with paper. These run in grooves, and by similar means the interior of the home may be divided into chambers.

The bridges, too, are of wood. They are built on piles, square joists again, driven into the soil beneath the water. The framework is covered with planks and the sides protected with rails. Sometimes they are extremely long.

The ceremonial arrangement of flowers, so frequently used in all branches of Japanese art, had a religious origin dating back to its introduction in the sixth century by the Buddhist priests. Having regard to the extravagant praise bestowed upon the flowers of Japan and the " viewing " as a favourite pastime of its people, the last part of this chapter contains a criticism written at Kyoto in 1910 by an English visitor who believed that the panegyrics had been overdone. Mean-

A PRINCESS VIEWING THE PLUM-PLOSSOM, AFTER YOSAI.

while, let us consider those scenes which painters and poets have so ardently, so repeatedly, depicted.

Before the winter snows have altogether vanished, the groves and avenues of plum-trees, planted in rural spots not far from the madding cities, are thronged with admiring crowds, who flock to view the pretty red and greenish-white blossoms, the emblems of the coming spring:

"Lo! in the middle of the wood The folded leaf is woo'd from out the bud."

There are as yet no leaves, and, soon for a short space, the paths are covered with " pearly-white clouds " of fallen leavesâ the petals of the primus. The next tree that flowers, the cherry, gives the signal for a short holidayâ cherry-blossom is the popular national flowerâ and fetes and merrymakings rule the pleasant days. Other minor flower festivals greet the wistaria, growing on other trees or trained upon trellis-work overhead, the peony, which often grows to the height of a tree, the many-coloured iris, the sacred lotus, maintaining its pristine purity amid surrounding mud, and in the autumn, the chrysanthemumâ emblem of imperial powerâ one of the crests of the Emperor. It forms the chief attraction at the annual garden-party at his palace in Tokyo, when the merits of each flower are discussed, "Sky at Dawn," "Moon's Halo," "Golden Dew," "Beacon Light," and many more with equally suggestive names.

A floral wealth ever changing is included in the decoration of houses and temples according to rules which avoid some flowers whilst using others. Vigorous growths with firm, young branches mark the coming of age; red and white flowers, but none of a drooping character, are used for weddingsâ red for the man, white for the woman. And so for other celebrations: farewell, old-age, and death, at the shrine, the sick-bed, and, above all, at two functionsâ the cha-no-yu, or tea ceremony, and the flower reception.

By the cha-jin, or masters of this ceremony, who were the arbiters of taste in the middle ages and after, the refined and indeed subtle flower-groupings were based on laws of composition. The literati, whose active service was finished, devoted themselves to the execution of these laws, which were perfectly arbitrary in their injunctions and prohibitions. It will be found that the earlier systems of arrangement allowed a greater crowding, a more miscellaneous choice, and a characteristic formality which disappears in the later period. It follows, then, that no painter or designer could illustrate a composition later than their own time, and this fact should be borne in mind.

The quaint forms and curious decoration of the vases, flower-holders, and baskets for flowers may be seen in stone and metal and pottery. The Chinese made precious vases in jade and other hard stones; the Japanese employed a greater variety of material, and devoted themselves more to form and design. Some flower-holders are specially adapted for the display of water-plants, so as to expose a free space of water. These are used in the warm season, when the sight of cool water is of itself refreshing. Sometimes stems of bamboo, of simple or fanciful form, are employed, without any outer covering, and they are associated for use in the home with quaint pieces of wood and bark, or even dried gourds.

Emblems in trees, emblems in flowers! The fir, the bamboo, and the plum are the " three friends " combined to form an emblem of longevity as in China. The lotus lily, upon whose broad thalamus the benign Buddha, seated, softly smiles upon the world, is his emblem. The Imperial badge, the chrysanthemum, was the Shinto emblem of the " way of the gods," as opposed to the " way of the Buddha." Then there are the fabulous animals. The dragon (no) rises amidst the clouds or from the sea with three claws extended, instead of the five upon the Imperial dragon of China. The Chinese feng huang becomes the ho-ho bird of Japan, the phoenix, which in both countries is the emblem of the Empress. The kirin, which, like the Chinese kilin, represents a near approach to the unicorn, having the body and hoofs of a deer, the tail of an ox, and a horn on its forehead, has a companion beast, the shishi (lion), called also the dog of Buddha, shows curling tufts of hair round the neck and on the limbs. The kame) the sacred tortoise, emblem of longevity, having a broad, hairy tail, and being sometimes represented with three legs, is another of the mythical animals immortalised in Oriental art. Yet these do not dim the fame of the Japanese as disciples of nature-study. Perhaps

VIEWING THE CHERRY-BLOSSOM.

the flowers and the birds are better rendered than the animals, yet the latter have a mythology of their own; curious tales are told of the foxes, which enter like evil spirits into possession of the forms of beautiful women, with intention to lead men on the wrong path, until some calm stream shows a reflection

VIEWING THE CHRYSANTHEMUM.

of their real nature, and the victims escape. We are learning something of Japanese myths, and long for more.

I set out below some criticisms, the first, written by a traveller in. Japan, whose name was not given but whose special article appeared in the Daily Chronicle, in June, 1910. His opinions differ from those which are usually current, but it is always advantageous to see all round a subject.

A LADY SEATED IN A NORIMONO UNDER THE CHERRY-BLOSSOM, PREPARING

TO SMOKE.

AFTER SUZUKI HARUNOBU.

"There is, save the temples and two or three palaces, little external Japanese architecture worth detailed mention â the earthquakes and fires are partly responsible. The existent and nascent efforts at new style are commonplace

French in character. The village scheme of structures is drab and unimpressive. Most of the houses are built of wood on the same pattern, as a rule, two storeyed, with roof of thatch, tile, or galvanised iron. There is little note of colour. Of the interiors it has been said that even the humblest endeavours to create its corner of Paradise. This is quite true, but while there is much attractiveness in detail, there is little variety in general design. Nearly all Japanese interiors have the same main scheme of construction and ornamentation. I know it is a prevalent idea that Japan is more or less a perennial feast of colour. It is nothing of the kind. It has its flower seasons, but the cherry blossom only lasts ten days at the most, and may be over in a third of the period; while the famous wistaria is only in its prime for a fortnight at the outside. As to the other flowers, such as the lotus and even the chrysanthemum, many countries can, nowadays, make very fair comparison. The leafage is, it is quite true, picturesque in autumn, but the tints are as good in most other countries. India is incomparably richer and wealthier in gorgeous colours. The birds and butterflies are much brighter in the tropics, and the dress, particularly of the women, is infinitely more picturesque in other sun countries, notably Burma. Indeed, the unrestrained eulogist of the Mousme and Geisha has much to answer for."

Mr. Ponting (" In Lotus Land: Japan ") describes a scene in more appreciative vein, a " viewing " in the temple park of Nara, "The Heart of Old Japan ":

"Giant wistaria vines have crept to the very utmost branches of the trees, and in May the tall cedars themselves seem to burst forth into clusters of drooping purple blooms. Through many an opening in the glorious arches overhead the sun throws long shafts of light which touch the pendant blossoms, and then, glancing downwards, melt moss and gravel into golden pools, or, searching out some spot on the brilliant lacquer, make it glow with ruddy fire as the great orb himself glows at daybreak."

SO seldom is it that the art of the potter, and still less of the Japanese potter, is sung by an occidental poet, that I shall be forgiven if I quote Longfellow in " Ke ramos."

"Cradled and rocked in Eastern seas, The islands of the Japanese Beneath me lie; o'er lake and plain The stork, the heron, and the crane Through the clear realms of azure drift, And on the hillside I can see The villages of Imari,

Whose thronged and flaming workshops lift Their twisted columns of smoke on high, Cloud cloisters that in ruins lie, With sunshine streaming through each rift, And broken arches of blue sky.

"All the bright flowers that fill the land, Ripple of waves on rock or sand, The snow on Fusiyama's cone. The midnight heaven so thickly sown With constellations of bright stars, The leaves that rustle, the reeds that make A whisper by each stream and lake, The saffron dawn, the sunset red, Are painted on those lovely jars; Again the skylark sings, again The stork, the heron, and the crane Float through the azure overhead, The counterfeit and counterpart Of Nature reproduced in Art."

The ceramic products of Old Japan are amongst its most precious art, which has been held in such great esteem that the enterprise of the European market has largely failed to attract it from the Japanese experts, though, singularly enough, skilful forgeries of old work, or the dregs of the factories, or the poor wares specially made for exportation, have a ready sale because they are cheap. Yet they have no more relation to the finer specimens than a common piece from a celebrated factory in England would have to its costliest examples. The first place in the making

ARCHAIC POTTERY RESEMBLING THAT OF THE HAN DYNASTY IN CHINA.

and decorating of porcelain is easily taken by China, and this is Japan's position with regard to pottery. The Japanese are the potters without rivals. Therefore it is to the pottery, rather than to the porcelain, that attention must be directed to discover the genius of the people whose picturesque conception, call it fancy if you will, delighted in quaint forms and in coloured enamels.

In both pottery and porcelain a multitude of objects were produced: vases, koros, dishes, tea- and water-kettles, chaire, chawan, chatsubo, bowls, rouge and incense-boxes, sake-kettles, bottles and cups, figures and groups, figures of animals, lanterns, hibachi, candlesticks, yatate sake and tea-sets, jars, scent-bottles (toyiburo), midzuire, cake-boxes, sake-pots, ash-pots, teapots, teapoys (midzusachi), and many more.

The " old Japan taste " of our forefathers, the plates, jars, and vases of Imari or Arita, in blue and white, or blue, red, and gold, were of quite secondary importance in Japan, which valued none of this so-called old Hizen. On the other hand, tons of Satsuma ware reach England every year, yet how few have seen a genuine specimen! The national products, the fine old pottery, not Satsuma alone, but Kyoto, Bizen, and the special wares of celebrated potters, Nomura Ninsei, Ogata Shinsho called Kenzan, Zengoro Hozen or Yeiraku, and others, these are loved in Japan.

The tea ceremony (cha-no-yu) had an influence upon the potter's art, but it was a conservative not progressive influence; the leaders (the cha-jiri) delighted in old things, as they followed old ways, but their utensils were simple, and such as did not admit of an exuberance of artistic imagination. Some slight repetition will not be amiss, it will be helpful. The most important objects required were tea-jars (chaire), in which powdered tea was kept, and tea-bowls (chawari), in which it was mixed with hot water, and from which it was drunk. Some of the most interestingâ not the most floridâ work of the artist-potters was displayed upon such pieces, which were highly treasured as the gifts of princes to favoured friends, being preserved in brocade bags, and carefully packed in small boxes, always handled with the most loving care.

The burning of incense was another function which brought into service certain utensils, fashioned in pottery by the master-makers under the supervision of the princes, their employers, who were the patrons of the potteries, and erected many of the kilns, as will be seen later. Incense was used in connection with the tea ceremony, and in the incense gameâ practised in the highest circles. Scent-boxes (kogo), in which little tablets of incense were kept, small covered vases on three or four feet with perforated covers (koro), in which these tablets were burned, and clove boilers (choji-buro) to scent the room when the water in them was boiled, were objects of nearly as much value as the tea utensils.

The flowers of Japan are more fully treated elsewhere, but the flower-vases for ceremonial bouquets were of the most delightful forms, upon which the decoration was applied so as to contrast with, not to rival, the beauty of the floral arrangement. In a recess of the living-room (tokonoma) or suspended from the ceiling or from a post the flowers brightened the daily life, but they were far more extensively used for ceremonies. In marriages, for instance, there was always the shimadai, a stand on which pine, bamboo, plum, were displayed with figures of the crane and tortoise, emblematic of virtue, happiness, and long life.

Before treating of the various potteries, which were shortly described in my "Chats on Oriental China," the pottery and the porcelain may be compared in a few sentences. Suitable clays for pottery were found in many parts of Japan, and the famous makers with few, very few, exceptions used it as the vehicle for expressing their genius, with no other tools

BOUQUET-HOLDER, UDZUME, BY OGATA SHINSHO (KENZAN).

than the hands or modelling tools â bamboo spatulae. The finger and tool marks may frequently be traced, and in many old pieces certain parts were left free from the enamel coating, exposing the baked clay; on the bottom part, outside the bowls and jars made for the tea ceremony, this was usual. The Raku tea-bowls were fashioned of clay which was soft and tender, specially suited as a poor conductor of heat for the purpose of holding in both hands whilst drinking the hot tea, and specially suited, too, because of the agreeable touch to the lips. The last point is often insisted upon and remarked in Japanese descriptions, but the foreign collector has only just begun to show equal appreciation of these.

The pottery of Nippon is referred by Japanese historians to a period about 660 B. C., when one Oosiu-tsumi made pots. Of course, doubt, in the absence of evidence, is cast upon this statement. It appears more likely that the common, fire-dried pot was made in many parts of the world, during very remote times, and that the first potters actually working in Japan came from Korea, about the beginning of the Chris-13

FIGURE OF A " NO " DANCER IN POTTERY, PAINTED AND LACQUERED BY RITSUO.

tian era. Further, the Chinese influence spread to Japan with the advent of Buddhism, about A. D. 550. Yet the government report ascribes the invention of the potter's wheel to a priest of Idzumi, nearly two hundred years later. The wheel was invented long before by the Chinese, so that, too, was imported. We next reach more definite statements, which commence the actual history upon which the authorities are agreed.

Gorodayu Shonsui, about 1510, travelled to China to learn the secrets of the manufacture at Foochou, or was it in the province of Fuchien or at the factory of Ching-te-chen? I will not labour the point, but we know that at Foochou Chinese lacquer was made at a very early date, and we also know that the province of Fuchien was the home of the Chinese potter, outside Ching-te-chen. Be this as it may, Shonsui remained in exile for some years, and returned with the knowledge necessaryâ the method and practice of mixing pastes, of painting in blue under the glaze, and of firing in the grand feu. The village which arose around his first kiln was Arita, in the province of Hizen, whose nearest seaport was Imari, hence we have the three names

Arita, Hizen, and Imari describing the same ware, which was, at first, more or less feeble imitations of Chinese blue-and-white porcelain, though later the decoration was applied in enamels over the glaze.

We see that the two influences of Korea and China resulted in two productsâ pottery from Korea, porcelain from China. Just as the Hizen factory was established by Gorodayu Shonsui, so from the earliest ages potteries were founded by Koreans. In various districts, near sources of suitable clays, under the protection of the feudal princes, kilns were built on Korean models. There was one at Karatsu, in Hizen, at the end of the seventh century; another, the Raku factory, at Kyoto, about the middle of the sixteenth century; a third at Seto, at the end of that century; and, somewhat later still, one at Hagi. The Koreans made no porcelain, and the finest pottery resulting from their work was, undoubtedly, that made for the Prince of Satsuma, cream-coloured or pale yellow ware, with a finely crackled glaze.

We now proceed with the chief factories in alphabetical order, but before doing that, a few words regarding Japanese writing and the marks of date will be useful, especially for reference.

In considering Japanese names and marks, I may note that the only safe guidance is to invoke the language itself, which may not in the future be quite impossible, or as an alternative the services of a Japanese. Failing those, the wisest plan is to learn the chief marks, and acquire ability to recognise them at a glance. In Nippon several styles of writing are in use, either Chinese or derived from the Chinese. Of the former, the seal, or chuan, and the common kiai shu characters are most often seen, especially upon pottery and porcelain. The katakana, a syllabic writing of forty-eight characters derived from portions of Chinese words, rarely occurs; but the hirokana, an abbreviated and running form also of forty-eight characters, from the same source, is more common, resembling very nearly to the unpractised eye the Chinese tsaou shu, grass text.

In the matter of date marks, Japan follows China in the adoption of an identical cycle of sixty years, and in the use of a special title for each reign, called in Chinese nien hao and in Japanese nengo. For the last two dynasties there have been but few changes in any one Emperor's nien hao in China; on the contrary, in Japan one Emperor has on frequent occasions taken more than one nengo, which rather distinguishes a period than a reign. Little reliance can be placed on any date marks, for you may be sure that no specimens are more ancient than the dates on them.

Two methods of measuring time, one arbitrary, from any special event marked by a nengo, one a cycle of sixty years, are accompanied by a third. This is a period of twelve years, each of which is distinguished by an animal, always in the same order as follows: dragon, serpent, horse, sheep, monkey, cock, dog, wild boar, rat, ox, tiger, and hare. The year 1688, which leads the table of the nengos following, was the dragon year. Sometimes the artist in his picture would insert the animal of the year in which it was painted, in such a manner as to show he meant it for a date, and when that date is accompanied by the nengo, the exact year can be ascertained, otherwise the animal is of little service for that purpose.

There is scarcely anything which looks more puzzling than the Japanese letters, or more properly ideographsâ that is to those who have not learned them. It takes an intelligent Japanese about seven years to learn them all, which is not surprising, considering they reach nearly thirty thousand. Only seventy appear to be needed in everyday life.

PERIODS OF JAPANESE HISTORY FROM GENROKU

Meiji. 1868 onwards.

This list covers the history of the art, especially of the old pottery, which would be at all likely to find its way into the Western world. It was during the seventeenth and eighteenth centuries that most of the " old Japan " was exported to Holland from Japan, and that ware was entirely unsuitable for the homes of the people, it was adapted to foreign taste.

Moreover, the period of Genroku resembled, if it resembled anything in Europe, the reign of Louis XIV. of France. The relations between Japan and Holland were at their best, and there is no doubt that the finest Dutch delft received its inspiration from the blue-and-white porcelain exported from the factories of Hizen, perhaps a few years before Genroku's time. It is recorded that in the second year of Shoho (1645) was commenced the export of pieces ornamented with coloured enamels and with gold and silver. Here, then, is the origin of the Western imitations, the delft ware, the gilded delft of Cornelius Keyser, Jacobus Pynaker, and Adrian Pynaker, whilst the designs of this old Japanese porcelain was copied at most of the early porcelain works of Europe.

A prunus tree and two quails, the sacred, hairy-tailed tortoise, the phcenix, a stork or two, and now and then a woman in court-dressâ what collector has not seen these designs on Dresden, where the imitations were very close, on Chelsea bearing the raised anchor mark, on Bow, St. Cloud, and other early factories, Japan patterns on Worcester, Derby, and what not? The West owes a deep debt to the East!

MARKS ON JAPANESE POTTERY AND PORCELAIN

In order to help as much as may be the collector of Japanese pottery and porcelain, numerous marks are given in the lists which may assist in identifying the ware. The first two lists follow the alphabetical order of the chapters, and the other two comprise a great many makers' names and factory names.

When you consider the conditions under which pottery was made, you will see that it is not yet possible to gather even the names of all of the old potters, because, in addition to the private kilns of many feudal princes, other kilns, many in number, were in operation in the country, producing largely, it is true, utensils for domestic use, but not limiting their output to those. Often, indeed, they made the tea-bowls and jars which now are highly appreciated in Japan.

Then, again, although the ordinary class of potters, the village workers, carried on their trade in the same place from generation to generation, it was otherwise with many of those who were great pottersâ Ninsei, for example. About the middle of the seventeenth century he established kilns at different places near Kyoto; for instance, at Awata, Woro, Kinkozan, which gave its name to the potter Kinkozan, and Seikanji. From these, other factories arose at Gojosaka, Kiyomidsu, and Iwakurazan. His name was subsequently given to the wares, but pieces marked Ninsei were made by his descendants and imitated by other potters.

These remarks apply almost equally to the Raku ware, made at first by Chojiro, and stamped with the seal character Raku (happiness), which gave its name to the pottery. The Raku system was extended to Ohi, that is Ohi-machi, to Tokyo, Osaka, Nagoya, and elsewhere. Certainly the descendants of Chojiro used the Raku seal through eleven generations. Hence that seal mark is not evidence of age. Further, the blue-and-white Chinese porcelain was copied in Japan at many factories. The Japanese potters never attained to the brilliant blue under the glaze, which was one of the glories of the Kang-he period of China, 1662-1722; the finest cobalt decoration of the Hizen factories, the beauty of the Hirato and Nabeshima blue, these had a different character. It is only by study and experience that the collector will acquire the ability to identify old ware, and to separate these blues, for example, independently of the mark, which is only to be relied upon when it corroborates the evidence of paste and glaze.

I have not traced any systematic marking for any long space of time, except in the Chojiro family, and the marks of date upon Japanese ware are few, though it was quite common for the potters or painters to inscribe their names or the place of manufacture upon their productions. These marks are found stamped in the paste or impressed with a seal, generally leaving the letters in relief, not always. Otherwise the inscription was made with the point of a bamboo spatula in the wet paste.

The Japanese rarely employed devices as marks, except when they copied Chinese designs. The Buddhist symbol, the swastika, or fylfot, one of the oldest emblems in the world, the badge of one of the feudal princes, is sometimes found. And amongst a few others are a leaf outlined with gold, two varieties of curved leafy branches, and a five-leaved flower. The blazons, or arms, given amongst the marks show some of the feudal princes, or Daimios, who had those private kilns, which were a distinct feature in Japanese ceramics. Since the abolition of the feudal system in 1868, the mere

MARKS OF POTTERS OR POTTERIES- 1.

I, AKAHADA; 2, 3, ARITA; 4, ASAHI; 5, 6, 7, BANKO; 8, 9, BIZEN; 10, FUJINA

II, IMADO; 12, KAGA; 13, KARATSU; 13, KENZAN; 14, KINZOZAN, 15, KISHIU 16, 17, KIYOMIDZU J 18, KUTANI; ig, MINATO; 20, 21, NINSEI.

MARKS OF POTTERS OR POTTERIES- II.

i, 2, OKI; 3, 4, 5, 6, RAKU; 7, 8, 9, SOMA; 10, TOYO-URA; n, TOZAN; 12, YATSU-

SHIRO; 13, 14, 15, 16, 17, YEIRAKU; 18, 19, 20, SEAL CHARACTERS FOR GOLD, PROSPERITY, FELICITY, (KIN, ROKU, KA). 261 manufacturer has arisen, whose aim is to make profit. The Daimios no longer emulate each other in producing the finest ware for the love of it and for the pleasure of presenting it to their friends, even sometimes to their faithful samurai. The samurai as a class are gone. These samurai were formerly the gentlemen-at-arms of the Daimios, or clan princes, and when the right of keeping private armies was abolished at the Revolution, there were thousands of them thrown on the country to live in poverty from want of suitable employment.

Following the Alphabetical Lists is this Third List of Marks on Japanese Pottery or Porcelain, which will be of Value for Reference.

(i) " Made in the period Genki, 1570-73." (2) " Made at Otokoyama in Southern Kii, in the first year of Kayei," 1848. (3) " Made at Seto in Great Japan "; Seto is in the province of Owari. (4) " Made by Sampo at the Zoshun Hall." (5) " Made at Himeji." (6) " Made by Hansuke in Great Japan." (7) " Enlightenment and civilisation," on porcelain coated with cloisonne enamel. (8) " Made in the period Taimix," a copied Chinese mark of the Ming period. (9) "Made in the period Semmio," another copied Chinese mark of Hsuan Te, Ming period. (10) " Made at the Togioku house or establishment." (n) Akahada yama, another Akahada mark, followed by the seal of the artist Bokuhaku. (12) Horaku, " profuse enjoyment," the name of a maker or a ware, stamped in an oval with letters in relief. (13) Seinei, a maker's name, stamped in a gourd-shaped panel on Raku ware, usually accompanied by the Raku stamp. (14) " Made by Jezan," stamped on rough red ware with a sugary glaze. (15) " Made by Kozan of Makuzu ": this is the mark of the fabric at Ota near Yokohama, established after the opening of the port to European trade to make imitations of Satsuma ware; Kozan, a potter from Kiyomidsu near Kyoto, who resided at Makuzu-gahara, here made many pieces of that kind. (16) " Made at Goraku house," stamped in a circle with characters in relief on ware sometimes attributed to Akahada. (17) " Original Minato ware of Kichiyemon (of) Sakai, Senshiu,"

MARKS OF POTTERS OR POTTERIESâ III.

another mark of this factory, one is given in the alphabetical list, and Minato ware is shortly described in the text. (18) Kagura, the name of a maker or a fabric.

Further Marks on Japanese Pottery or Porcelain. Fottrth List.

(i) " Made in the period Yempo," 1673-81; a Nabeshima mark. (2) Made in the period Bunkwa, 1804-18; a Hizen mark. (3) " Made by Toyen in the Meiji period' 1868, to our own times; a mark on blue-and-white. (4) A copied Chinese mark of the Ming period. (5) "Made at the Fuji kiln of Makuzu." (6) "Made by Kozan at the Makuzu kiln," which was near Kyoto. (7) "Made by Giyokusei of the Fukushun house." (8) " Made by Gosuke at the To-giyoku house." (9) Koto, "East side of lake "â i. e. of Lake Biwa. (10) " Made by the honourable Gorodayu Shonsui"; this is improbable as a mark of the old potter, (n) " Made in imitation of my ancestor Gorodayu Shonsui"; a Hizen modern mark on blue-and-white. (12) Made by Hokuhan at the Kyoto house." (13) Made by Kosai of Great Japan. (14) Mi-kuni, "Three kingdoms "; name of a place. (15) " Made by Kiyen." (16) " Hizen pottery," in Chinese characters, probably made by Kizo of Nembokuan. (17) Sanhan, a maker's name. (18) Kwabo, a maker's name; Bizen ware. (19) Ki, part of a maker's name, in Katakana character, made at the Takatori factory. (20) Sei, a maker's name. (21) Kwanriyo, a maker's name. (22) Maiko, name of a place near Kobi. (23) Yuko, a maker's name. (24) Asahi, another mark of the factory; it means " morning light," and is said to indicate the colour of the ware. (25) Kitei, the name of a firm of potters who also made porcelain. (26) Rokubei, a maker's name. (27) Tami, part of a maker's name, used on green-glazed earthenware. (28) Minpei, a maker's name on yellow-glazed Awaji ware, not unlike Awata.

(29) Rissai, a maker's name, probably an Awaji pottery.

(30) "Banko of Japan," on Banko ware, made by Datei.

(31) Itusai, a maker's name, on ware like Akahada ware.

(32) Riyozen, a maker's name. (33) Shiosai, probably a maker's name. (34) Bunki, a maker's name, sometimes used with the Raku stamp. (35) Shuntei, a maker's name. (36) Shungetsu, a maker's name. (37) Masaki, a maker's name, Kyoto ware. (38) Bokuko, a maker's name. (39) Oike, the

A. D. 1673-1681. "A. D. 1804-1818. A. D. 1868-

M101 j i6i-j. Id y â Â; y. z.?. cr:.

MARKS OF POTTERS OR POTTERIESâ IV.

name of a street in Kioto. (40) Two stamped marks: Taihei above, meaning peace; Hozan, a maker's name, below; Awata ware. (41) Makusu, a place near Kyoto. (42) Seishi, a maker's name. (43) Akashi, a place in the province of Harima. (44) Inuyama, name of a factory in the village of Inakimura in Owari province. (45) Nikko, the name of a place near Tokyo, famous for its temple. (46) Shuzan, a maker's name. (47) Sobai tei, "the Sobai house." (48) Zen, part of a name, like Zengoro, used by a maker. (49) Hozan, a maker's name, painted on pottery coated with red lacquer at Kyoto. (50) Kikko, a maker of Raku ware, modern. (51) Jusan ken, "The Jusan house." (52) Another Kikko mark. (53) Kwankei, a maker's name. (54) Horaku, the name of a fabric or ware made by Toyosuke, and coated with lacquer at the town of Nagoya, in Owari.

A K AH AD A ware was made at Koriyama, in the county Ji. of Soishimo, province of Yamato, now the Nara Ken, or Prefecture, famous for the old city with the temples, Nara. With the Kondo or main temple of Horuji; the celebrated Chu-monâ the gateway to the inner enclosure of the temple of Horyu-ji; the east pagoda of Yakushi-ji, the temple of Todaiji, and many other famous buildings, it was a marvel.

The Akahada ware dates back from the middle of the seventeenth century. The factory, like so many others, was under the protection of the feudal prince of the province, whose orders were carried out. The making of vessels for the tea ceremony (cha-no-yu) occupied the early years of the pottery. Such was the furnace (furo), or cylindrical fire-vessel (hi-ire), usually having three legs, or feet, in buff ware covered with a thickish white glaze, or pale-brown ware with a dark-brown glaze. Of the same clay were the water-vases (midzu-sashi), the tea-jars (chaire), the tea-bowls (chawari) â numerous examples of which are shown in the illustrations, rudely made on purposeâ varied in shape, some shallow, some cylindrical, but all designed with edges smooth to the lips; ash-pans (hai-ki) unglazed; shallow saucers, with incurved edges; water-jars (midzu-ire), and other vessels, for the Koi-cha or the Usu-cha forms of ceremonial tea-drinking.

In addition to these and accompanying them was the incense burning. The vases (korcs) had the most varied forms, as vases usually supported by feet, and there were figures of men, animals, and birds, usually with perforations in the covers. Upon the inside of these koros a fine white ash was spread, which supported the lighted charcoal and the incense, which was contained in an incense-box (kogo). The incense game was a favourite pastime in the olden days; forfeits were paid for failing to guess the name of the perfume which was burnt.

At Akahada the old ware was inscribed with the name by means of a bamboo point, used upon the wet clay, not stamped. Later the mark was stamped in a curved, heart-shaped panel, used as a seal, with the letters in relief. Two pieces at the Victoria and Albert Museum have this mark. One is a cylindrical fire-vessel, on three small feet of buff ware, having a crackled, whitish glaze, and the other is an incense-box, in the form of the god of contentment, the children's friend, Hotei.

Arita, Hizen, or Imari Ware: Kakiyemon

Arita, a village in the province of Hizen, now the Nagasaki Ken, was one of the early homes of the Koreans, the potters brought from their own country by princes of Japan. Ri-sanpei, about the end of the sixteenth century, was first settled at Taku by Prince Nabeshima. Gorodayu Shonsui soon used the materials he had secured in China, and the Arita factory was decaying when Ri-sanpei, removing from Taku, found good feldspathic rock in a valley near Arita, with the long-wanted white clay (shiro tsuchi). Here, then, were the two substances necessary for the making of porcelainâ the kaolin and petuntze of the Chinese, china clay and china rock. From them was made the old Imari ware, which included not only that of Arita and its branch kilns, but the wares of Okawiji, Shira-ishi, Shida, Koshida, Yoshida, and Matsugaya.

There were other kilns in Hizen of which the oldest was Karatsu, which seems to have been established in the seventh century. Ko-Karatsu, old Karatsu, ware is very rare. The first productions of pottery were followed by stoneware, which about A. D. 1600 was rudely painted with scrolls, after the Korean manner. Imitations of old Korean ware, called

FIRE VESSEL, AKAHADA. BRAZIER, IMADO. TAKATORI. OKAWAJI.

Oku-korai, were also made about this time, especially tea-bowls (chawan), of a reddish-brown colour covered with drab, pinkish-drab, or yellowish-brown glaze. The later ware, following the Chiu-ko-Karatsu, the middle old Karatsu of the period A. D. 1600-54, is known as Karatsu yaki.

The works of Arita, now the most important centre of the porcelain trade, were founded shortly after those of Karatsu. Ri-sinpei seems to have made a defective kind of porcelain, but he got no farther than did Shonsui with regard to decora-

BLUE-AND-WHITE PORCELAIN BOX ATTRIBUTED TO SHONSUI.

tion. Both painted in blue under the glaze, and whilst the latter sometimes used the seal character Fuku (happiness) as a mark, it is doubtful whether pieces were ever signed with his name. Neither of them understood the process of enamel painting. Having been fashioned, their ware was baked to the biscuit state and painted with blue, then glazed and burnt at the temperature of the grand feu. The necessity for firing enamels in a muffle kiln, after the colours and gilding had been applied over the glaze, had, no doubt, been appreciated, but neither of them knew how to do it; the

Koreans suffered from the same lack of knowledge. The honour of making this great addition to the decorative resources of Japanese potters was reserved to Higashi-shima Tokuzayemon, who in 1648 went to Nagasaki with the object of visiting China, but, receiving the necessary information from the captain of a trading junk, to whom he had explained the purpose of his intended visit, he returned to Arita, and began the new method of decorating with enamel

PAPER-WEIGHT IN IMARI OR HLZEN PORCELAIN.

colours, imitating, probably, rather the earlier Ming ware of Ch'eng Hua than the later of Wan Li, who began to reign in 1573. The imitative results were not satisfactory, the enamels lacked that brilliancy which alone made them acceptable, but soon the native instincts prevailed over the desire to follow a copy of diapers and archaic designs.

Kakiyemon, who worked with Tokuzayemon, is sometimes credited with the introduction of decoration by means of verifiable enamels relieved with gold; but what he really did was to develop a native style of the type known as chrys-anthemo-pceonienne with chrysanthemums and peonies in blue, red, and goldâ a lilac blue, a lustreless red, and a somewhat dead gold. This old Imari became essentially an article of commerce with the Dutch, who settled at Deshima in 1641, about four years after the Portuguese had been expelled, and from seven to ten of their ships entered the harbour of Nagasaki annually. The Dutch at Delft set themselves to imitate the Imari decoration in its general character. But another type, created by Kakiyemon, was more remarkable for its delicacy); its ornament was simple almost to severity. Upon a paste of fine white porcelain, covered with a soft yet brilliant glaze, no less fine, medallions of flowers were painted in red, blue, and grass-green, so that each little picture was surrounded by a wide frame of white having no decoration. The colours were few, the subjects many; the dragon, the ho-ho bird, the bamboo, the plum or prunus, landscapes, and various diaper designs are common. From specimens of this type the factories of Meissen and Chantilly, amongst others, copied their earliest designs, which have therefore evidence of Kakiyemon's influenceâ not of the old Japan ware still copied and exported to please the taste of those who like the violet and the red with gold in strong tones, and with an intense blue under the glaze, not the Chinese blue of the famous Kang-he blue-and-white, but a "Mohammedan blue," resembling the Hsuan Te blue of the early part of the fifteenth century. The best Japanese blue belonged to another factory.

Asahi Ware

The pottery of Asahi has some additional interest, because it is made in the centre of the tea-growing district of Japan, at Uji, in the province of Yamashiro in the Kyoto Ken. There in the tea-gardens, under "the hot sun of May," crowds of women and girls, wearing kimonos and tall sun-bonnets, gather the leaves of the shrub which has been cultivated in Japan for centuries as a native plant of that country. The Japanese say native, but it was an exotic from China.

The pottery has been in existence from the Shoho period (1644-47). Whether the name Asahi ware is derived from its colour or from the mountain to the east of Uji is a matter of opinion. The colour is said to resemble the morning light. As a matter of fact, it is a grey ware, covered with a greenish-grey glaze, belonging to the Yaki class. The word Yaki occurs frequently in this section. Asahi Yaki, like all the other ware called Yaki, is pottery sometimes termed Yaki-mono. The crackled wares are Hibi Yaki; the celadons, whether native or Chinese, belong to the Seiji class, and stoneware is Shaki.

Asahi was famous from the commencement for making vessels in which the ground tea was stored, but it also produced those objects which have been described as being related to the tea ceremony. So famous were these vessels, that a noted chajin, leader of the ceremony, no less a man than Kobori Masakatsu, son of Kobori Totomi-no-Kami, the founder of one branch of these ceremonies, encouraged the potter by honouring him with a seal for marking his ware. The presentation of a seal for this purpose was a distinct recognition of merit. The tenth Zengoro received a gold seal from the Prince of Kii in 1827, and a silver seal inscribed Yeiraku.

At the present time the factory produces tea-jars, vases, etc., of every description. Close by, at Tawara, is another factory, founded at about the same time, whose speciality was teapots. As a rule, the tea was ground, and hot water poured upon it in the "bowl from which it was drunk; but teapots of several forms were in use. One form had a pannier handle like a kettle, from the spout over the cover to the back, where the second form, like those we use, has its handle. The third form has a hollow handle and the spout at a right angle to it towards the left.

Though these are called teapots, many of them were used with small cups for sake" drinking.

Awata faience: Kinkozan

The Awata kilns were established about 1620, and an artist, Kuzayemon, tried to copy the work of Ninsei, using black and other colours for decoration, and also using coloured enamels. Ninsei visited the factory and worked there and made many fine specimens, although he was hindered very much by the inferior quality of the materials at his disposal; the paste was poor, and so was the glaze. The early body of the Awata-yaki was close and hard; the glaze, though lustrous, had a greyish white, semi-lucid appearance, quite different from the usual fine glaze of the Japanese pottery. The crackle was curious, showing the edges, which are not palpable in fine crackle. It was uniform and fairly small. The obvious remedy was soon found, the decoration was lavishly applied, and it became extravagant.

Kinkozan, a workman-artist, like Ninsei, set about the work of improving the ware, and succeeded so well that he, again like Ninsei. takes his place amongst the master potters. The glaze, too, was perfected, and its lustrous, creamy tone formed a suitable ground for coloured enamel decoration. Amongst these, grass-green and deep blue were chief, but red was also used, and gold is nearly always associated with the colours upon the soft glaze, for these colours were applied over the glaze. Purple, yellow, and silver occur but rarely. Kinkozan's work commenced early in the eighteenth century.

Some specimens of Awata faienceâ Awata-yakiâ are marked Awa-ta, but this mark is more uncommon than the name Kinkozan, and most are not marked, so that it is very difficult to identify old Awata, except by four rules, which may be applied with some measure of success to all of the wares of Kyoto, of which this is a suburb: the paste, that is, the body where there is no glaze, is close and hard, the glaze is lustrous, the crackle fine and uniform, and the enamel decoration is clear, brilliant, and carefully applied. The last remark, "carefully applied," may read better "artistically applied," for the old artists took time for their work; the modern ones are in haste, and haste speaks. At the same time, in noting these tests, due regard should be given to the difference between Kinkozan's improvements at Awata and the early ware, in the making and decorating of which Ninsei was for a short time engaged. The type created by Kinkozan may be described as a homogeneous, very close-grained, almost black body or biscuit serving as a ground for ornament in sharp relief and for regular designs in enamels, amongst which the deep blue was prominent, accompanied by grass-green, yellow, and white.

Awaji Ware

BOWL FOR TEA (CHAWAN), BY MINPEI. AWAJI WARE, LIKE AWATA WARE. THE FACTORY STILL EXISTING DATES FROM ABOUT 1830.

OZAYEMON, a merchant of Kuwana, came under the Jf influence of the cha-no-yu ethics, and was inspired with a desire to make objects, such as those used in the ceremonies. He was a wealthy amateur, whose influence obtained admission to the Kyoto potteries, and whose wealth enabled him to obtain the best materials for his experiments, which were largely limited to copying, during his first period, the Raku ware, of which something more will be said, and even the Korean ware. His progress was marked in his imitations of the delicate work of Ninsei and the bold designs of Kenzan, so that when the Shogun lyenari, about 1785, sent him a commission, the results were so satisfactory that he was summoned to Yedo (Kyoto). Here he pursued his labours under the patronage of the nobles; the Shogun himself visited his factory, and admired the results which Gozayemon produced.

The natural effects were to create a demand for his works and to spur him to further efforts, which carried him on to imitate the Chinese models, which under Kang-he had reached the highest excellence in the famille verte, and under Yung-ching and Keen-lung equal superiority in the famille rose. Side by side with the magnificent wares, Japanese ceramics in polychromatic decoration were plainly inferior. The Shogun, so it is said, sent to the Imperial factory at Ching-te-chen, asking for the recipes and for a supply of materials, and when both had been procured, Gozayemon entered upon the second period of his work, the imitation oi the Chinese, in which his success was soon remarkable; but the pieces he imitated do not appear to be of the finestâ they could be scarcely distinguished from the enamel pieces of Wan-li (1573-1620). He also copied Delft ware, and, indeed, he seemed to have a genius for imitating all kinds of pottery and porcelain.

His greatness was not founded on these imitations, except as far as they evolved his own styleâ a purely Japanese oneâ of brilliant glazes and tasteful floral ornament. Many of his pieces were marked Banko, meaning everlasting, and others Fuyeki, changeless, but the seal Banko was also used by Yusetsu, under circumstances which are related in a note regarding that potter. Gozayemon returned to Kuwana, in the province ofjse, where he died in 1800. His comparatively scanty output was absorbed by Japanese collectors, so that they have escaped the copyist. He took no pupils, and though one of his relatives endeavoured to trade upon the mark, the Banko seal, he obtained only a modified success during the utilisation of the materials which Gozayemon had accumulated, and which were soon exhausted. Whilst he lived, none but the favoured few could obtain examples of his art, and when he died, but for an accident his secrets would have passed away too.

Banko, or Ise Banko, Ware: Yusetsu

Thirty years after Gozayemon's death, his precious formula for the making of enamel colours fell into the hands of a dealer in curiosities, pottery, lacquer, etc., whose son, Mori Yusetsu, had gained some distinction by making the Raku pottery and another kind which was finished off with the finger and thumb before firing, so that the impression of the skin was left upon the surface. He too lived at Kuwana, in Ise" province, and, after acquiring the recipe, he bought the Banko stamp from the grandson of Gozayemon, and proceeded to imitate the work of the Ise merchant and potter, so through his copies that work became much more familiar than it otherwise would have been to the ordinary buyer. And perceiving that some of the Chinese modellers applied the moulds to the interior of certain pieces, he adopted that method and added a novelty to Japanese pottery. Under such a method the inside would be sharp and clean, but it appears doubtful whether the fingers could secure an equally sharp impression on the outside. The Kyoto artist, Mokubei, had also copied the Chinese, fashioning his clay in the mould, and I cannot think that, if Yusetsu had to use from six to twelve longitudinal sections, he would have adopted any other plan than that of building up the piece from the strips of clay in the usual way with the moulding outside. However, I can only give my opinion on the statement, that his modelling was always done from the inside.

Yusetsu's Banko ware was finely modelled, in spite of the opinion given, and the designs from his school, which ranks as a modern one, have been much appreciated for their artistic excellence, which was combined with skilful potting. Storks and dragons, etc., moulded in high relief, and clever arabesques, in coloured slip or liquid clay on rich grounds of green or red, were notable amongst much good work.

All the pottery of the Gozayemon type is interesting, even as imitation. The pieces stamped Yusetsu are, of course, distinct, marking a complete change in the character of Banko ware. The variety which is most desirable is a finely crackled faience of a cream tint, decorated with blue under the glaze, and above it with numerous diaper designs, upon which are reserved panels containing landscapes or mythical subjects. Next in merit as an artist to Yusetsu was his younger brother, Yuyeki, who also worked at the factory, which is still in existence.

Bizen Stoneware

In the sixteenth century Hideyoshi, a potter at Imbe, succeeded in imitating the red ware of China, generally known by the name boccaro ware, which was also copied by

Bottcher, at Meissen, and by Dwight and Elers in England. The valuable pieces of this old Bizen ware were stamped with a crescent or with a cherry blossom.

Towards the end of the seventeenth century improvements displaced the old brick-like pottery, which had three varieties, glazed, unglazed, and marbled. Two new pastes were found: the Ao-Bizen, a slate-coloured or brown clay, a very fine, hard stoneware, whose choice specimens of deities, mythological figures, birds, fishes, and animals, are ranked with the best works of plastic art in Japan; and, a little later, a red clay, having a texture of equal quality. This red paste, when glazed, shows bronze-like tones, closely resembling the metal sentoku â the golden bronze. Before me is a good specimen of this early Bizen, a figure of Hotei, the god of contentment, standing on a wind-bag with a pierced hole. His round face, with jovial smile, his rotund, uncovered body, draped over the shoulders and below the waist, illustrates a type of native art which has a great attraction for collectors of Japanese figures; the colour is delightful, the metallic sheen astonishing, and the bell-like ring most unusual.

It is scarcely possible to praise too highly the skill, the individuality, and the effect of these fine, old, salt-glaze figures. I say salt-glaze, though there is no proof that salt-glazing, as understood in England, was so practised in Japan; the thinness and closeness, the thorough incorporation of the glaze with the paste, and the general appearance of the ware set it apart in a class similar to that of salt-glaze. Rarer than either the slate-colour or the red is the white Bizen ware, which has a similar dense paste, strongly baked. It is said that the ware was left for days, or even weeks, in the kiln with the object of securing the entire fusing and incorporation of glaze with paste.

The modern ware has a soft glaze and quite a dull ring; none of those qualities which characterise the old products are seen in the paste. The degeneracy is even more marked than in some of the other modern wares, which have a certain charm; but the red clay figures of the seven gods and the poor imitations of the mythological monsters are only interesting because of the histories attached to themâ they show nothing of the potter's craft in comparison with the Ko-Bizen, that is, Old Bizen, which gave way, about A. D. 1580, to Bizen-Yaki, the later work. The old red ware, covered with a thin glaze, is really a stoneware, resembling in texture the brown stoneware, also slightly glazed. Their unusual qualities render them easily recognisable.

Fujina Ware

This was made at the private kiln of the Prince of Fumai, in the village of Matsuy6, province of Idsumo, and it has similar qualities to the Idsumo Yaki, being manufactured from a soft, tough clay, which, when fired, gave various shades of dull red, grey, drab, pale, and dark buff. Then glazes of various colours were applied, such as sage-green, sea-green, white, buff, brown, brownish-red, and yellow. These were decorated with streaks of other colours, with flowers, etc., in white slip or painted and gilt. The Idsumo ware properâ the old ware, which Fujina was notâ had the same character as the Hagi ware, varying from a pale brown to chocolate in colour, covered with a crackled glaze. When, early in the seventeenth century, a Korean potter named Rikei came to Japan, he settled at Hagi, and adopted the name of Korai Saiyemon. His ware, like others from Korea, has a triangular space cut out of the raised edge at the bottom.

The Fujina ware resembled Idsumo, and Idsumo was like Hagi, though the last is sometimes known by the potter's name. The later work at Fujina, owing to the influence of Kobori Masakatsu, imitated Satsuma, and this is still manufactured.

Hirato or Hirado White Porcelain or Decorated in Blue

Though the old white Hirado porcelain is highly esteemed, it was never able to reach the wonderful softness of the old blanc de Chine, the white porcelain made at Tehua, in the province of Fuchien; to which a reference has been already made. That had a paste of smooth texture resembling ivory, upon which the rich, thick glaze lies, as if it were part and parcel of the paste itself, so closely is it blended. The Hirato factory at Mikawa-uchi-yama, " the hill between three rivers," was founded by another Korean, about 1600, who made pottery, decorating it with blue under the glaze. The discovery of Ri-sanpei at Arita, by which material for making porcelain was placed at the disposal of the neighbouring potters, affected this factory, whose other name was Mikochi, but he retained the secret of the enamels, so that here the only decoration applied was blue under the glaze. The work declined, the factory was closed, until in 1740, Matsura, the chief of Hirato, an island near Hizen, started it again under conditions which recall the early days of the Meissen factory; the workmen were forbidden to sell or give their productions without special permission. The supervision was strict, the products were not for sale; Matsura made presents to his friends, or to the Court of the Tokugawa at Yedo.

Brinkley held the opinion that the old Hirato porcelain showed the highest degree of excellence and perfection to which the ceramist ever attained. Without altogether accepting this judgment, which is too sweeping, I may say that some of the Hirato which I have seen is very wonderful, the blueâ the colour mainly employedâ being exquisitely soft and clear, seeming to float in the milk-white glaze. Then, too, what a choice, a variety, and an excellence of forms! Incense burners (koros) as vases, pigeons, ducks, and other birds, figures of gods, goddesses, animals, and birds modelled with great skill, worthy to figure in the choicest collections. The long period extending from 1740 to 1830 produced the fine porcelain called Hirato yaki, which had a very fine paste equal to the Chinese, whiter and purer than the Imari yaki or the Nabeshima yaki. This purity was attained by the most careful attention to the preparation and refinement of the materials used for paste and glaze, so that, on the one hand, it is free from the grit so common in Imari ware, and, on the other, it closely resembles in granulation the porcelain of China. But the blue-and-white is best in combination.

Amongst the finest productions of this factory were large plates or tables, some feet in diameter, called sometsuke, painted with Chinese boys playing under a palm-tree. These were specially made for the prince, and, as in the case of other private factories, sales were prohibited. Sometimes, however, a piece may be bought. Its value depends upon the number of boys, three, five, or seven, the last being most valuable. The smaller dishes, of saucer shape, may have similar boys chasing butterflies under the tree, but their value is very small, relatively, though the age, about 1770, and the colour of the beautiful greyish blue under the glaze are the same. Other products consisted of cylindrical flower vases, ornamented with bands of medallions, containing symbols, and cf ornaments or okimonos in the forms of men and animals. These old porcelain pieces were made at Mikawaji, the full name of which was cited above.

It may be necessary to remark that, though some old ware, ornamented in relief and in slip, is rare, there are factories still at work in the district. Notably, an egg-shell china was made about 1837, which, though at first white, was more recently enamelled in various colours. At the Victoria and Albert Museum there are a few old and some modern specimens. The contrast between them is striking. In the old ware the blue is incomparable; in the modern, painting in enamel colours and gilding are used with ornament in relief, such as the sho chiku bai, fir, prunus, and bamboo trees, the three friends; two keeping green and flourishing throughout the winter, and the prunus, the Taoist emblem of immortality, throwing out spikes of flowers from its leafless stalks up to extreme old age. Or again, a conventional lion amongst waves and clouds may be accompanied by ho-ho birds or phoenixes on a gold ground.

No mistake is likely to occur on the part of the collector if he fixes his mind upon the blue; a note follows on Nabes-hima blue, but this even is not so fine. Mr. W. G. Gulland, whose gifts to the above museum will be remembered, presented some fine specimens of Japanese ware to the Brighton Museum, and amongst them are a few examples of the famous

Hirato blue, which are full of interest. To the ordinary collector I would say, "If you get a piece of fine quality, hold it." And note that in the old porcelain if another colour was used with the blue, that colour was brown.

Only within the last few years have the Japanese owners been induced to sell, and the skilled collectors who used to exploit Japan have been withdrawn. Little arrives here now but modern imitations, which are not quite white, but greenish, and they are not perfectly potted. I saw a short time since a fine figure of an eagle perched on a rock; it might have been modelled in the finest bronze, so perfect was it, and on the white ground the lovely soft clear blue decoration was applied and covered with a glaze of the finest quality. Some pieces have other decoration of delicate pictures etched in the clay before firing, and I think in this Hirato easily takes the first place. It is surprising that through all the operations of potting, firing, and glazing this finely executed ornament remained uninjured, bearing in mind that much of it was also in relief.

European potters modelled many of their pieces from old Hirato ware; Plymouth and Worcester and Bow copied the raised shells and seaweed; Dresden no less imitated the figures, and copied, too, the birds and flowers in relief and openwork. American and European collectors have quite a passion for Hirato blue-and-white, more so than for the rarer polychromes and even these are very rare; but old Hirato is also highly valued by the rich Japanese!

Imado Ware

This ware was one of the few made in Tokyo, which had only a number of small kilns producing inferior pottery for domestic use and roofing-tiles, except in the Imado-machi district, where attempts were made about the middle of the nineteenth century to make mottled ware by mixing clays of different colours, red and black, white and black, and so on. The name of the maker, Gosaburo, was applied to the ware as a seal-mark impressed.

Tokyo does not appear to have been favourably situated for the making of either pottery, faience, or porcelain; notwithstanding its position as the capital of Japan, with a population of over a million and a half, the absence of suitable clays appears to have presented obstacles which have not yet been overcome, though Kozawa Benshi, a modern potter, has long been engaged in making Raku ware, and more recently in modelling figures in terra-cotta, using only the bamboo spatulse and knives which resembled those made by a Kyoto potter named Miura Kenya, who settled in Tokyo. The pottery record of Tokyo for collecting purpose may be disregarded by those who require antiquities.

OGATA SANSEI, commonly called Kenzan, was born in 1663 and lived till 1743. He was trained to be a painter, like his elder brother, Korin. Korin eventually devoted himself to lacquer, and Kenzan to pottery; in each case the art education received opened the road to eminence, and it is notable because such instances are quite uncommon. Kenzan took a further step which had great influence on his careerâ he went to various potteries and mastered the technical work, the manipulation of clays and glazes, so that his equipment was complete; his use of the brush gave the finishing touches to the pottery he made. Very quickly he proved a perfect exponent of the teachings of Japanese art, combining great boldness of design with an original style, producing fine decorations, which, in the native taste, were only meant to convey limited impressionsâ a branch of prunus or cherry blossom, birds in the bamboos, perched on a bramble over a flower, or flying over a rice-field. Such conceptions distinguished the work of the early painters, and were entirely suitable to the limited space at the disposal of the potter.

Kenzan preferred to paint his designs in Shibu-ye and Ai-ye, black, russet-brown, and blue; his decoration in Kin-ye, coloured enamels and gold was no less effective.

His best work is found on Awata ware having the usual poor glaze of its early period; yet even that could not disguise the master's hand, and to prevent all errors he marked his pieces with his name, "Kenzan." But his name is not reserved to one factory; even the coarse clay of Shigariki, with a gritty body inferior to that of Awata, ornamented with his bold sketches, became a thing of beauty. Later, he went to Yedo, now called Tokyo, and, though there the materials were only suitable for the application of coloured glazes, he founded the kiln of Imado in that city and was successful in a new styleâ brilliant glazes upon a poor clay â beauty of a different order, an evolution in colour.

In the Victoria and Albert Museum there is a Kenzan

JAR FOR RICE-POWDER, BY KENZAN.

bowl whose decoration is typicalâ snow-laden pines expressed with severe simplicity, with such masterly handling, that nothing more could be added without destroying its effect. Genuine examples by the oldest Kenzan are very rare and valuable. His son and grandson copied his style with much success, and they also used his mark; the inferiority of the work and the nature of the body supply the needful tests.

Bold impressionist sketches, coarse body, and extraordinary freedom in the application of massed colour, distinguished by the presence of a brilliant emerald green in rich harmony with the other enamelsâ these qualities are not difficult to recognise on any piece which has the family mark.

Kishiu Ware

Although history records the establishment of kilns two hundred years ago by the Prince of Kii at Wakayama, now the name of the ken or prefecture then known as the province of Kii, no particulars reach us until the first years of the nineteenth century. No pottery that can be identified has been found, and the earliest specimen of porcelain at the Victoria and Albert Museum is dated about 1800. It has the mark given in the list. For the improvements wrought by Zengoro Hozen reference should be made to Yeiraku ware. Although the old ware is so ill-defined, the modern, moulded in raised outline with enamel grounds of purple, yellow, and blue, is not uncommon.

Kiyomidzu Ware

In order to follow the list of marks a few words on the Kiyomidzu factories will emphasise the importance of Kyoto as a pottery centre. Ninsei, the great potter, erected kilns here and elsewhere, but his chief work will always be associated with Kyoto. The Awata district of the city, or perhaps, more correctly, the Kinkozan, gave renown to another potter, Kinkozan Sobei, and amongst those potters in the Seikanji district who worked in the factory of Kiyomidzu no name is more distinguished than Takahasi Dohachi, whose career is set out under the heading " Kyotoâ 'Dohachi'

Before, however, his advent occurred, the Kiyomidzu kilns at Seikanji had produced some fine pottery, which was marked at first with the word Seikanji in an oval, and later with the name Dohachi, both of which are given. The former occurs upon a buff-ware incense-burner of globular form, standing on three small feet covered with a crackled cream-coloured ground painted in green with a diaper of hexagons, and having two heart-shaped panels containing a dragon and a lion. The second is marked, stamped upon a square cup of yellowish ware covered with a grey glaze and roughly painted in black. The first piece was made about 1800; the second about 1830.

The Kiyomidzu factories flourishâ another Takahashi Dohachi holds his place amongst other descendants of. the eld potters, such as the second Wake Kitei. They produce the same patterns as their fathers copied from the old Arita vareâ the Sometsukeâ blue under the glaze, but they have learnt the art of applying coloured enamels in the decoration, and some of them have adopted the word Kiyomidzu as their first name.

Kutani Porcelain

If you look at the map of Japan, you will find the province of Kaga on the west, separated from Kyoto by a lofty range of mountains. Here, at the village of Kutani-mura, probably a few years before 1660, the feudal Prince of Taichoji built a kiln where tea-jars and water-vessels of common ware were made until 1665, when his son, Toshiaki, sent Goto Saijiro to Arita, to learn the methods of making porcelain; when he returned, the Kutani yaki underwent a complete change.

The paste at first was only clay, and not good enough to make pottery free from faults. Indeed, the defective body of these early pieces could not be hidden by lustrous glazes or rich enamels, therefore clay was imported from Imari; but this was sometimes mixed with the local refractory material, and often neither sufficed, so that white biscuit ware from other factories was bought and decorated at Kutani. Hence, it is rather upon the style of the decoration and the quality of the enamels that attention must be devoted in order to be certain of identification, though some pieces have marks which, with the other characteristics, are undeniable.

During the last forty years of the seventeenth century, and about as many years following in the eighteenth century, the wares produced were of two distinct kinds, of which one, the Ao kutani, derives its name from a green (ao) glaze of wonderful brilliancy and depth. A large dish lies before me, the sloping rim of which has a ground of dark aubergine enclosing panels

DISH, PAINTED BY MORIKAGE, IN KUTANI PORCELAIN.

with white frames containing alternate yellow and green grounds, the former covering a scale pattern, the latter a swastika trellis; on the fall of the dish is a border of aubergine, covering a Greek-key design. This encloses the central large round panel, decorated with a wonderful three-clawed dragon, with dark aubergine mane and scaled body, in shades of green, amongst clouds in aubergine and shades of green.

This decoration lies upon a seeded, yellow ground. The back of the dish, covered with an iridescent green glaze, over vermicular scrolls in black, encloses the yellow base, covering a stoneware, in the centre of which is placed the mark known as the open-window mark, in black under green glaze. This may be accepted as indicating the special features of the Ao kutani. The green is scarcely less fine than the finest Chinese; the yellow and aubergine, lustrous and full-toned, are enamels painted over designs traced in aubergine and black upon the biscuit.

The other class resembled the Imari, with one difference which is distinctiveâ there is no blue employed under the glaze in combination with coloured enamels over the glaze. Otherwise the colours were similar; but the enamels, which include a soft Prussian blue, were finer, and the red, soft, subdued, and full-toned, varied from rich Indian red to russet-brown.

The designs were those of an artist, the noted Kuzumi Morikage, who painted simple but effective scenes from nature, differing altogether from the masses of brilliant blossoms so notable in Imari ware. It is well to note that the work of Morikag6 remained as the standard of Kutani decoration, though conventional diapers, scrolls, and medallions, enclosing symbols, may decorate many of the finest examples to the exclusion of figure subjects, with the one exception of the Chinese karako, children at play. Modern Kutani, like modern Satsuma, is ornamented with peacocks, chrysanthemums, and peonies, saints and lange lijsen or graceful damsels, and many other subjects.

Bearing in mind that the paste furnishes no safe guide when Kutani blue-and-white is under consideration, it is evident that a judgment must be made on the tone of the blue and the nature of the glaze. The latter has a peculiar softness, the blue is poor; inferior to Chinese and the best Hizen, totally different from the delicate blue of Hirato, it is an inferior colour, and will never, I think, be valuable. But the coloured pieces, notwithstanding what has been said of the paste, have so much of distinction in their enamels, and in their style of decoration, that they stand alone, and the more so because of the beauty of the soft glaze.

By comparison, it may well be said that Ming blue-and-white is old; so it is, but the pale grey-blue of the fifteenth century pales in interest and value before that of the sixteenth, which itself is only a herald of the triumphs of the reign of Kang-he, a specimen," specimen, of which, at the sale of the Louis Huth collection, realised 5,900 guineas. When Japanese blue-and-white porcelain becomes the vogue, large sums will be secured for fine specimens of Hirato and Nabeshima ware, and then Japanese collectors may be tempted to sell. Till then, the princes, the nobility, and the rich collectors, who have secured the finest productions of these private and renowned factories, will rejoice in their rarity, and in the high prices which they have already reached, as much as in their beauty, which has a richness qui pent lutter avec celui des pierreries elles-memes.

The earliest examples at the Victoria and Albert Museum of old Kutani porcelain are a shallow bowl (hachi) and a square dish (sara), both painted in yellow, green, and purple, and both made about 1620. They are marked with a seal character, Fuku (happiness), known as the open-window mark. Other specimens, two saucer dishes (sara) and a similar cake-box (kwasi-ire), are one hundred and fifty years later, and two pairs of flower-vases only date back to 1875.

It is evident again that genuine Kutani ware may be modern, but the only modern products which may excite the interest of the collector are those made under the direction of Zengoro Hozen, who, about 1840, settled at Kutani and taught the style of ornament known as Kinrante, of which something more is said under "Yeiraku Ware." It will suffice here to notice that he was the twelfth generation from the great potter Yeiraku in direct descent.

The peculiarity of this Yeiraku Kinrante consisted in its imitation of brocade patterns for the grounds, which were diapered in lozenges, mosaics, broken sticks, and patterned with the Greek-key, with trellis-work, with scrolls, stars, flowers, or scales. Nishikite ware, which resembles Arita ware, has similar brocade diapers. It will be seen that this Kinrante ware resembled the Ao kutani already described, only it was much later.

The work of Kuzumi Morikage lost its influence with time; the factory, for about twenty years before the nineteenth century commenced, produced scarcely any good work, and, although efforts were made by a potter named Yoshidaya, about 1804 to 1812, and by a porcelain painter, one Shozo, it was not until the advent of Zengoroâ that is, Yeirakuâ that real progress was made. Now, in the district, there are several kilnsâ not in the Kutani village itself, because that is high up in the mountains, but nearer the place where the clay is found, Kutani-mura. Some ware made from imported clay is perfectly white and transparent, but the genuine old Kutani ware was made from the clay found close by, and it has a uniform, rather dark-red tone, differing from the greyish-white, which was made also from clay brought from elsewhere.

The later products are, in decoration, noted for red grounds and rich gilding, gold grounds and painting in red. They have little resemblance either to the old enamelled Japanese patterns, or to the imitations of Chinese porcelain, which were made about 1750-70, just before the close of the Meiwa period.

Kutani appears to have lost the patronage of the feudal Prince of Taichoji, for we read that the Prince of Kaga and the Shogun Tsunayoshi gave some encouragement to the potters, which, however, was not sufficient, for nearly all of the finest old work dates back to the century preceding 1770, and it is scarcely necessary to remark that this has the greatest value.

Kyoto â Dohachi

About the time when Zengoro Hozen was adding to his laurels at Kyoto, another noted potter was also making a wreath. Dohachi (Takahasi), about 1825, commenced his career, and soon exhibited such technical skill that some of his glazes rivalled those which Ninsei had discovered, and some of his designs were as graceful as the best of the Japanese work. The most coveted glaze is an unusual dull white, with a tinge of pink, which appears to have been reproduced from a Korean model, which was called the gohon or " pattern ware," the tinge of pink being sometimes broken by flecks or spots in the glaze.

In 1830 Dohachi's reputation was established, and his sphere of action was enlargedâ he became a teacher of the potters in various factories, a position which nearly all the great masters had assumed. Dohachi accomplished the fusion of the Korean and Japanese style of decoration, which had been an idea in the Taiko's mind two hundred and fifty years before, when he had imported a quantity of Korean pottery for copying. In his old age the artist-potter took the name of Ninami, with which he marked some of his wares, though, in general, Dohachi was used for that purpose.

Amongst the modern potters, Kyoto boasts of Kiyomidzu Rokubei, Seyfou, Taizan, and Tanzan; Tokyo, of Inouye; Osaka, of Ma isan; and Yokohama, of Makuzu. Rokubei painted landscapes resembling those of Tannyii, who painted the wares made by his family long ago; he preserved the old style. Seyfou was a master of coloured glazesâ violets and aubergines, corals and cobalt blues. Makuzu for some time flooded the market with the mock Satsuma, which is both a snare and a sham. He, too, had extraordinary skill in glazes, and did better work on ancient lines later. Maizan's modern Satsuma was noted for the fine paintings of flowers, butterflies, and figures, which will be treasured as time goes on.

Some modern Japanese productions, such as vases and other objects incrusted with cloisonne" enamel, are fine, curious and interesting. The porcelain, to which the cloisons or metallic filets were fixed, was fired first, then the enamel colours as glassy fluxes were applied and fired until the whole surface was covered, the surplus glaze was filed away, and, lastly, the surface was polished. Numerous firings were necessary to fill the spaces between the cloisons evenly.

The Japanese also cover faience with lacquer, chiefly dark

KENZAN TO KYOTO WARE 299 green or black, decorated afterwards with colours and gold. The well-known basket-work, enclosing curious fragile specimens of Sheba egg-shell porcelain, may be old or modern.-The beauty of the interior painting and the fineness of the basket-work appear to be the best tests of age; the modern examples are not equal to the old.

Kyotoâ Yeiraku Ware

In 1878 Franks wrote: " There is an ancient pottery at Kyoto, founded by a family called Yeiraku, a title bestowed upon them by the Prince of Kii. The present maker is of the thirteenth generation. They make both pottery and porcelain, especially the latter." Yeiraku is amongst the most illustrious names which dominate the history of ceramics in Japan, which is a record rather of individuals than factories.

The early products were tea-bowls (cha-wan) and tea-jars (chaire) for the cha-no-yu. In 1594 the family removed to Kyoto, and in the eleventh generation was represented by Zengoro Hozen, who at first devoted himself to meet the requirements of the tea ceremonies, under the advice of the cha-jin y in which he showed remarkable skill, blending pastes of different colours with great dexterity, and acquiring a high reputation for his work, to which he added imitations of Korean faience.

Porcelain soon attracted his attention, and ultimately he produced fine celadons of the sea-green tint, and admirable blue-and-white, with the blue, as usual, under the glaze, lyenari, the eleventh prince of the Tokugawa dynasty, governed a land at peace, where wealth was devoted to art, and the feudal princes, who followed his example, sent gifts of pottery and porcelain to the Shogun, a custom which established a whole-hearted emulation in their factories. Zengoro's deserved fame induced Harunori, feudal Prince of Kishu, to appoint him, in 1827, as the manager of his kilns, where he made the Oniwa-yaki, the celebrated Yeiraku ware, in imitation of the Chinese, though it scarcely ever equalled it. The ware was stamped with his seal, and it. attained au immense popularity amongst collectors. He made a close study of the composition and application of glazes, and his aubergine porcelain, his rich combinations of turquoise blue, purple, and yellow, applied to faience, were some of his achievements. Another colour, the coral-red, again imitated from the old Chinese, was no less successful, the names Kinrante (scarlet and gold brocade pattern) and Akaji-kinga (gold designs on a red ground) being sufficiently distinctive. This success brought many honours to Yeiraku; Harunori gave him no less than three seals, which may be found upon the ware he made. One, Kahin Shiriu, was devoted to the very finest pieces, and to them sometimes is added the second seal, Yeiraku, and many of the specimens imitating the

Chinese turquoise blues and purples are stamped Yeiraku-yen. In addition to pottery and porcelain, a hard stoneware was produced and decorated with rich single colour and variegated glazes.

The great potter worked for Harunori at Nishihama, for eight or nine years; when he retired, Yoshehei, a potter from Kyoto, was appointed director of the works, which were closed in 1844, when Harunori died.

'THHIS factory, near the town of Sakai, in the province X of Idsumi, is interesting because of its antiquity. A Buddhist priest named Goghi, or Giyogi, who returned from Korea in the seventh century, founded, it is said, the Todai-ji temple in the city of Nara, the old capital of the empire. He is credited with the invention of the potter's wheel, but there appears no evidence to substantiate such a claim. No doubt prevails in my mind, the Chinese invented that wheel, as they invented many things which were discovered by other peoples. Giyogi probably brought it from Korea, and he might have worked with it at Minato, or instructed the potters in its use.

Archaic pottery, such as that ascribed to the early centuries, is very rare, and as far as I know, none of our museums have any specimens of the first Minato ware turned upon the wheel. It was centuries later when the factory made the brittle biscuit ware, which for a long time was left in the biscuit stateâ a yellowish earthenware, unglazed, eminently suited for ash-bowls (hai ki), which were used in the tea ceremony, but useless for tea-bowls (chawari), because pottery unglazed allows water to percolate.

In the seventeenth century a thin glaze was adopted. About this time another pottery was started by Hachita Gensai, who confined his attention to the production of ash-bowls for use at the cha-no-yu. They resembled the unglazed Minato ware, though known by the name of the maker as Gensai ware.

This later ware gives distinct evidence of turning upon the wheel; but much of the early ware, the oldest of the tea-bowls, including many of those most precious to collectors, was moulded by hand, leaving marks upon the clay even if it is glazed, the impressions of the fingers. One difficulty, a grave one, in attempting to classify early pottery such as the Minato Yaki in the absence of marks, is to be found in the number of potteries, some of them carried on by a small family, and many producing the same articlesâ tea-bowls, ash-bowls, and ordinary household utensils. For this reason, amongst the other marks not arranged in alphabetical order, will be found some which are common, some very uncommon. The mark "Minato Yaki," which is given, dates about A. D. 1770. The old kilns are still in use, but the pottery of Gensai has ceased to exist.

Nabeshima Porcelain

The factory was the property of Nabeshima, feudal Prince of Hizen, who, at Okochi-yama, produced porcelain distinguished for its paste and glaze, as well as its blue, though it scarcely approaches Hirato in either respectâ 'the blue has the curious " Mohammedan " tone. Whereas the colour at Hirato used sometimes, but rarely, with blue was brown, at Nabeshima it was red or green, and this distinction aids recognition, for at the private factories of porcelain no factory marks were used, though copies of Chinese pieces might be marked with the marks appearing on the original. For the same reason Nabeshima porcelain never appeared upon the market, being, as we have stated with regard to Hirato, reserved for the feudal prince. Again, like Hirato, specimens are rareâ even the museums are often lacking. Amongst the marks will be found the blazon of the prince of this house who employed Ri-sanpei when he returned from the Korean War in 1592. Ri-sanpei was a Korean potter, but he met with indifferent success in his search for materials.

The removal of the factory in 1710 to Okochi or Okawaji, after two trials at Taku and Arita, was attended with success, and it is to the prince of the later period that this was due. There is one hint that must not be overlooked. The lower edge of the saucers for the cups is painted in blue with a design resembling the teeth of a comb, hence its name Kushite â that is, the ware with the comb-teeth. This, then, marked the ware produced and sent by the Prince in presentation to the Imperial Court and to the Shogun, in plates, cups, and ornaments, which are amongst the objects most desired by Japanese collectors, though two varieties of celadon were also much admired. I have a pair of vases, probably made for a present to the Emperor, whose three leaves and flowers of the Paulownia imperialis are treated conventionally in relief on a celadon ground. These are in imitation of Chinese celadon. The other variety was a fine crackled ground of peculiar tone.

In the Victoria and Albert Museum there is a quadrangular incense-burner (koro) consisting of a tray with four feet, supporting a trough, over which fits a cover of pierced network; at the sides are alternately a tree and a koi fish at a waterfall; borders of leaves and cinquefoil on a red ground. This early piece is assigned to 1740. There are other specimens of later origin. One, a saucer dish (sara), is painted with fern-like branches and leaves in green and blue, on the inside, whilst outside are scrolls in blue surmounting the blue comb-teeth (kushite"), which form a border to the foot rim.

Again I have to note that Okawaji ware may be modern, for amongst the objects in the Museum is a pair of flower-vases (hana-ike) which are not earlier than 1875. Like much of the modern ware, the vases are richly ornamented in brilliant colours and gilding, with flowers and leaves. Round the neck are storks in a red ground; at the base a band of green scale pattern with two sacred tortoises amidst conventional waves.

But the Okawaji porcelain which the collector seeks is the best of the ware which is painted with the blue, the Nabeshima ware with the Kushite" design as a mark, the white or buff ware covered with the notable celadon glaze.

Ninsei and Kyoto Faience

The name of Ninsei, Nomura Ninsei, must ever be honoured amongst the great potters of Japan. If the three elements, Chinese, Korean, and Japanese, blended in him, from that

FLOWER VASE, BY NINSEI.

blend he evolved a product which was national, and this, in spite of the fact that the making of pottery was not his profession; yet, somewhere about 1650, having possessed himself of the secrets of the Hizen factories, he set himself to manufacture enamelled pottery. Omuro-yaki, the name given to his first successful efforts, was made in the district of Omuro, for he had no kiln of his own, only a keen logic, an inventive spirit, and a fine tasteâ and these were enough.

Working in the neighbourhood of Kyoto, at Awata, Iwakura, and Mizoro, he practised and imparted, giving to his fellow workmen of his knowledge, and probably acquiring from them practical skill, until his influence wrought such a vital change that the natural style proclaimed itself Japanese. It was then that the faience of Kyoto assumed a new character, a beauty which before had been lacking, for, though the works of Ninsei belonged to various styles, each seemed to be the outcome of a special process, though all of the buff, fawn-coloured, and cream-coloured ware was crackled with a circular crackle almost regular. This is, of itself, a trustworthy test of this ware.

The paste or body of the pieces made and decorated by him varied, as we should expect, in view of his migrations. The most common is a hard close-grained clay nearly brick-red in colour; then another clay was yellowish-grey, with a texture as close as pipe-clay. The most popular was the pottery with a finely crackled glaze decorated with flowers, in which blue and green enamels were used with gold. His monochrome glazes, black over green, pearl-white, golden-brown, chocolate, and buff, were often painted with coloured enamels in floral designs and gilt. His skill as a modeller was almost as great as that shown in other directions.

The test of the crackle, the test of the paste, the quality of the decoration, and of the modelling, should be applied to every piece, even though it is marked with his two characters, engraved in the paste, for his designs were imitated at Kyoto, where decorated faience was very popular, and many of them are marked with his name. Genuine specimens realise high prices in Japan, and though the demand for fine old Japanese ware has not yet arisen in England, it will come, and whoever owns any old Kyoto ware, the work of Ninsei, will rejoice thereat and be glad. Two other noted potters, Kinkozan and Kenzan, were associated with Kyoto and its neighbourhood later, but we have already read something of Ninseiat Awata, which was Kyoto too.

Ohi Ware

Near Kanawaza, in thekaga province, a kiln was established about the end of the seventeenth century by a potter, Choza-yemon, on the Raku system. Each piece was shaped by hand and fired separately. The ware of Ohi was encouraged by the leaders of the tea ceremonies, which, of itself, is a testimony to its excellence. There are numerous wares called Raku, which vary, it may be slightly, but the best must have two qualiticsâ thcy must bc smooth to the touch of hand and lip, and they must retain the heat. Some clays possess these qualities more than others, and the Ohi clay was redder and denser than manyâ the glaze was a very smooth yellowish-red lustre. The fourth Chozayemon used a seal which is shown in the list by the side of the name of another maker scratched in the paste. This name Sen-ki is one amongst many. Nearly all the villagers are potters possessing their own kiln.

Raku Ware

An old Korean potter, Ameya, settled in Kyoto about 1560, and introduced the Raku ware, which was named Juraku, before the Shogun Hideyoshi honoured his son and successor, Chojiro, by giving him a seal to mark his ware. This seal is shown as the fourth Raku mark in the list. The descendants of Chojiro, the Ameya Chojiro, who is known as the first of the family whose generations have descended to the present day, used their own seals, as the gold seal was lost by the second Chojiro, but the character was always Raku. This mark is represented in the Museum at South Kensington by a series extending from about 1650 to 1840, from the third, to the eleventh Chojiro. The successive names are: (i) Chojiro, (2) Chojiro, (3) Do-niu, (4) Ichi-niu, (5) So-niu, (6) Sa-niu, (7) Cho-riiu, (8) Toku-niu, (9) Riyo-niu, (10) Tan-niu, and (u) Kichizayemon.

The other seal, mark 3, is associated with Kichizayemon's seal in a double mark upon a tea-bowl. It reads " Made at the Senraku Garden." Mark 4 is found upon a papier-mache

STATUETTE OF FUKUROKUJU IN RAKU WARE.

tea-bowl covered with brown lacquer, and 5 shows the name of a potter, Kikko, a modern maker of Raku ware whose kilns are at Osaka. These pieces are in the Victoria and Albert Museum, with others from various Raku potteries.

WHILST pottery is known as yaki, and the crackled ware as hibi-yaki, the celadon variety is named seiji and the stoneware shaki. It may happen that all these varieties may be traced to one factory or one district, or the wares may be limited. At Sanda they were yaki and seiji. Kuki, feudal Prince of the Setsu province, established kilns at Sanda at the close of the seventeenth century, but ordinary ware only was made until a hundred years later, when two workmen returned from Arita, where they had succeeded in learning how to make porcelain, and, by the aid of some pupils of the famous master Rokubei, on their return they produced an excellent celadon, the Sanda seiji, which became so noted as to be used as a generic term for Japanese celadon, though a much finer product had long before been made at the Hizen potteries, especially at Nabeshima.

The Nabeshima celadon had a tone of much delicacy, the Chinese was a little warmer in tone, but the Sanda seiji was a brighter green. This ware was produced in large quantities, whilst that of Nabeshima was only made for presentation or for special use. Some princes reserved the whole of the products of their factories; others were content to allow the sale of what they did not require for themselves. The abolition of the feudal system led to the decline of many of the privately owned kilns, and Sanda celadon ceased to be. In the Victoria and Albert Museum are two specimens of this glaze. One is an incense-burner (koro) shaped as a cock looking backwards, made about 1710; the other is 1. CUP, MINO WARE. DISH, VEDO BANKO WARE. SAKE CUP, YEIRAKU WARE.

2. VASE, OTA WARE. VASE, ARITA WARE. CANDLESTICK, TOZAN WARE.

a curious reticulated cage, oviform in shape, which might have been used as a koro or as a receptacle for the leaves of fragrant flowers. This is ascribed to 1767, and is a piece of unusual character, resembling in form a piece of Seto ware in the same museum, though the pierced work is of different design.

Satsuma Ware or Faience

Whatever opinion may prevail regarding Japanese porcelain in comparison with Chinese, there is a general agreement that the pottery of Japan is pre-eminent, and foremost stands the old Satsuma. So-called Satsuma, sent in loads from Tokyo, may be brilliantly decorated, it may be perhaps artistic â all the large vases and jardinieres, for instance; but it is not the Satsuma which is so highly valued by the connoisseurs of Oriental Art; in fact, it is nothing like it in size, colour, texture, crackle, or decoration. In size pieces of real Satsuma are small; in colour they range from cream to old ivory; in texture they are hard; in crackle, minute; in decoration, enamel colours, matt gold, and raised ornament are of the greatest delicacy. There are other varieties still rarer;

but we quote Mr. Ernest Hart: " During the whole of my stay in Japan, in private and public collections, and in all the collections which I have seen in Europe, fine Satsuma of the older dates is the rarest and least attainable, while spurious imitations are the most abundant and disfiguring features. But of some thousands of pieces of so-called Satsuma offered me elsewhere, and at other times, I have hardly ever found one that was both genuine and of any art value."

The feudal Prince of Satsuma, in 1598, returned from a war in Korea with a number of workmen, some of whom were potters. Shimazu Yoshihiro employed these men in copying from Korean models, having first selected the most skilful and removed them to Chiusa or Chosa. Ware having a fine paste was made, some covered with green, yellow, or black glaze, some parti-coloured or flambe. The Prince of Sasshiu, by name Mitsuhisa, set up a kiln in his own grounds, in which verifiable enamels were employed by workmen, who were furnished with designs by a noted painterâ Tangen, possibly.

Tangen decorated some of the ware himself, for a beautiful enamelled specimen might well be Satsuma-Tangen, and, as such, would be recognised by the Japanese collector, because of the fashion of its decoration. At a later period, after the closing of this and another private kiln, came another Prince of Sasshiu, who, at the end of the eighteenth century, took the Satsuma factory under his protection. This Prince Yeio sent two men to Kyoto, and, on their return, the manufacture of hard Satsuma was resumed and decorated with diapers, floral subjects, and landscapes, in addition to the mythological ho-ho birds, the shishi lion, the dragon, and the kirin, a kind of unicorn commonly called a kylin. The productions were presented to the Shoguns and Daimios, and to the friends of the prince. They were not for sale.

The enamelled faience having decoration in colours and gold upon a hard, white paste is very rare, so are the monochrome glazes, especially yellow and black. Olive-green, associated with dark mustard-yellow or with chocolate brown, really comes into another class of the flambs or transmutation glazes, and not the monochrome.

SAKE-BOTTLE IN OLD SATSUMA WARE.

These splashed pieces have a different paste, forming a fine, hard body, nearly a stoneware, and they had a high reputation in the cha-no-yu ceremony, in which you will read that a distinct function in that ceremony was the admiring of the old utensils, especially the tea-bowls. The stimulus given to the potter in this way was considerable, the cha-jin was the arbiter of taste, as he was the ceremonial chief of the tea-club, the leader of the cult of the cha.

Old Satsuma is exceedingly rare. It is said that there are

PERFUME-BURNER IN SATSUMA WARE.

no genuine specimens having a mark, and none painted with figures. One curious class " mushroom " Satsuma is highly valued in America, where it is described as resembling a bed of mushrooms, in curious, round crackle, with ivory brown undertints. Imitations? Why, yes! Tokyo and Kyoto and Ota. These are all yellower in tone than the real old ware. From Ota, Kozan, a modern manufacturer, has issued a great quantity of pottery commonly sold under the Satsuma name. The old decoration and the old ware are aptly described by Franks: "The Satsuma ware, made at Chiusa, known as ko-chiusa, resembles a very smooth ostrich-egg in texture and colour, and is very delicately decorated. Another ware is grey inlaid with white, like the pottery of Yadsushiro, and is closely copied from Korean." The decoration may be seen upon a few pieces in the Victoria and Albert Museum. It is sparse, not crowded, consisting of a few sprays or branches of flowers in colours and gold, which was applied in outlines as early as 1630. Another style of decoration consists of panels or patches of different diapers and conventional ornament, also painted with enamel colours and glit. A koro, or incense-burner, about A. D. 1660, a vase to hold a tea-ladle (shaku-tade), about thirty years later in date, in the Museum, are both ko-chiusa. Another koro, a tripod vase with handles and a cover, surmounted by a lion, made at Nawashirogawa, about 1720, marks the later home of the factory. Both Chiusa and Nawashirogawa are in the province of Satsuma.

Seto Ware

Many villages in the province of Owari had their kilns, and produced ware which bore the name of its place of originâ Seto, Shino, Oribe, and so on. The old Seto ware was reddish-buff stoneware, covered with a brown glaze, streaked with lighter or darker tones of brown, and marked at the base with curious, irregular, concentric rings, caused by the thread or wire used to detach the object in its clay state from the wheel resembling the markings on the outside of an oyster-shell. These itoguiri marks appear especially on the early Seto wareâ the stoneware, not the porcelain. The most famous potter, whose work distinguished the village of Seto, was Kato Shirozayemon, whose other name was Toshiro. On his return from a visit to China, early in the thirteenth century, he, after trying kilns at several places, found here the clay he wanted.

It was used in making vessels for the tea ceremony, which need no description, because they have been noted before. The tea-drinkers gave the name of Ko-Seto to the much-prized ware made by him from the native clay, though other ware, made from clay which he brought from China, named Kara-mono, or Chinese ware, was even more highly valued. We read of one small tea-bowl which cost thousands of dollars in the days of the Shogun Hideyoshi. Japanese collectors account the first Toshiro's ware as priceless.

Toshiro's descendants took his name, prefixing the second, the third, and the fourth, but they appear to have had other names, which, however, are not recorded as marks, and need not be given. Another potter, Kato Tamikichi, settled at Seto, after working at Arita, early in the nineteenth century. He produced the sometsuke porcelain, painted in blue under the glaze. This is still made in plates or tables of large size.

Ki-Seto ware, the yellow Seto, was produced at another pottery. The buff-coloured stoneware was covered with a yellow glaze, at first thin and transparent, afterwards opaque. The latter glaze was often marked by transparent green spots, and decorated with flowers and grasses. There is one resemblance between this and the Seto ware proper, on the base, the itoguiri marks may be tracedâ not in the earliest fifteenth-century work, made by Haku-an, which is excessively rare, but in the ware made two centuries later. It depends for its value upon the depth of the yellow glaze; the specimens having a dark-yellow colour are amongst the objects most valued by the tea-drinkers.

Soma Ware

Amongst the blazons given in the lists will be found that of the Prince of Soma, a kicking horse, ascribed to the painter Kano Naonobu. This ware derives its name from the feudal prince, so the decoration of it in later times was associated with the horse; though the older ware only bears his coat-of-arms, the early nineteenth-century products were painted with a horse, or a herd of horses, galloping. The pottery made at Naga-mura consisted chiefly of small cups, probably sake"-cups, with a rough indented surface outside, npon which the horse was sometimes represented in relief. Heraldic badges occur upon examples from many factories, but, when we bear in mind that princes made presents to their friends, it would not be safe to conclude that the blazon always indicated the pottery where they were produced.

Toyo-ura Ware

Of the old potteries at the foot of the hill of Toyo-ura, in the province of Nagato, little is known. Unglazed ash-bowls, like those described elsewhere, were the chief objects made. The mark given, "Toyo-ura yama," the name of the factory, is found upon pieces made about the middle of the nineteenth centuryâ pinkish-yellow unglazed ware, with black marks at the side.

Tozan Ware

The feudal prince of the family of Sakai, in the province of Harima, founded the pottery for the purpose of imitating the Arita ware of the class known as sometsuke, painted- in blue under the glaze. The early ware appears to have no mark; the one given dates about 1820, when the imitation was successful. Porcelain, painted with symbols, landscapes, etc., was produced, as well as celadon porcelain, also after the Chinese style. Like many of the other private factories, when the power of the Shogun ceased, the interest of the princely patron in the fictile art, the personal element, diminished and expired; so that, in many cases, even if the kilns were not closed, the work degenerated, as was the case here. I have not been able to find why the ware received the name Tozan, for the mark indicates the place of origin in this caseâ " Made at Himeji."

Yatsu-shiro Ware

Potteries existed in the province of Higo, south of Hizen, from very remote times, centuries before the arrival of a Korean potter, best known as Uyeno Kizo, a vassal of the feudal Prince Kato Kiyomasa, but only common articles for household use were made until about 1600, when he settled at Toda, near the port of Yatsu-shiro, opposite the island of Amakusa, noted for its potter's clay, which yielded a fine, iron-red paste, for pottery known at first as Toda-yaki, afterwards as Yatsu-shiro yaki, one of the most delicate faiences of Japan.

The paste had a close texture of admirable quality, and a pearl-grey glaze was used upon it, which in the older pieces is uniform, lustrous, and minutely crackled, producing a combination of rich quality as a ground upon which the decoration of storks flying in the clouds, of various diapers, or of simple lines in combination was applied, not in the usual way by the painting of enamel colours, but inlaid with white clay before glazing. A tea-bowl (chawan) which I have has the hard red paste, a pearl-grey glaze, finely crackled and ornamented with lines, diapers, and flowers in white inlays, also on the base inside. The red clay is splashed on the base where there is no glaze, and above it where it is mingled with the pearl-grey glaze. This ware was copied from the Korean, but the copy is far superior to the original. It represents the Henry Deux or St. Porchaire ware of Japan, and is very rare. The modern ware is pretty, but collectors have no use for modernity.

Another very desirable variety of the Yatsu-shiro yaki is the streaked pottery in white; the design engraved and filled with white is intended to represent brush marks from a very coarse brush, used with boldness and rapidity. The potters of this factory never used enamels; their decoration, the colour of the glaze, and the texture of the clay varied, but the ornament was always inlaid pate sur pate. The storks and clouds (unkaku) formed the usual design, the paste varied from iron-red to dark grey, the glaze from pearl-grey to dark brown, and the crackle in the degree of its fineness; but as the inlaid decoration was constant and peculiar to this factory, it is easy to identify the ware when familiar with its distinguishing features, and here, as always, one careful glance is better than a page of description.

Yet the study, apart from actual specimens, is full of interest; the bowls, such as the one described, show how great was the influence of the cha-jin, and the cha-no-yu, for the vessels employed in the tea-clubs were compulsoryâ coarse and archaic bowls, not turned on the wheel, were preferred to all others. We should say that they were thick, perhaps unshapely and little decorated, but they were highly prized for one qualityâ they were very smooth to the lips, as I have before noted several times.

FOR those who have learnt to love Japanese prints, their charm is immense, their fascination extreme. In the finest of them, the colouring, quiet as it may be, is serene and mellow, in perfect harmony. In others, where the tones are rich and glowing, they are still harmonious. For grace and beauty of composition, and for excellence in the sweep of the lines, they surpass all other coloured prints, forming a class apart.

The wonderful advance in public estimation, which has led the Western collector to place them amongst his treasures of art, has affected their value so much, that they may soon be beyond the purse of those of moderate means. Now, when it is too late, the Japanese, who have only lately shared our appreciation, realise that they have made a great mistake in selling them out of their own country for a mere trifle, and with characteristic sagacity they are hastening to supply the market with reproductions, so that, at the outset, a danger awaits the beginnerâ he may be tempted to buy these forgeries, which are worthless.

Fortunately, there are tests which will minimise this danger. Look at the paper and feel it. If it is stiff and springy and thick, the print is modern; the old prints are upon soft paper difficult to describe, because it in texture resembles nothing that we use, but so peculiar as to be easily recognised with practice. Hold the print up to the light; if it is old, you will see the whole picture through the back; if it is modern, the colours only will be shown. Then, again, as the engravers worked at home in the living-room, the paper is often very brownâ that is, the old paperâ because the engravings were hung up in that room to dry, though some of the old paper had a natural brown tone.

The old colours were soft and mellow; they may be faded, but the harmony is still thereâ the fading has affected them equally. The later German pigments, especially an offensive violet, may easily be detected as work not earlier than about 1880, whilst the latest colours, the aniline dyes, differ, owing to their lack of capacity. Comparisons must be made to emphasise these differences, but the task is not a hard one. The colours used in the best period, mineral and vegetable, the reds and yellows, the curious lacquer colours, the quality of the blacks, may soon be identified, and should never be mistaken. The earliest prints were tinted by hand, and this should be specially noted. In fact, in one lesson under proper teaching, the beginner would acquire such ability to distinguish the old from the modern prints, that it seems a pity not to have practical lessons for this purpose, rather than books, though these have their valueâ they furnish material for interesting study.

As in the West, so in the East, the first books were printed from wood blocks; but, whilst the Western world progressed in adopting movable types in the fifteenth century, the Oriental practice of engraving was maintained until the last few decades, and still exists. This produced a continuous succession of skilled wood-engravers, to whom much of the credit for colour-printing in Japan is due, but even their names have been forgotten. Probably they were never recorded, yet their work will never perish, and, though the artist, the print-designer, receives all the credit, many of the painters had nothing at all to do, either with the engraving or the printing. So that when we speak of a fine colour-print, by Kiyonaga, or Utamaro, we must distinctly remember that the design only was supplied by them; the engraving was always done by another person. And we must remember, too, that when the engraving was completed, thousands of prints received impression from the blocks.

The Ukiyo-ye school of genre painting never equalled the Tosa and Kano schools, upon which we need not dwell here, except to note that the former was the earlier by hundreds of years. Considered from an artistic point of view, the paintings of the later genre school excited less interest than the colour-printsâ there was but little demand for them in Japan, where the artists devoted themselves to the preparation of illustrations for books and of subjects for prints, to the exclusion of painting proper. This is one of the causes why such genre paintings are rare. Nobody valued them. Yet they were always superior to the colour-prints in which most importance was attached to the harmony of colouring. No print can equal the original in the quality, which, for lack of a better word, may be termed the lustre of the colours, neither can it be equal in life and freedom of touch.

When the engraver pasted the design, face downwards, upon the block of soft cherry-wood, he proceeded to carve the block until that design was left in bold relief, thus destroying the original entirely. The process is referred to later. I am inclined to doubt whether coloured drawings were thus destroyedâ first, because there would remain no guide to the printer; second, because illustrations of actual print-making show the picture upon the wall; and third, because Fukuba's collection of Ukiyo-ye paintings at the Japan-British Exhibition included every artist of eminence, from Iwasa Matabei and Hishikawa Moronobu, to Hokusai, Kunisada, and Hiroshige.

I cannot do better than quote Mr. Arthur Morrison's introduction to Mr. Happer's catalogue, to which I refer elsewhere. It is very appreciative and interesting.

"No process of printing has ever brought forth such another body of pure art as was put forth in Japan in the eighteenth century and in the early part of the nineteenth; though in fact one may hesitate to use the word ' printing' to describe the process whereby Japanese colour-prints were produced, since it conveys to European minds ideas of mechanical facture such as had no part in the art we are considering. Each print, indeed, may be considered a water- colour picture produced by hand pressure; for there was no press, and the printer was an artist rather than an artisan, mixing and spreading his colours on the blocks and tinting his sheets by a dexterous, simple, but delicate use of the ten fingers he was born with.

"Perhaps it is scarcely necessary, at this time of day, to reiterate the details of the process; but it may be stated shortly that the original drawing, in black outline on very thin paper, was pasted face-downward on a wood block, and then cut through by the engraver with a precision which left on the block an exact reverse of every brush-stroke of the original, Proofs were taken, by hand pressure, of this outline block, and were pasted in their turn on fresh blocks, one for each colour in the design. Each of these colour blocks was then cut in a manner to leave a flat surface of the correct form to receive the pigment proper to it; and the finished print was the result of a careful and extraordinarily skilful rubbing on all the blocks in succession, beginning with the key-block. Such, broadly, was the procedure, though many refinements were used, the colours being graded and varied on the blocks, tints being printed over tints, and wholly uncoloured and uninked blocks being employed to effect a gauffrage or ' blind-tooling which often has a charming effect in prints of the finest period.

"This process, in its perfection, was of course not evolved except after intermediate stages of experiment and advance; and here it may be well to glance for a moment at the history of the school of artists to whom we owe this delightful chapter of the world's art. It must be understood that there are and have been many diverse schools of painting in Japan, and one of the latest evolved was that of the Ukiyo-ye, or school of ordinary life.

"The founder of this school was one Iwasa Matabei, a man of noble birth, who lived at the end of the sixteenth century and through the first half of the seventeenth. Matabei was one of the greatest artists produced by Japan or any other country, though his work is now exceedingly rare; he was a painter purely, and produced no colour-prints, but by combining the characteristic features of the two great classic academiesâ the Tosa and the Kanoâ with much that was wholly his own, he originated the manner which was followed, with individual variations, by the school of artists who produced the colour-prints. The school was maintained by Matabei's son and other followers, still as a school of painters merely, till the time of Hishigawa Moronobu, in the latter half of the seventeenth century. Moronobu, a painter of genius, widened the scope of the school, and was the first of its members to produce prints, although in plain black only. His book illustrations had great force and character, and his detached sheet prints are rare and much sought.

"From the time of Moronobu the Japanese print passed through a period of development culminating in the decade 1760-1770, when Harunobu put forth an extraordinary succession of works in which the printing process was pushed to its furthest and most exquisite limits. First the prints in plain black were roughly embellished by hand with touches of a red-lead pigment called tan; these tan-ye, as such prints were called, soon received touches of other colour to reinforce the red, and presently gave place to prints coloured by hand in a fuller manner, the red tint being now given by beni, a beautiful pigment which was used in divers ways all through the classic period of colour-printing. In a little while it came to pass that black lacquer was used to reinstate the moderately full palette used in the hand-coloured print, and the prints distinguished by this feature are known as urushi-ye. The urushi-ye was the final form of the hand-coloured print, and was immediately followed by the simplest form of the print in which colour was applied by pressure, in the manner which has endured ever since.

"These first sheets wholly produced by printing appeared early in the eighteenth century and were the production of Torii Kiyonobu, who with his younger brother, Kiyomasu, drew many designs illustrating scenes in the theatres of their time. The first colours used were a rose-pink (beni, in fact) and a soft green, and extremely beautiful arrangements of colour were effected with this simple palette.

"Presently other tints were added and secondary colours were produced by superposition of blue over red, red over yellow, and so forth. All through the early part of the eighteenth century, prints of increasing complexity and technical accomplishment were given to the world by painters of the Torii and Okumura sub-schoolsâ Torii Kiyohiro, Torii Kiyotada, Torii Kiyoshige, Torii Kiyomitsu, Okumura Masanobu, Okumura Toshinobu, and Nishimura Shigenaga, till at last Suzuki Harunobu, a pupil of Shigenaga, and an artist of extraordinary delicacy and distinction, carried the process to its highest possibilities.

"From that moment the ukiyo-ye studios of Yedo sent forth a succession of the most exquisite colour-prints which the world has seen. Harunobu's pupil Koriusai and Kiyomitsu's pupil Kiyonaga made designs of great sweetness and dignity, and Katsugawa Shunsho, pupil of a sub-school which had hitherto confined itself to painting, began a series of portraits of actors and women in powerful line and strangely delightful colour. Kitagawa Utamaro, from about 1780 to 1804, poured forth his splendid series of beautiful women and groups, while Yeishi, Yeisho, Shigemasa, Shuncho, Shunman, Kitao Masanobu, Toyokuni, Toyohiro, and Sharaku enriched the world with many prints of the first order, with individual excellencies peculiar to each master. Then came Hokusai, the marvellous ' old man painting-mad' and Hiroshige, the extraordinary landscape painter, who with the simple and restricted means of the Japanese colour-printer, and a direct audacity of technique surprising to analyse, caused the natural aspect of old Japan to live before our eyes for ever.

"Many other painters contributed to the history of the art, but in so hasty a sketch as this even their names must be passed over; almost all of the least importance were represented in the very splendid Happer Collection. Mr. Happer's extraordinarily complete series of prints by Hiroshige had been well known for some time, but the collection as a whole was scarcely less noteworthy for its remarkable series of the finest work of Harunobu, a master whose works become more and more the object of the best collectors, and command prices many times greater than those of even a few years back. It had also a special feature in its hachirakaki â those tall, narrow prints which were used to decorate the hachira or supporting parts of a Japanese house.

"Owing to the use for which they were designed, prints of this form were destroyed in large numbers, and so are now uncommon in any state, and especially rare in the brilliant condition of many in this collection. Prints by the rare primitive artists made another striking feature of Mr. Happer's collection, and included such rarities as specimens of Nishi-mura Shigenobu, Torii Kiyotada and Torii Kiyoshige; while examples of that especial prizeâ the complete uncut early triptychâ figured among them, and there was a complete set of Hokusai's ten tall prints of the Shashinkio â the only set I had ever seen together."

I have put the last two paragraphs in the past tense.

The paintings of Japan show no appreciation of the roundness or modelling of things; they are circumscribed by lines enclosing gradations of colour, which may compensate, in some degree, for the absence of chiaroscuro, but which are what we should term flat washes for fabrics, and monochromes or polychromes of the " blob " type for all other objects. Infinite use was made of the black line applied by the brush whose point was held vertically.

The earliest prints, the sumi-ye, the black-and-white, were impressions from wood blocks, upon which a tracing of the original sketch, or the sketch itself, face-downwards, had been pasted, and cut through from the back, an easy process enough when the toughness and thinness of Japanese paper are considered. The one object of the engraver was to preserve the exact touch of the original. Impressions from the blocks were facsimiles of that original, and they were used in the preparation of colour-blocks, just as in the modern process colour-printing; each block was cut away, so that a flat surface remained for the printing of each colour separately, having always due regard to its relation with the key-block.

The two-colour printing in redâ i. e. rose-pink and greenâ the beni-ye, required three blocks, two for the colours, one for the key, and to this class were ascribed those prints with a third colour, yellow. The polychrome prints, the nishiki-ye, are distinguished from those in which the predominant colour is a rich tone of orange-red, free from varnish, which are the tan-ye. The other class, in which a glossy black and colours â varnish or lacquer coloursâ appear, forms the true urushi-ye.

The sizes and arrangements of the prints give the biyobus or screens with six pictures as the largest, though all screens are not large. The kakemonos also vary in size, the standard being 29 inches long, 10 wide, made up of two full sheets joined in the middle. The long, narrow prints, about 5 inches wide, are the hachirakaki, which were used to decorate the hachira, the inside pillars supporting the roof of the house. Lastly, the smaller pictures of kakemono form are known as hosso-ye. The makimonos were horizontal, not vertical, like the kakemonos.

The surimonos resembled nothing so much in English art as the " admission" and " benefit" tickets engraved by Bartolozzi, mostly after Cipriani. They were souvenir or commemorative prints of small size with decorative designsâ little picturesâ upon which the artist had lavished colour, silver, and gold, with a profusion which is somewhat surprising when contrasted with the artistic effect, the simplicity of design and colour, so marked in the larger and earlier works.

'Gauffrage is a process of raising in relief, which was often applied to prints so as to secure certain fluting or crimping, without colour. To effect this a special block was cut and so adapted to the key-block that, on application of the usual pressure, the parts affected stood out from the surrounding design; thus the feathers of a crane treated by gauffrage would show, not only the exact form designed by the artist, but a relief, which in Western art would be treated by shading; and we have noted that shading, as we understand it, was not practised by Oriental painters, in gauffrage, slight shadows were naturally cast by the parts in relief, according to the angle at which the light fell.

In the making of the surimono the gauffrage is usually heightened by extreme pressure, giving a high, sharp relief on both the plain and the coloured parts. The print rarely covers the whole of the ground, because a space must be left for the poetry which conveys the good wishes, for the New Year especially. The design is suitable to the occasion, if it be only a group of symbolical ornament, or a single spray of flowers. "The Ship of Good Fortune with its Seven Gods of Good Luck and its Cargo of Treasures," the animals representing the year of the cycle of twelve years, and a host of other subjects were utilised, not only by the designers of colour-prints, but by a multitude of amateurs whose signatures ire attached to their work. These are puzzling to the collector who thinks only of the professional artist who furnished designs for other people, and in addition supplied them to the publishers just as they did the ordinary colour-print designs. Perhaps their origin scarcely dates back further than 1750.

BEFORE resuming the consideration of the colours, let us glance for a moment at the men who produced the coloured print designs. The painters, almost without exception, belonged to the lower ordersâ they were members of the most humble, but best-known school. Again and again writers on this subject insist on " the low degree " of the Ukiyo-ye painters. To us that fact is only interesting in passing. It is the work that matters rather than the man, though it strikes us with surprise that such a mass of fine work should be consistently produced through two hundred years, by men who lived on the verge of poverty, as in the case of Hokusai. At the best the painters appear to have been of the artisan class, earning from fifty to seventy sen a day, equivalent to from a shilling to eighteenpence.

They lived with the people, and painted those subjects with which they were most familiar; their constant association with the Yoshiwara women is evident by their workâ the most flagrant examples of such association are rightly banned. This statement can be revised in the case of some, whose work also speaks for itself. But the rival portraits of famous courtesans is as much a feature of the colour-print as the Geisha girls, who belonged to another class. The former can always be distinguished by their flowing robes, immense sashes, and especially by the amazing coiffure with its rows of giant pins. Utamaro and his school revelled in depicting them.

Then the engravers and the printers were men again of the artisan class, even lowlier in position. Their work was usually carried on in their homes, and, though skilful beyond compare, it was mechanical in its interpretation of the artist's designs. The latter, when he made a correction, did so by sticking in its proper position upon the design a piece of paper, on which the correction was drawn. Such was the ability of the engraver that it is sometimes difficult to separate the drawing from the print without the most careful inspection.

This is a testimony to the skill of the printer as well. He copied the colours with absolute fidelity, increasing the colours of his palette as the artist himself enlarged his scheme of colouring.

Japanese names are rendered into English by words of varying form, though the sounds, when pronounced, are closely allied. I have endeavoured to keep to one standard, but have not interfered much with what other people say. This will account for differences which you will find in the spelling. Mr. Happer thus describes the prints:

"The terminology of prints varies, and, in order to avoid reiteration, the following explanation is offered.

"The earliest prints, usually in books, were black and white, called sumi-ye. Beni-ye, a term originally limited to the pink and green two-colour print, is also loosely applied to prints with a third colour, usually yellow, achieved with only two colour-blocks, as distinguished from the multiple colour-printâ the true nishiki-ye. Owing to the dominant orange-red, called tan, the hand-coloured print, without the addition of lacquer, is termed tan-ye, and where the glossy black, and colours mixed with lacquer appear, urushi-ye is the correct term.

"The term kakemono-ye is rightly restricted in this catalogue to the vertical diptych or two full-sized sheets joined to make a picture 29 inches long by 10 inches wide. The narrow long picture of about 5 inches wide is called hashira-kake, from hashira (the inner pillar of a Japanese house), on which it was designed to hang. Often in one sheet of paper, usually they are joined about the middle."

During the tentative stages the colours were soberâ we have noted the black and white, with soft tints applied by hand; soft flame-colour reds, faded greens, tawny browns, dull blacks, darkened violets, formed the palette which, in all subjects, as in the theatre compositions, gained strength as it was enriched with purer, vivid tones, which in later times were carried to excess. It is Shunsho's name which stands pre-eminent amongst the artists of Katsugawa. Designer of great power, colourist of fine taste, he lifted figure painting from its lowly place in art, and placed on a level with all that was best in landscape and classical painting, the genre of his day; the work he did received but slight recognition from the arbiters of taste, the aristocratic critics at home, but to the Western world it was comprehensible and popular, it was a revelation of attitude, gesture, width of treatment, and colour.

These artists of the Ukiyo-ye were not, as I have elsewhere remarked, the learned products of the classical schools of Tosa and Kano; they came from the people whose lives they chronicled, they painted what they saw, what they knew, and, if they erred, they did so in company so notable, so celebrated, that error ceased to beâ hence the everlasting formula for drawing a face. But the brilliant and refined examples of Shunsho's actors in female characters had qualities which the face, formalised as it was, could not diminish. The actor stood before the toilet-glass in robes of neutral tints indescribable, enlivened by orange-pink and apple-green. Apple-green formed the ground, too, and a pale, buff dado carried a fungus design in white. Other actors were in four or five soft colours, emphasised with gauffmge, all finely printed, with perfect register. Charming compositions, refined colouring! Reminiscent of Harunobu in the pale lavender skies and deep-red tree-trunks in the series of Rokhasen, where girls are types of " The Six Poets." His other chief works are " The Fans " (3 vols. 1769), "The Mirror of the Beauties of the Maison Verte " (3 vols. 1776). These are all illustrated with colour-prints, forming perhaps the best books of this kind which the country has produced.

I must not forget one point in connection with the colours used, and that relates to the key-block, which was not always in black. The outlines of the face and the undraped figure were rendered in red, in prints after Utamaro especially, and Shunman. Utamaro lived with his publisher and the effect was probably the result of a successful experiment.

The colours used in colour-printing were numerous, and included: tamango, clear yellow; toka, dark chestnut; at, dark blue; kusa, lettuce-green; yama buki, clear orange; yubana, mastic white; tatsutsi, silver white; chiai, vermilion; talcha, red-brown; sumi, black; and the celebrated btni, rose-red. These have been described elsewhere, but one style in which blue is predominant, perhaps in imitation of the old Nankin blue porcelain, is known by a special name, aizuri â that is, blue print. Mr. Happer had one marvellous example of this style on the wall of his room, which I could not help admiring. It was by Hiroshige, "Twilight Moon, Ryogoku Bridge," one from the earliest set of views of Yedo, having that decorative border which appears to indicate a first impression or proof, being omitted in the later issues. Blue, a wonderful shade, gave an indescribable effect. Whistlerian in the extreme! Shall we ever know how much this great artist was influenced by Japanese coloration?

The story of Claude Monet's purchase of a bundle of colour-prints at Zaandam from a Dutch grocer who used them as wrappers for his butter and cheese only goes back to 1856 or 1857, an d that was about twelve years before Japan opened her eyes to the world. Yet those prints helped Monet, Manet, and Degas, the Impressionist school, as they helped Whistler. Would it be claiming too much to say that this art owed its origin to that?

All the charm and grace, the simplicity and truth, combined with strength, which mark the best period in Japan are lost in the base, inferior modern work which the tyro often buys in ignoranceâ ignorance of the old colours and the free outlinesâ ignorance of that refinement which was no less than marvellous, when we consider that this art was designed for the masses, and ignorance, too, of the defective colour and mechanical lines which distinguish the gaudy prints of to-day. The simplicity and directness of the old traditions require some study, but an ordinary observer can soon train himselfâ and in this self-training lies the secret of successâ can master the points which form the tests, not alone between the ancient and the modern, but between the old masters themselves. Collectors must judge by the best standards, and study those standards in the libraries of the great museums. Then they can buy! Or they can go to Sotheby's during a big sale!

I do not propose to pass each artist of the Ukiyo-ye school in a review that shall be historical and critical. By kind permission of the Controller of His Majesty's Stationery Office, I am able to provide an authentic list of signatures of the artists, and, by Mr. Mapper's good consent, another list with the approximate dates when they lived and worked. I have in front of me a list which I had copied from actual examples, but I came to the conclusion that, for reference, the others were fuller and better than my own. I think these two lists will meet the requirements of nearly all collectors. I repeat my previous remark about variations in the English spelling.

In the following pages I have selected some of the most distinguished artists, and dealt with them in a desire to give some added interest to a subject which is now receiving such attention, that monographs on individual painters and print-designers have already appeared in France, and Mr. Happer has, I know, one ready on Hiroshige; but Hiroshige is near the close.

Moronobu has been mentioned, and his work up to the time of his death in 1695, in block-printing, was a revelation of strong, firm line, in fine composition, where the massing of the black and white is singularly effective. These prints were sometimes coloured by hand, and the next step, that of printing in colour, soon followed. In connection with that step we see the foundations of the great Torii school by Kiyonobu, with whom I deal later. Kiyonobu had a number of pupils who may be identified by the use of a part of his name, which was something like a certificate of merit. Hence, using Kiyo, we have Kiyomasu, Kiyotada, Kiyotomo, Kiyo-harn, Kiyoshige, Kiyonobu II. (or Shiro), Kondo Kiyonobu (son of Kiyoharu), Kiyohisa, and Kiyofusa. And, using nobu, we find the famous Masanobu, Okumura Masanobu, who, like his master, made black prints, hand-coloured prints, and mechanically coloured prints. More remains to be said of him.

Careful note should be made of this factâ when an artist became the head of a school, his name stood in the same relation to his pupils as did that of Kiyonobu. It must also be remembered that many of the print-designers were distinguished painters, and that the early masters owed much to the Tosa and Kano schools indirectly, and for colour more than for designâ indeed, nothing for design, which in the older schools was entirely regulated by tradition, was, in fact, governed by rules, which gave no scope for initiative. In them, the pupils imitated their teachers in a continuous succession.

Space forbids the inclusion of many of the lesser masters except in the listâ indeed, some of the greater ones have less than justice done to them from the same reason. A kind of claissfication, founded on that of Fenollosa, will give useful indications in a summary of the Ukiyo-ye masters.

I. Its birth. Matabei and his successors, painters, seventeenth century.

II. Its babyhood. Moronobu, ink-prints, end of seventeenth century.

III. Its childhood. Chosun, painter, Kiyonobu and

Masanobu; ink-prints coloured by hand, early eighteenth century.

IV. Its youth. Kiyonobu and Masanobu, colour-prints in two colours, invented about 1743; Kiyo-mitsu, Shigenaga, and Toyonobu added a third block. V. Its manhood. I. Harunobu inaugurated complete colour-printing, 1765.

2. Toyoharu, Shunsho, and Shigemasa shared with Koriusai the honours which followed.

3. Kiyonaga dominant about 1780.

4. Yeishi, Toyokuni, and Utamaro to 1880.

5. Hokusai, Kunisada, Hiroshige, and the end. From the print-designers' point of view only, there are two names in the list which may be excluded, Matabei and Chosun, who were purely painters. The list given coincides with one that was furnished to me by Mr. Happer, who added one modern name, Kuniyoshi, who drew a series of " Views of Yedo " in the old style without much success. It is in landscape where the European influence is evident that he has great success.

The decay of the colour-print in art led to reproductions of the old subjects, which form a kind of burlesque in which the original subjects are remotely treated in more or less glaring, poor, muddy colours, which can easily be distinguished from the old.

The classical Chinese style of painting, including the Buddhist, the schools of Tosa and Kano, which in their turn became classical; the Shi jo and the Ukiyo-ye, which probably will rank as classical, failed when the spirit and beauty of them were lost in conventional formalism. Colour-printing failed, too, from the same cause. Yet there is hope. If the nimble, clever fingers of the Japanese, guided by the great minds which in modern national life have worked miraclesâ if those minds and those fingers, in unison, grasp the new developments, a renaissance of art may carry glad tidings to a world that will never forget the glorious past.

The artists of the early schools, Buddhist, Tosa, Chinese, and Kano, which can be distinguished by the variations of style and method, were the intellectual men of their generation, and they received honourable recognitionâ the reward of learning and poetic fancy embodied by the brush. On the other hand, the Ukiyo-ye painters, though the best products of the artisan class, were ignored. This is one reason why Japanese colour-prints could be bought so cheaply at first. They cost little to produce, and were sold in large numbers. So we may say that Ukiyo-ye, the vulgar, or common art of the people, was a protest, great and successful, against the exclusiveness of wealth and position. True, each of the other schools has its followers, so clearly have the traditions of the past been maintained. But these followers axe the classes who failed to appreciate this later work until recently. The masses hailed it with joy. Portraits of actors and beauties, theatre programmes, fairy tales, stories from history, were produced in thousands, amongst a host of other subjects, such as the Seven Gods of Good Fortune, which, with the exception of Benten, the goddess of wealth and fertility, were treated in a broad, jocular spirit. Truly for them, the people, the Ukiyo-ye, which depicted "the passing world of every-day life," was a boon.

The Daimios and their Samuria patronised Hishikawa Moronobu, who, about 1659, had made twelve drawings for a. book of instruction for women, all about etiquette and hygiene, with these as illustrations, printed from one block in blackâ the sumi-ye. When these were coloured by hand they became Otsu-ye, because Matabei, the founder of the school lived at Otsu.

Naturally, the first efforts of block-printing were crude, but progress and time worked hand in hand, so that, from that period onwards, the single-sheet picture, the cheap print, grew from strength to strength, and from one sheet to five or more; only seldom, however, more than five. About 1675 Moronobu developed, to an extraordinary degree, his power as a designer of ink-prints. From his time, comparisons can be made in the style of the women's robes, and, above all, of their coiffure. I thought I had made a discovery in tracing the changes in the fashion of hair-dressing, but in talking it over with Mr. Happer, I found that Fenollosa had fully dealt with that subject, and on reference, I came to the conclusion that the best determination of dates is to be found in the recognition, of the artist's style, which, even in the print, is as distinctive as our penmanship, and which, like it, requires a considerable amount of study. Fortunately, most of the prints have the signature, which was engraved with the design, yet the signature cannot be trusted apart from the style.

THE new men cared nothing for the traditions, even of their teachersâ they worked upon the material which was always before them. They vied with each other, they passed from imitation of the best which their masters had done, to the development of the plenitude of their own powers; and the utilisation of a large number of blocks gave opportunities, freely used, for harmonious and nearly infinite design and colouring, which, though imitated, in cheap copies, reveal qualities which worn-out or retouched blocks can never show. And here let me state that too much stress is often laid upon the signature. In all ages the signature has been the readiest, easiest forgery, and amongst all nations, in all branches of art, this fact remains. In Japanese prints the signature was, as I have said, cut in the ink-block from the first. But we return to the men amongst whom Koriusai and Kiyonaga share the premier honours with Harunobu.

Koriusai did his finest work during the period 1770-1781. In the latter year he devoted himself entirely to paintingâ another example of popularity relinquished, perhaps, for love of art. In his prints, which are distinguished by the prevalence of brilliant blue and orange, also by a new dark chromium green, we recognise the master of the long hachira-kaki, the strip pictures for the posts inside the house. Harunobu usually confined himself to one figure as the subject of such narrow prints; Koriusai has successfully introduced three, and the coiffures of the women show curious changes of fashion, which some collectors crystallise into distinct dates. I have said something elsewhere on this point, which is a very attractive one.

Kiyonaga, like all the pupils of the Torii school, is distinguished in the list by Torii in brackets after his name. He was the last great artist of this school, and his works are valued for their fine qualities; the perfect brushwork, the bold, varied, and expressive line, and the rich colouring, displayed all the resources of colour-printing. His creations were ever fresh, beautiful, and unhackneyed. Here he differed from Koriusai, whose frequent mannerisms were in a measure responsible for his defeat by his younger rival, Kiyonaga, who found himself pitted also against Shunsho and Shigemasa, and the emulation was altogether good, it stimulated each, though, as we have seen, Koriusai retired from the contest. Kiyonaga matched himself against each, his power of drawing, his perfection of composition, and group of colour, making of him a formidable competitor. Shunsho drew actors, yet, when Kiyonaga entered this field, the elegance of his lines gave Shunsho, great artist as he was, no chance, " alive with motion, vitality, and open-air"! Shigemasa was the exponent of the delicate, the elegant line, yet when Kiyonaga adopted his style, he, in it, reached perfection in line, delicacy in texture, combined with matchless brilliancy in colour. From 1780 to 1790 his influence permeated Ukiyo-ye art; even the rival schools felt his power and yielded to his charm. When he himself became conscious that both were leaving him, he severed himself from colour-printing at one stroke, retiring into obscurity for more than twenty years before he passed away. Shuncho, of all the many whom he taught, alone approaches the high plane of his master. At first a pupil of the Shunsho school, he was attracted like his confreres to Kiyonaga, and unsigned works of the two men are difficult to separate, except in one particularâ the pupil shows the greater effeminacy.

When in 1765 full colour-printing was invented, the school of painters, headed by Chosun, maintained the traditions of the art of painting, and Shunsui, son or pupil of Chosun, founded the Katsukawa family or school, the pupils of which were adopted and distinguished by the prefix Shun. Amongst them was Shunsho, who made successful inroads upon the actor-printing preserves of Torii Kiyomitsu, which was but justice when we note that Toyoharu and Harunobu had both invaded Shunsui's. Evidently, these were endeavouring to escape from the actor and all his works; the vulgarity, which Harunobu denounced, was welcomed by Shunsho, who, in 1765, started his series of actors, full of dramatic force, wonderful in colour, and interesting in costume and coiffure. Every line of the kimono, of the obi, of the feather-like pattern, is pure and harmonious, and his great picture-book, the " Seiro Bijin Awase Kagami" (1776), a collection of actors and theatre scenes, is almost the most elaborate ever printed. After running a race with Koriusai, after even comparing favourably with Harunobu, Shunsho was beaten by Kiyonaga, and, like Toyoharu, retired, and devoted himself to painting. Shunko and his rival, Buncho, were the greatest artists of his school, but Shunroâ that is, Hokusaiâ the future great master, only received his early training in it. Again, referring back to 1765, another name deserves distinction amongst many whose names appear in the list, but whose work marks no epoch. Kitao Shigemasa, like Toyoharu and Shunsho, follows his line of work parallel with those of Harunobu and Koriusai; but whilst they came into collision with Kiyonaga and were beaten back, he, though scarcely a rival ever, because Kiyonaga was too strong for him, was, in a measure, his fellow worker; certainly he was not a pupil, not in any way a follower. While Koriusai produced portrait after portrait of the beauties of the Yoshiwara, Shigemasa appropriated another class, the professional singing girls, the Geisha, and, as a draughtsman, he suffers nothing by comparison with him or with Shunsho. Indeed, in simplicity of design and softness of colour, he is the greatest. Some of his tints are secured by hatching one colour in lines over another. The deliberate power and finish of Shigemasa can only be appreciated by actual study of his prints, where his painting of cloth, of solid embroidery, of drapery, reveals textures of much beauty. In painting, print-designing, and book-illustra- tion he achieved well-merited success, he stands almost unrivalled for perfect beauty. Shunsho's great book, the " Seiro Bijin Awase," owed much of its distinction to the collaboration of Shigemasa, amongst whose many pupils Kitao Masanobu was eminent. He must be differentiated from the early Masanobuâ Okumura Masanobuâ as the latter was one of the founders of the Ukiyo-ye, whilst Kitao Masanobu was contemporary with Kiyonaga and his rivals. In his illustrated book, the designs for the Yoshiwara beauties are marked by great complexity, his paintings have the same character, and even a single chrysanthemum carries its maximum number of blooms.

Before considering the Utagawa school, the difference between Shunsho, and Shuncho, Shunko, etc., may be noted. There are other artists of the Katsugawa school whose names are likely to deceive if the second syllable is not carefully noted. Shunman belonged to the Kitao family, not to the Katsugawa, and he changed the form of the character Shun in his name so that he should not be, in error, ascribed to it. Shunsho we have seen as the founder of a school for actor prints; Shuncho has been noted as the closest follower of Kiyonaga; Shunman started an original style, treating outdoor groups in tones of pure grey, yet withal brightening the neutral tints with red or yellow upon the flowers, and green upon the leaves. His powerful curves and strange, odd touches are distinctive, and he it was who began a fashion, which, on Kiyonaga's retirement, merged into something of extravaganceâ that was the inordinate height of the female figures, which sprang from the petite to the grande, and the difference is very striking when comparisons are made between the early and the late Ukiyo-ye.

The people loved the theatre, the nobility shunned and banned it, but the advent of the great actor Danjuro gave to the three men who excelled in the production of prints after Moronobu's death, to Torii Kiyonobu, Torii Kiyomasu, and Okumura Masanobu, a new incentive, a popular subject upon which they displayed the resources of their art. From tfie few prints of Moronobu came the stream of productions introducing the ever-varying scenes of the theatre by his great successors, whose wonderful grasp of mass and line, coupled with marvellous facility of execution, fully met the popular demand for Danjuro in his robes and roles. The Tokugawa rulers tried expedients to check the enthusiasm of the people for the theatre, but, whilst abolishing some abuses, they seemed to stimulate the theatre-going habit and the popularity of colour-prints which had, in the Ukiyo-ye school before, represented the manners, customs, and history of the nation, and the amusements of the women, now deserted themâ the theatre was triumphant.

In early eighteenth-century prints the colour applied by hand was tan (red lead), hence the name tan-ye. About 1715 Torii Kiyonobu substituted for tan another red extracted from saffronâ fugitive, but beautiful. This was the red beni which was associated with greenish-yellow and low-toned blues and purples. Before that date black and white ruled supreme with the hand-colouring already mentioned. Colour and detail received much more attention both at Kyoto, where Ukiyo-ye had its home, and at Yedo, where it became fashionable. The discovery of urushi, or thin lacquer, as a vehicle for the colours gave rise to the urushi-ye, a new style, in which parts of the design were heightened in effect by metallic powders, souffle or blown on through a bamboo tube, and some parts were painted with black lacquer; but this was a little later. Without undue emphasis it will be well to note the hair-dressing, and the fashion, say, of the obi or sash.

Up to this point the print had a black outline, the colour was applied by hand. Impressions in colour from flat woodblocks are assigned to 1743 or thereabout. The long delay in colour-printing seems to have been due to the failure to find a vehicle for the colour in such mechanical work; some genius suggested rice-paste, and though the hachirakaki or long prints for the pillars were still hand-paintedâ why is not clearâ the beni-ye prints in red with green formed, with the superimposed black outline, a very delightful colour scheme, with delicate shades of the two colours applied by the aid of two colour-blocks. This process, in spite of re- peated experiments, was in vogue for about seventeen years. Even now, though the red has often failed and turned to yellowâ still, however, beni-ye â and though the green merged into russet, these rare two-colour prints are amongst the most charming productions of old colour-printing.

The art of the three masters, all of whom utilised this process, can scarcely be differentiated, except that Masanobu confined his attention largely to the delineation of women, whilst Kiyonobu and Kij omasu devoted themselves to theatrical scenes. They were painters as well as print-designers; and Masanobu, as a painter, for a time did little for prints, setting himself to rival Chosun, who will receive notice presently.

It was Kiyonobu who founded the Torii school, which took the first of his personal names, Torii Chobei. If Masanobu's style is soft and feminine, Kiyonobu's is severely strong, simple, and round. His faces are long and oval, with curved noses, and eyes having the pupils in the corners. These points are distinctive. About 1756 he began to use a third colour-block, but whether its invention should be credited to him or to Nishimura Shigenaga remains doubtful. In any case the invention had far-reaching results, for which the practical skill derived from the two-colour system had been a worthy preparation. The simpler means were displaced by those of greater complexity, but the method was the same, and, with the new system, new men appeared furnished with powers in no whit inferior to their mastersâ indeed, so close is the resemblance, that without the signature one might well be mistaken for the other. None of them were engravers or printersâ it must be remembered, they were designers.

Suzuki Harunobu, pupil of Shigenaga, gave early promise of success which was more than justified when, about 1765, he became the most popular artist of his time. Two of his sayings are worth quoting. " Why should I degrade myself by the delineation of actors? " indicated uncommon independence in those days, but then his desire was, as he said, to be " the true successor of the painters in the department of printing." He meant that his prints should be fit substitutes for paintings, and his coloration has been described as " a correct conception of saturated harmony." The number of colour-blocks were by him only limited by the effects which he wished to produce, and many of these were the result of the superposition of coloursâ green and purple, for exampleâ by pairs of primary colours. Harunobu founded a school whose most celebrated pupil was Koriusai, who ranks amongst the most able designers of his country, sharing the honours with Kiyonaga, with Harunobu in a class apart.

THE early colour-prints made at Yedo were called Yedo-ye, though later, when more colours were employed and another style adopted, a new name, Nishiki-ye, expressed the change, indicating brocade pictures. Harunobu was well served by his printers, whose pigments were as good as the method of their application was admirable. The new art of 1765 astonished and delighted the people of Japan, though Ukiyo-ye was only a natural growth, the fruit of training and experience which liberated the palette to painter and engraver, and gave work to the schools, which was increased by the process of sheet-printing in diptych and triptych.

So that the school of Chosun, with Shunsui and Tsunemasa, and later with Shunsui's pupil Shunsho, the schools of Okumura and the Torii, flourished side by side for many years. Shigenaga and Toyonobu, branching off from Oku-mara, shared with all the others in the progress of the period, aspiring to the glories of a full palette, leaving the old traditions, and passing onwards from the print coloured by hand, from the early printing in red and green, and from the three-colour process, to multiple colour-blocks and coloured grounds, the special features of the development. The Torii school provided a great artist, Torii Kiyomitsu, whose best work might be ascribed to Harunobu, in the absence of signature, though before Harunobu died, in 1770, his prints had reached a high level of excellence which is properly estimated by collectors now. The competition of the schools was keen. Koriusai succeeded Harunobu, and closely imitated him; Kiyonaga followed Kiyomitsu, and brought 18 success to the Torii school; whilst Shunsho, the disciple of Shunsui, founded his own celebrated school, and Toyoharu appeared upon the scene as the pupil and successor of Toyonobu. Such an array of talent, such a struggle for supremacy, had never before been seen. When these died, the decadence commenced, though it was arrested by several individual artists, who are deservedly placed amongst the foremost masters of the art, which was just perfected when the Utagawas, the greatest group of individuals in number and productiveness, took prominent positions as print-designers. Though the schools of Harunobu and of Koriusai were in the ascendant before Kiyonaga's genius drew all under his influence, or nearly all, the other schools fought on with varying fortunes. The Utagawa family had furnished two pupils to the first Toyonubu, and the Utagawa school founded by them was destined to play a great part in the subsequent history of the Ukiyo-ye. The elder Utagawa, Toyonobuâ again note how the Toyo in the master's name is carried onâ died young, and his works are scarce in painting and colour-prints alike. Toyoharu, who became the leader of the school, showed no sign of decadence, but he only spent a few years in print-designing, retiring to practise the more congenial art of painting; yet, in that short period, he displayed very uncommon talents. His finest work is a set of four prints illustrating the elegant accomplishments, which, for perfect drawing, for combined strength and expressiveness of touch, show qualities which place him, for the moment, side by side with Kiyonaga; and his early retirement was followed by the advent of his greatest pupil, Toyokuni, whose style was not unlike that of Kiyonaga. He was a popular artist without much originality, but he saw what the public wanted, and met the demand. The colour-prints of actors by him have but little worthy of praise, being for the most part coarse and careless. On the other hand, some of his works in triptych and pentaptych, some of his groups of very tall girls, and some of his night pieces may contend with those of Utamaro, with whom he appears in competition, for when he published a series of " Beauties of the Yoshi- wy d r:-7 wara," Utamaro issued a similar set, and this happened more than once.

Toyokuni was influenced by the Dutch manner through his master, Toyoharu. Evidences may be found in his prints of unusual light and shade, modified European curves, and so on. Toyokuni's brother, Toyohiro, was an able designer who worked in the same school, sometimes upon the same subject, who had pupils of his own, amongst whom was the famous Hiroshige, one, and not the least, of the trinity of the renaissance of Ukiyo-ye, which included Kunisada and Hokusai, of whom Kunisada was taught by Toyokuni with another pupil Kuniyoshi. These two became leaders, and lived till about 1860, being followed by Kuniyoshi's pupil, Yoshitoshi, the head of the Ukiyoyeshi, until he died a few years since. Of Kunisada, it is said that no artist produced more prints, and that in none is the decline of art more consistently displayed. He employed several names on his colour-prints, as additions to either Kunisada, Toyokuni or Toyokuni II., or Utagawa, his school or family name; such were Kachoro, Gototei, Kio, Kokuteisha, Ichiyosai, and Ichiyusai.

Yeishi was at his best from about 1786 to 1800, when Utamaro and Toyokuni also flourished, though the last lived on for twenty-five years in the new century; the exact dates are given in the list. Yeishi, for a painter and print-designer of the Ukiyo-ye, was quite an aristocrat, being of good birth and some education, and more, a recruit from the classical Kano academy. If we consider his full names we secure an index of his career. Kano Yeisen, the Yedo Court painter, was his first master; from this we get an acknowledgment of his influence in the prefix of the name Yeishi. His further progress was made under Okumura Bunkaku of the Torii, or, in another form, the Cho school. Both school and master were commemorated by Yeishi in his brush name, Chobunsai. His personal name was Hosoda Yokitomi; hence his school, a small one, was the Hosoda school. Such variations as these can be traced in the names of many artists. From the Kano manner, with the landscape in a formula, the gods in a formula, and with everything formalised, the exchange to notes of nature-study was new life. In such infusion of new blood the decadence of the art of Ukiyo-ye was for the moment arrested. The artist saw what was around him, and he represented it just as he saw it.

Still, Kiyonaga was the force, and that Yeishi put forth his own strength and made his own standard is a testimony to his judgment, no less than to his skill. Here a subject or its treatment might suggest Kiyonaga, there the blossoming greys have more than a touch of Shunman; but in the force of drawing and design, the largeness of the massing, the purity of the colour, and the clear sharpness of expression, all this was Yeishi, and not another. Yet there were blemishes not belonging to him alone, but to the period; the almost absurd elongation of the figures of men and women, the deterioration in the lines of the faces, were only two faults, and there were many more. The subjects were often vulgar, the treatment was correspondingly vulgar, and liberty became licence, because the ideals were lost, the social and artistic standards had been swept away.

Soon after the beginning of the nineteenth century, Yeishi relinquished the drawing of designs for colour-printing. Was it due to chagrin at well-merited reproof for degrading his art, or was it annoyance at the superior success of Toyokuni and Utamaro? Whatever was the cause, its effect was to send him back to his painting, and from 1805 onwards, for ten years, he issued large numbers of sketches in brushwork of Yedo beauties. His most famous pupil was Yeishoâ some say Gokei, but nearly all those whose prefix is Yei had been pupils at his school, and all except Yeisho followed the later manner of Utamaro.

Utamaro, like Yeishi, was of a different class from the ordinary pupils of the Ukiyoyeshi, but with him and Toyokuni the popular craze for novelty spoilt, in a large measure, that which would have made for improvement. Then the foreign influence of the Dutch, the issue of cheap, not always good, illustrated books, the persistent theatre-going, and the general unrest, were elements which evolved the coarser feelings.

New tastes were easily met by artists having such power and facility as Utamaro, and that his work obtained an immense popularity is a testimony to his ability to provide just what was wanted. In Ukiyo-ye art, realism was the breath of its existence, but when the vulgar delighted in the revelations that passed far beyond the bounds of propriety, not to mention good taste, that breath was far from pleasing.

Utamaro was a geniusâ a wayward one, it is true. His father, a painter of the classical Kano school, was hopeful for his son, and placed him under the care of Sekeyin, a celebrated artist, who devoted himself to illustrating fine oooks. There he acquired a mastery over brushwork. Under the name of Toyoaki he painted Chinese subjects in the Kano manner, but about 1780 he was attracted by the success of

Kiyonaga, with the result that, after a few years of study, he amalgamated some of that artist's strongest qualities with his own. For some reason he dropped the iirst of his two names, Toriyamaâ Toriyama Toyoakiâ and assumed that of Kitagawa. It is said that his father disowned him for this, but I cannot ascertain the reason. However, Kitagawa Utamaro, about 1786, advanced to a richer and more lavish composition of numerous figures or detailed landscape. He ceased to use the thick stroke shown in his previous work, and for a time substituted a delicate hair-like line, which yielded to a firmer line in Kiyonaga's manner. This sends on the story some five years, during which time he lived with his publisher, Tsutaya Juzaburo, and produced some of his best work. The year 1792 was remarkable for the fine work of all the great artists then livingâ Shuncho, Yeishi, Toyokuni, and Utamaro. The prints of the last artist were distinguished by some fine reds, especially a beautiful rose-red sometimes used in his outlines, and a no less brilliant black appeared. Then about 1796 he issued some of his finest books, illustrated with drawings of birds and flowers in colours, but the criticism upon his women of about this time is so severe, that I will not venture an opinion upon it, but set it out in extenso in the next paragraph.

Fenollosa criticises a large colour-print, "Girls under a

Wistaria Arbour ": "Who can deny a certain kind of beauty and charm to this characteristic print? In the faces there is still a trace of Kiyonaga, as if his style had been distorted in a bad mirror. The eyes have become short slits, the nose as long as a horse's, the mouth not big enough to swallow the ladies' pipe, the arm hardly twice as thick as its stem. The balloon has become as big as a modern sleeve, and seriously challenges comparison with a neighbouring lantern. What I mean by the looseness of drawing can be seen in the flabby folds about the neck. The ladies look as if their clothes were tumbling off. One wonders, too, what sort of ungainly thing they are carrying in their obis. And yet the technical beauties of the print and its handling of colour are as fine as ever."

Another criticism of Monsieur T. Duret is no less interesting: " Utamaro is the last of the great artists who have specially devoted themselves to representing, with exquisite lines and skilful composition, the women of Japan. After him the art changes. Hokusai applied himself to other subjects. Hiroshige devoted himself to landscape. Kuniyoshi to battles and soldiers, and crowds of people. Utamaro, by his own genius and the charm of his subjects, wields a veritable fascination over the Europeans, who learn to appreciate him. The engravings we owe to him are at the present time in the very first rank of the possessions a- collector covets. It may be as well, however, to utter a word of warning to connoisseurs, to put them on their guard against imitations and copies."

Not only is this word of warning necessary with regard to Utamaro and his colour-printsâ it applies to all of the noted artists whose names we shall give in some kind of merit later. Now in Utamaro's case there were the pupils, Hidemaro, Kikumaro, Michi-maro, with Toshimaro, and Kikumaro's pupils, Yoshimaro and Yukimaro, amongst others; there was his widow, who married one of them, who always made use of the master's name, and there were the publishers, who appear to have employed the pupils, who made use of his name. The collector's businessâ I should add, pleasureâ is to sift the true from the false. The best of these prints are very charming. Women at work and at playâ mainly at playâ with the music of the samisen, and the refreshment of sake, or walking in the street or garden! Women in a famous series, "The forty-seven Ronin represented by the most beautiful women! " Utamaro, the " decadent," died at Yedo in 1806.

Yeizan was the son of Kano Yeiri, a pupil of the painter Nansei, and a friend of Hokkei, with whom he sometimes worked in the style of Hokusai. But he began his career as an artificial-flower maker, and his early designing appears to have been connected wth the surimono prints which were so popular as commemorative and New Year's cards. Then he set himself the task of imitating Utamaro's work. That artist had just died, and Yeizan's imitations were so close that they have been accepted as originals, especially in those cases where Utamaro's signature was attached. The difficulty of detection in the colour-prints of this class is considerably increased because the same engraver, the same printer, and the same publisher were often engaged upon their production.

Yet his own designs, in either the style of Utamaro or Toyokuni, whom he also imitated, have sufficient merit of their own to enable him to rank with them and with Shunsen, whose work of the same period was of considerable excellence. Like other artists, Yeizan had several names, the personal one being Chokiusai Mangoro, and the other Tamegoro and Toshinobu. We have noted that several of the designers oi colour-prints after a time gave up this branch of art. To these must be added this painter, who, about 1829, became an author of illustrated books, for which he furnished the designs.

Many painters, from Utamaro onwards, devoted themselves to the drawing of women, exaggerated into tall, slender models upon which were displayed brocaded drapery, in graceful folds and manifold patterns. And more, some of themâ and in this, Yeizan was equal to Utamaroâ gave a great amount of attention to tfre headdress, in whjcjj the hair was built up into wonderful curves, and ornamented with a striking array of large supporting pins of extraordinary shape. Many of the courtesans were painted in half-length portraits, in which these pins are especially conspicuous. These portraits were as popular as the full-length ones of these " beauties of the Yoshiwara," and they characterise the colour-prints of Utamaro, Yeishi, and their followers, as much as they do those of Yeizan. Their contemporaries in the Torii and Utagawa schools, together with the pupils of Shunsho, occupied themselves in depicting the actors and scenes from the theatreâ in fact, the later Torii did but little else. And we have seen the great master Harunobu refusing to touch the subject, though, amongst his many drawings of women, a few actors appear to have crept in.

We have by no means reached the point when we can say we know Japan and all things Japanese. At the best, we are only on the fringe of a subject teeming with interest, and with all that lore which awaits the revelation, hoc opus, hie labor est, to cast aside preconceived ideas, to divest ourselves of cast-iron prejudicesâ social, religious, and political â and in the true spirit of scientific inquiry to endue ourselves with strange and unknown customs, national and local feelings and conceptions, and altogether with an atmosphere foreign to our own in every way, but supremely attractive, inconceivably subtle, and exceedingly brilliant. Again and again I have insisted upon the necessity for a mental attitude commensurate with the importance of the subject, which, at this point, is colour-prints, though the same need governs every branch of Oriental art, of the craft of the workman, whose poor pay and wretched daily food in no way affected his devotion to his master or to his art, whose claims, though never ceasing, were met by persistent endeavour, by life-long service, and by a ceaseless surrender of self to art, which yielded some fruit during life, but only the full harvest when the passage of time embalmed with sweet memories the names of those who in silence and forgetfulness had fought on to victory, having no regard to fame or fortune, or to those things which move the hearts and minds of meaner men.

SUCH volumes have been written about Hokusai and his works, that a short account such as can be given here will be far from doing justice to him. Passing away in 1849, at the age of ninety, he left behind him such a mass of drawings, so many thousands of engravings after subjects drawn by him, and so many books illustrated with his work, that one is simply overwhelmed with wondering astonishment that one hand could accomplish so much, when we know that he was always a poor man in trouble from the age of twenty-six until his death, after he had for the last time signed himself " Manjorin," or rather, "Gwakio Rojin Manji," " the old man mad about drawing," a signature used since 1835. The variations in his style matched the varieties of his subjects, of which a mere list would occupy pages of this book. Rather would we answer the question " What did he paint? " in another way. He drew the likeness of everything in heaven above, and in the earth beneath, and in the waters under the earth, which gives three divisionsâ the mythical, the territorial, and the marine. He attached himself to the school of Shunsho, the popular schoolâ Ukiyo-yeâ and signed himself " Katsu Shunro," and this part of his life seems the only one in which he was free from pressing care. Then he studied several of the old masters, notably Iccho, and from the two stylesâ the ancient and modernâ his own had birth. He had served a long apprenticeship; now, in the year 1795, he signed his pictures " Hokusai " or " Hishikawa Sori," but in the next year, at the age of thirty-six, he changed his name again to Hokusaiâ maturity had arrived. It will no doubt be noted by the collector, that the signature " Hokusai" is given allied with other names. Katsuchika is one of these, and indicates his birthplace, the quarter of Yedo where his father made mirrors in metal for the Shogun. Gwakio Jin is another, which he prefixed to Hokusai about 1800, to indicate that he felt " mad about drawing." A later inscription reads: " Zen Hokusai aratami I-itzu," formerly Hokusai, changing to I-itzu."" Zen Hokusai Manji, Tokimasa, Zen Hosukai Taito, or Katsuchika Taito are a few more.

A description of some of his drawings, not the prints, from the catalogue of the Blondeau Collection may have some interest.

"ORIGINAL DRAWINGS BY HOKUSAI

"The Collection is mentioned in De Goncourt's work on the Master, published in 1896.

"A Wood Cutter seated on a bundle of faggots, with another on his back, his axe lying behind him; in colours on paper, full-size, oblong; signed HOKUSAI. " An Ox laden with bundles of reeds, being driven by a boy on the far side, half hidden by its haunches; in colours on paper, full-size, oblong; signed HOKUSAI. " A Black Crow flying across a red sun streaked by mist; in colours on paper, full-size, oblong; signed HOKUSAI. " A Hake with a stalk of bamboo through its gills; in colours on paper, full-size, oblong; signed HOKUSAI. " A Dragon Fly, Egg Fruit, and three Shells; in colours on paper, full-size, oblong; signed HOKUSAI. " Passion Flower, a trailing branch with three clusters of blooms of the hardy blue variety; in colours on paper, full-size, oblong; signed HOKUSAI. "Floral Study. A large-leaved trailing plant with purple berries; in colours on paper, full-size, oblong; signed HOKUSAI. " Plum Blossom. A closely-pruned branch just bursting into bloom; in colours, on paper, full-size, oblong; signed HOKUSAI. " Cock and Hen of domestic fowls side by side, pecking on the ground; in colours on silk, mounted in brocade and framed; signed ZEN

HOKUSAI TAITO."

The opinions held by expert critics on Hokusai are very well worth quoting. Therefore I append them, with acknow- ledgments to the writers for the excerpts. Fenollosa says: " He drew a variety of things, more rapidly and more vitally than any other artist of his day; he saw pictorial relations freshly, and created them with individuality and spontaneity. This power over line, notan, and colour was almost endless when he chose to exercise it. There is nothing out of which he could not make a composition. His illustrated books together compose an encyclopaedia of the world. And yet he never rose to the level of those great ideas which have made of Oriental civilisation a force that can never die out of human culture. His was a world cut off from all standards, except the intensity of its own impressions, of its pleasures. No artist ever so revelled childishly, genially, humorously, in pure externality."

F. M. Gookin, whose collection was sold at Sotheby's in May 1910, remarks: " Hokusai, who lived and worked until he reached the age of eighty-nine, produced a mass of works which, in all probability, has never been equalled in extent or variety by those of any other man. No other Japanese artist ever had so many different manners, or so many pseudonyms, or essayed so many different themes, or was more daring in his compositions, or displayed more originality. Like Shakaru, he belongs in a class by himself. His art, wonderful in its versatility and masterly qualities, is in many respects sui generis. The personal equation is always dominant. This was his salvation. More than any other thing, it helped him to steer a straight course and avoid the rocks upon which so many of his contemporaries were wrecked."

E. F. Strange, in " Japanese Colour Prints," art handbook of the Victoria and Albert Museum, which is now out of print, writes as follows: " The position of Hokusai in Japanese art is generally misunderstood. As a painter, he is not in the first rank outside of his own school, that of the Ukiyo-ye. He lacked the loftiness of idea (from the Japanese point of view) and the refinement of classical training. With us, who do not understand these things, he is, and always will be, one of the great artists of the world. But we must not make the mistake of considering his greatness as typically Japanese.

The qualities that ensure it in our eyes do not count in its favour among the artists of his own country. As a personality he is also great. Poor, but of an indomitable pride, he held on the way of his art with supreme perseverance."

The prints, in a few examples from the same source, are quite amongst the best that Nippon has ever produced, but from a wealth of information I can only give here a very few particulars of the works of Hokusai (Katsushika), 1760-1849.

"An Iris Garden. Three Ladies, one seated on the planks over the marshy ground, another standing in conversation with her, and a third attending to the plants, under the bough of a pine tree; oblong print about Hashirakaki size; signed SORI. c. 1795

"Two Ladies by a River, facing the entrance to a tea house, standing conversing, each with a pipe, and a boy beside one carrying parcels and an umbrella; near by, two boys going fishing; oblong print about Hashirakaki size; signed ZEN SORI HOKUSAI. c. 1796

"Enoshima. View of the Island with Fuji in the distance, from the Seven Ri Beach, where two women are standing conversing with a girl bearing a baby on her back, and beside them a man resting his load balanced on an upright staff; YOKO-YE form; signed HOKUSAI SORI. c. 1796

"A Lobster for the New Year; a long narrow print about Hashirakaki size, for a Surimono; signed GWAKIO JIN HOKUSAI. TOYO DOKURIN, i. e. ' Yedo Old Style." Written in the corner is the date of purchase by a former owner; Kyowa 2 = 1802.

"At the Temple Gate. A Little Girl who has been to a Shmto temple for the MIYAMAIRI ceremony, seated on a man's shoulders, returning, with two women by the side of the man; pigeons on the angle of the Temple roof; extra large sheet, upright; signed KATSUSHIKA HOKUSAI. c. 1807

"New Year Dancers. A Group of three outside a house, one with a mask, carrying a MOCHI pestle with GOHEI and a fan, another with straw hat and fern leaves beating a gong, and a third dressed as a woman on high clogs; full-size, upright; signed KATSUSHIKA HOKUSAI. c. 1807"

Finally, in order to give a fair idea regarding the Views, I give the Japan name of the series, its English translation, and other particulars, about which one only regret moves meâ that is, the time is not ripe to produce the publisher's seals.

"Riukiu Hakkei (Eight Views of the Loochoo Islands). Seven Prints of the First Edition, published by Moriji of Yedo, c. 1820; full-size, oblong; signed ZEN HOKUSAI, ARATAMI I-ITZU, ' formerly Hokusai, changing to I-itzu."

"Shokoku Takimeguri (Travelling around the Waterfall Country). Complete set of eight full-size, upright; signed ZEN HOKUSAI I-ITSU. Publisher's seal, Yeijudo of Yedo. c. 1827

"Shokoku Meikio Kiran (Views of the Bridges of Various Provinces). Nine of the set of eleven full-size, oblong; signed ZEN HOKUSAI I-ITSU. Publisher's seal, Yeijudo of Yedo. c. 1827-30

"Settsu Gekka (Snow, Moon, Flowers). The three friends of the Poet. Complete set of three; full-size, oblong; signed ZEN HOSKUAI I-ITSU. Published by Yeijudo of Yedo. Original edition, c. 1830

"(The Imagery of the Poets.) Five of this set of ten plates, extra tall size, upright; signed ZEN HOKUSAI ARATAMI I-ITZU. Publisher's sign of Moriji, 1830.

"Hiakunin Isshu Uragawa Yetoki (The Hundred Poems explained by the Nurse). Twenty-five out of twenty-seven known sheets of this series; full-size, oblong; signed ZEN HOKUSAI MANJI. First edition, published by Yeijudo of Yedo, 1839.

Hokusai had his peculiaritiesâ what great artist had them not? He drew everything in the world about him that was worth the trouble, and apparently few scenes of men and beasts and flowers were outside the bounds which he set for himself. Rather did he enlarge his scope into the world of the unseen, the creations of ghosts and monsters, which told of the superstition of his fellow countrymen, also into the realm of the grotesque, which revealed another side of the national character.

With what unfaltering skill, the result of an endless capacity for taking pains, did he describe the curves of wave and mountain! What a contrast between the heavy blocking of the largest mass, and the almost microscopic care in the slightest detail. In all the troubles that dogged his footsteps, in all the worries of his family life, never for a moment did he lose sight of the idea that he was a student.

In his own words he described his career: " From the age of six I had a mania for drawing the forms of things. By the time I was fifty, I had published an infinity of designs; but all I have produced before the age of seventy is not worth taking into account. At seventy-three I have learned a little about the real structure of nature, of animals, plants, trees, birds, fishes, and insects. In consequence, when I am eighty, I shall have made still more progress; at ninety, I shall penetrate the mystery of things; at a hundred, I shall certainly have reached a marvellous stage; and, when I am a hundred and ten, everything I do, be it but a dot or a line, will be alive."

He wrote this when he was seventy-five, and he lived for fifteen years longer. Upon his tomb at Asakusa, a northern suburb of Tokyo, was the inscription: " Tomb of Gwakio Rojin Manji," which means, ft the old man mad about drawing," and this, too, was the last of his signatures upon his works.

When we consider that, in order to live, he was compelled to keep on drawing by day and night, for his patrons were the poor, who could pay only a few sen, his devotion to his art is truly marvellous, as his love for it was undying. Now he has received some recognition as one of the greatest painters, not only of the Ukiyo-ye, which he particularly affected, but of the nation which now appreciates his genius.

T T IROSHIGE was, as we have seen, a pupil of Toyohiro, 1 1 who was a fine landscape painter, with a wonderful eye for composition, and yet a poor one for colour, with the usual mannerisms of Ukiyo-ye, such as the bars across the landscape representing cloud effects in rose-pink, and the small figures in the view, just colour dots, yet effective withal. The young Hiroshige had tried to enter the school of Toyo-kuni I., but it was full; however, he was fortunately adopted by Toyohiro and worked for him till, in 1828, he died, and the pupil became the master. He was then thirty-two years old, and from that year onwards to 1850 his best work appears to have been done, though he lived eight years longer.

His wonderful power, softer and more charming than that of Hokusai, places him at the head of the Japanese landscape designers, and among the greatest and most original of the world. At first he suffered from the prevailing taste for tilings theatricalâ actors, and scenes from the plays. Leaving Yedo he went to Kyoto, but after publishing a set of views of that city he returned to Yedo and produced landscapes and books of views which were so excellent as guide-books, that the scenes of many of the pictures may be recognised on the spot to-day. Mr. J. S. Happer, the greatest living authority on Hiroshige, has very kindly allowed me to use some most valuable notes which have not appeared before in any book, only in the sale catalogue of the second portion of his collection. My hearty thanks are hereby tendered to him, and my readers will recognise the spirit which prompted him to permit their use. We must hope that his monograph on Hiroshige will not be long delayed. For other help due acknowledgment is made elsewhere.

The notes are given in full, and the information on the use of an adopted name in the third paragraph will assist in solving a proposition which has puzzled many minds. Another point worth remembering is that, as Hiroshige worked for Toyohiro till 1828, and the master received the credit derived from his pupil's early work, so Shigenobu worked for Hiroshige, who, in all probability, utilised his services in his later works. The term "school" may read "family," and " worked for " must be modified in this senseâ the pupil was adopted by the master and assumed a part of his name in ordinary cases. The successor to the headship could, on the death of the head, take the whole name, as Mr. Happer shows clearly in this chapter later.

Hiroshige was almost as versatile in his choice of subjects as Hokusai himself. Landscapes were undoubtedly his strongest and best subject; in them he ranged the face of nature in all her moods. But he also painted the ordinary Ukiyo-ye subjects, the graceful beauties of the Yoshiwara, and the prints of his paintings might well be ascribed to other artists who appear to have devoted their lives to the production of this class of work, which has a tendency to stale upon one's taste.

Mention is made of three prints designed as advertisements for a dealer in shell-work, which consisted of intricate, clever groupings of the different objects the dealer had for sale. His humorous designs are not uncommon. Before me is a picture of one from a print.

This print includes representations of the Seven Gods of Good Fortune (Shichi-fuki-jiri): viz. Fukurokuju, with tall head, a rough staff and scroll, and the robes of an ancient scholar; Hotei, with a bag, containing sometimes the Sacred Treasures, here shown separately; Daikoku, with his mallet and bales of merchandise; Yebisu, with fishing-rod and tai fish (in this instance, in a jar); Jurojin, with a fan, and the robe of a scholar; Bishamon, in armour, with a trident; and

Benten, the only female of the group, with a musical instrument, the biwa. The ship in which they travel is called the Treasure Ship (Takarabune), and sails into every port on New Year's Eve, with the Seven Gods as crew, and the Sacred Treasures (Takaramono) as cargo. At the prow is the Dragon, and by the side swims the hairy-tailed Tortoise, symbolising success and longevity respectively. The chief of the Sacred Treasures are: The Hat of Invisibility, the Lucky Rain-cloak, the Inexhaustible Purse, the Peaches of Longevity, the Sacred Jewel (at the mast-head), the Clove (Choji), the Scrolls, the Hammer, the Weight, and the Shippo, a flat disc, probably a coin. Mount Fuji, the Pine-tree, and the Crane are all emblems of longevity. The character on the sail is Jiu which has the same meaning.

Ando Hiroshige was represented at the White City by several drawings, "A Yedo belle, promenading under cherry-trees," "Mount Fuji, from Kara stage," "A ferry boat on Sumida River," amongst others; but it is impossible here to say more.

Mr. J. S. Happer, the collector, sets out in the pages which follow, the results of his investigations, and it is with much pleasure that I give them welcome in this book.

"In collecting the colour-prints of the Ukiyo-ye school of Japan, the work of Hiroshige early attracted the admiration and interest of the collector. Finding that little was known about the artist, and that there was more or less uncertainty regarding his work and that of two of his pupils, who used the same brush name, it was decided to acquire everything obtainable bearing his signature, in the hope that hitherto unknown gems of art might be discovered, and that from aumerous examples some definite knowledge of the artist might be attained.

"This purpose, kept steadily in view for years, was attended with unexpected success. By comparing thousands of prints, by the possession of some three thousand, and by the careful scrutiny of every character and seal on each print, important data were obtained, which are now given to the collectors of the world for their information, with the hope that the works of Hiroshige the First (in the writer's opinion the only one of the name worthy of note as a print artist) will receive their proper recognition. If this will enhance the fame of Hiroshige and give him a lasting place in the Ukiyo-ye school as the greatest interpreter of Nature in all her moods, this collector will feel amply rewarded for his labour.

"The statement made in some excellent and painstaking works on Japanese colour-prints that two or three artists worked simultaneously and used in common the name Hiroshige, seemed to the dweller in Japan utterly contrary to all the customs of Japanese artistic or ordinary life. The adoption of a name is a serious matter in Japan, whether in the world of art or literature, whether at birth, at important epochs of life, or at death. The succession to an honoured title was not to be carelessly or unwarrantably entered upon. It seemed, therefore, incredible that a name so esteemed by his contemporaries as ' Hiroshige ' should be the common property of, at least, two individuals. When there was no son worthy to continue the name of Danjuro, the actor, a prominent actor pupil was adopted and took the name of Danjuro, but there were never two Danjuros acting simultaneously. When Hokusai gave one of his many names to a pupil, he ceased to use it himself. Toyokuni was a name borne by three individuals, but by each the strict etiquette of the age was carefully observed; the son took the title on the death of the first Toyokuni, and not until he left the world of art did Kunisada, the artistic heir, come into the full enjoyment of the title to which, as the abler artist, he had the better right. By analogy, and by all the customs of Japan, it seemed incredible that a direct violation of traditional usage should have taken place in the case of Hiroshige. As his death occurred in comparatively recent times, it seemed not impossible to discover the truth, and by the facts now stated for the first time, with proofs afforded by prints, it is hoped that the mooted questions are now satisfactorily settled.

"In searching for information from the prints themselves, a discovery of the utmost importance was made: On prints issued in the Kokwa era, 1844-1847 (perhaps even two years earlier), and the following eras, are imprinted the zodiacal ar imal signs for the subsidiary cycle of twelve years, followed by a number. The theory that this was a device for year and month dating was confirmed by eagerly inspecting hundreds of prints, not only by Hiroshige, but by his contemporariesâ Yeisen, Kuniyoshi, and Toyokuni (Kunisada).

"This discovery was a particularly valuable one, for it was during the years 1848-1858 that the works appeared which caused the confusion regarding the Hiroshiges. There may be a latitude of twelve years, for a seal date of the snake year may apply equally to the year 1845 or 1857, Du w h such an interval it is easy to determine which is the likely date. Occasionally is found, in lieu of a number for the month, the character uru, either in full or abridged, meaning intercalary, for, as students of chronology are aware, Japan in pre-Meiji days followed the Chinese lunar calendar, and had, at varying intervals, years of thirteen months. These intervals did not coincide with the zodiacal cycle signs, hence the addition of the uru character to the seal made the date absolutely correctâ e. g. ' Rat, uru," could only be 1852, as that was the only rat year in the period between 1842 and 1858 which had an intercalary month. This discovery, the seal date, prepared the way for the final discovery, and that was the finding of a sheet dated 1859, 2n(month, with the signature Shigenobu aratamete ni sei Hiroshige, meaning ' Hiroshige II. changed from Shigenobu a form of signature made familiar to the collector from its use by Hokusai (Hoku-sai aratame litsu), Kunisada (Kunisada aratame Toyokuni), and others.

"This Shigenobu has been confused with Yanagawa Shigenobu; in fact his work ascribed to Yanagawa Shigenobu was cited by one very eminent authority as ' imitative as might be expected of Hiroshige I. to some extent But Hokusai's son-in-law does not break away from Hokusai's style to follow Hiroshige.

"In brief, and to avoid elaboration, it is claimed that the prints completely prove that Hiroshige, the Hiroshige who is famed for the Tokaido set which has the masterpieces of the ' Rainy Day at Shono," ' Snow at Kambara etc., is the Hiroshige whose name appears on all prints issued up to the date of his death (the 6th day of the gth month of Ansei 5, 1858), that his pupil, Shigenobu, did not take the name Hiroshige II. until the beginning of 1859 J that all the work appearing during the Ansei era and prior to that era, was the work of the master, though it is reasonable to think that in some of his lengthy series he may have allowed his pupil to assist, as Hokusai's pupils assisted in his great work, the Mangwa; but he did not resign, nor did his pupil take, the name Hiroshige till after the death of the man who made it famous.

"Especially has the noted set of YEDO HYAK'KEI â Hundred Views of Yedoâ (118 in all) misled collectors; but the seal date, together with contemporary comment, conclusively points to the authorship as that of Hiroshige I. Each plate is dated, and the seal dates show that the prints were engraved (probably drawn a month or two in advance) during the years 1856, 1857, and 1858, the latest date being 1858, loth monthâ one month after the master's death. The seal dates are confirmed in two instances by character dates: On one plate, inscribed in the upper left-hand corner are the characters Ansei 4, 1857, while the seal date reads ' Snake 8," 8th month; on another ' Ansei 4, Snake 6th month' appears on the flag, and the seal reads ' Snake 7'â i. e. a month later; still other plates have the character uru in the seal, fixing the date with certainty. If further proof were needed, it may be found in the fact that, after the first edition was issued, another edition appeared, omitting one of the plates of the first edition, and containing one plate signed Ni sei Hiroshige (Hiroshige II.), but this plate is dated Ram 6, 1859-66, and the signature is negative evidence that the other plates, as is the fact, were by the first Hiroshige. Probably some accident happened to the blocks, and the aid of the pupil was invoked to supply the deficiency.

"Other notable sets often ascribed to Hiroshige II. are: VIEWS OF SIXTY PROVINCES, THIRTY-SIX VIEWS OF FUJI, and the VERTICAL SET OF THE TOKAIDO, issued by Tsutaya; but all these plates are the work of Hiroshige I.

"With the foregoing facts it is hoped that others may produce supplementary information from prints not included in this collection, when a monograph on Hiroshige, equal to that on Hokusai, may be written. At present it is futile to attempt authoritative dating of prints issued prior to 1842."

Hokusai and Hiroshige may be accepted almost as modern artists, certainly the masters of the Ukiyo-ye of a late period. They excelled in landscape painting, and Hiroshige deserves much credit for his persistent efforts to popularise this art in coloured prints, when one remembers that portraits of actors, scenes from the drama, portraits of Yoshiwara women and Geisha girls, were so easy to sell, everybody wanted ihem. He lived to see the success of his endeavours, and his colour-prints have a rare distinction, which Mr. Happer has properly expressed. Some think that Hiroshige's landscapes are less striking than Hokusai's, but no one amongst the Japanese artists has surpassed Hiroshige in rendering the idea of distance. In fact, they are scarcely comparableâ their methods were different, each was supreme in his own way.

Utamaro painted a few landscapes and some plants and insects which were very remarkable. So did Keisai Yeisen, Shunsen, Hokkei, and a number of other men, too numerous to mention here. In the catalogue of sale prices a kakemono-ye after Yeisen will be duly noted. It realised the large sum of Â 84, and depicted a moonlight scene with unusual and striking effect. So much of useful information is contained in the catalogue, so much that embodies great expert knowledge of the subject, that I cannot do better than advise a careful study of itâ not for the prices alone, though nothing has been inserted that did not sell for Â 10 or more. By adopting such an arbitrary plan, many most useful prints are not mentioned, but even the diminished list is almost excessively large for a book like this.

For a similar reason numbers of the lesser men who designed for colour-blocks are omitted, but that is partially remedied by the lists, especially by the signatures. One last consideration will close this section, and in my opinion it is important.

What rule is to be the standard for these colour-prints? Shall certain subjects always sell well? Shall the works of certain painters demand high prices? The answer to the first question depends upon the general demand of collectors. The answer to the second must be modified by the fact that the painter only furnished the design; otherwise the print is not at all his work.

Rather am I inclined to a standard in which subject and aesthetic merit shall form the main considerations. The beauty of the design, the refinement and harmony of its colouring, and all those qualities which appeal to the artistic sense, are above other considerations, and the mere signature is not enough to satisfy those whose chief desire is to possess fine colour-prints.

The order of merit of the artists of the Ukiyo-ye school has been thus estimated by Fenollosa. I give it because whilst it is very difficult to divide artists into classes, the process is easier where, as here, they were engaged in work very similar in character. " Of first rank, five, namely: Matabei, Okumura Masanobu, Harunobu, Kiyonaga, and Hokusai; of second rank, eight, namely: Moronobu, Kaiget-sudo, Kiyonobu, Kiyomasu, Koriusai, Shigemasa, Shuncho, and Utamaro; and of the third rank, fourteen, namely: Chosun, Shunsui, Shunsho, Toshinobu, Mangosaburo, Shigen-aga, Toy-onobu, Kiyomitsu, Kiyohiro, Toyoharu, Buncho, Yeishi, Toyokuni, and Hiroshige."

Some of these are not mentioned in my notes; one, at least, does not appear in the lists of Mr. Strange or Mr. Happer.

What one would like to know is this: is the judgment to be given upon the work of the painter as a painting, or upon the labours of the engraver and colour-printer? It is certainly possible that the same craftsmen might have been employed upon the work of several painters. And the solution appears to lie in the direction of the publisher. Efforts are being made to collate the publishers' seals. When that is done, I think that a new standard may arise, founded at least in part upon the merits of the colour-prints themselves. Fenollosa's merit list does not refer specifically to these at all. He classifies them as painters, yet in the third rank he places Hiroshige. I should feel inclined to rank Hiroshige next to Hokusai in the first rank. Differences of 1 " â.–Â-fcÂ â Â lÂ–5F C f Â â-W- â 7 r

SIGNATURES OF PAINTERSâ I.

opinion, differences of taste in art, breed no ill feeling, and those who collect colour-prints are content to acquire the best possible specimens at as reasonable a rate as may be.

The signatures on this page may include the school name, which was often prefixed to the personal name, as Kano Masanobu, the founder of the Kano school, or put in parentheses after the name, as Shunsho (Katsukawa). The latter is prac- tised in English catalogues, etc., but the former is the Japanese practice. The essential part of the name is given in every case in this list.

(i) Kose-no-Kanaoka, (2) Chodensu, also called Myocho or Mincho, (3) Josetsu, (4) Shubun, (5) Kano Masanobu, (6) Kano Motonobu, (7) Tosa Mitsunobu, (8) Sesshu, (9) Shugetsu, (10) Shukwan, (n) Shukwado, (12) Sotatsu, (13) Naonobu, (14) Yasunobu, (15) Kano Tannyu, (16) Mitsuoki, (17) Matabei, (18) Hishikawa Moronobu, (19) Iccho, (20) Koetsu, (21) Tsunenobu, (22) Korin, (23) Kenzan, (24) Ritsuo, (25) Mitsuoki, (26) Go-shun, (27) Okkyo, (28) Ippo, (29) Sosen, (30) Gan-Ku. Others follow on the next page. None of the authorities which I have been able to consult give a complete list, and the lists in this book do not pretend to be anything more than suggestive, as indeed indicating the chief amongst many great painters.

The latest authorities, the British Museum catalogue and that of the Japan-British Exhibition, do not agree, and I have followed the latter rather than the former, as this is the first occasion in which there has been an opportunity to study native paintings with the aid of a guide, drawn up under the auspices of the Japanese Government. The dates given are taken from the same source, which shows that the primitive school which culminated in Tosa Mitsunobu (1454-1525) was only opposed by the organised Kano school on the advent of its founder, Kano Masanobu (1454-1550), though Chodensu, a century earlier, by breaking away from the traditional style, may be regarded as its virtual originator. Sesshu, an independent, went to China accompanied by his disciple, Shugetsu, and again the Chinese influence over Japanese art was reinforced. When attention is called again and again to this influence, it must be remembered that the Buddhist priests had in their ranks many philosophers and poets who were also painters, and that these looked to China as the mother-country of religion and art. Thus it is that for long centuries the Tosa school under the influence of its neighbours represented much from religion and from the Court, and very little from nature, whilst nature, becoming more important in the Kano school, ruled other independent schools, such as the later Shijo and the Ukiyo-ye.

In the signatures continued on this page will be found several artists closely associated with colour-prints. These were essentially of the Ukiyo-ye school. The Shijo school, so called from a street in Kyoto, though modern,

SIGNATURES OF PAINTERSâ II.

was not attracted to the art which aimed to supply pictures to the people for a few sen. Hokusai stands apart as a master-painter of landscapes, figures, flowers, and animals. His pupils followed his style, and like him supplied subjects for colour-prints. His various signatures show his change of names, and their names, as derived in part from him, are set out in what may prove to be a helpful form. A long list of painters is given in the section on colour-prints. The last list concluded with number 30.

(31) Hoitsu, (32) Sukenobu, (33) Chosun, (34) Shunsho, (35) Shunro (Hokusai), (36) Sori (Hokusai), (37) Tokimasa (Hokusai), (38) Sesshin (Hokusai), (39) Hokusai, (40) Taito (Hokusai), (41) Katsushika (Hokusai), (42) Manrodjin (Hokusai), (43) Itsu (Hokusai), (44) Issai (pupil of Hokusai), (45) Hokuju (another pupil), (46) Hoku-un (a third), (47) Hokkei (a fourth), (48) Hokuga (a fifth), (49) Teisai (a sixth), (50) Hokuba (a seventh), (51) Hokusai's signature as (52) Keisai Kitao, (53) Keisai Yeisen, (54) Hiroshige, (55) Kunisada, (56) Kuniyoshi, (57) Kiosai, (58) Zeshin, (59) Yosai.

I am fortunate in being able to add a very complete alphabetical list of facsimile signatures from colour-prints, under special circumstances.

The Controller of His Majesty's Stationery Office has given me permission to use the marks and signatures in Mr. Edward Strange's "Japanese Colour Prints," the excellent Handbook of the Victoria and Albert Museum. I am deeply indebted to the Controller and also to Mr. Strange, and tender to both my sincere thanks.

Note. â The supplementary names are those in parentheses; that in larger type being the one by which the artist is generally known.

I ASHIHIRO, 2 ASHIKIYO, 3 ASHIKUNI, 4 ASHIMARO, 5 ASHITSURA, 6 ASHIYTJKI (Kegwado), 7 BAIKOKU, 8 BAISHU, 9 BOGETSU, 10 CHIKAMARO, u CHIKA-NOBU (Yoshu), 12 CHOSO, 13 FUSATANE (Isshosai), 14 GAKUTEI (Yedo), 15 GAKUTEI (" Year of the Rabbit," with seal), 16 GEKKO, 17 GEPPS, 18 GOKEI (Yeishi's pupil), 19 GOSHICHI (Harukawa), 20 GYSDAI, 21 GYOKUHO, 22 HANZAN (Kakio), 23 HARUNOBU (Suzuki), 24 HIROKAGE, 25 HIKOKUNI.

26 HlrOKUNI, 27 HlrONOBU, 28 HlrOSADA, 2Q HlrOSHIGE (I.), 30 HlrOSHIGE (II. Ichiysoai), 31 HIROSHIGE (II. Ichiryusai), 32 HIROSHIGE (II.), 33 HOKKEI (Shunyosai), 34 HOKUBA, 35 HOKUBA (Teisai), 36 HOKUCHO (Shunshosai), 37 HOKUGA, 38 HOKUI, 39 HOKUJIU (Shotei), 40 HOKUMYO (Sekkotei), 41 (Hokusai) SHUNRO, 42 (Hokusai) HISHIGAWA SORI, 43 (Hokusai) KATSUSHIKA TAITO, 44 HOKUSAI SORI, 45 (Hokusai) SAKINO HOKUSAI TAMEKAZU, 46 HOKUSEI (Tohosai), 47 HOKUSHU (Shunkosai), 48 HOKUSUI, 49 HOKUTSUI, 50 HOKUYEI (Shunkosai).

51 KADZUSADA (Hishikawa), 52 KAGETOSHI (Gokotei's pupil), 53 KASETSU, 54 (Keisai) YEISEN, 55 KEISEI, 56 KIKUMARO, 57 KIYOHARU (Hishigawa), 58 KIYOHIRO, 59 KIYOKUNI, 60 KIYOMINE (Torii), 61 KIYOMITSU (Torii), 62 KlyONAGA, 63 KlyONOBU (Torii), 64 KlyOSADA, 65 KORUISAI, 66

KOYEN, 67 KUNIAKI, 68 KUNICHIKA, 69 KUNIHARU (Arashi Tokusaburs, changed to), 70 KUNIHIKO, 71 KUNIHIRO, 72 KUNIHISA I., 73 KUNIHISA II., 74 KUNIKANE (Ichihosai), 75 KUNIKAZU.

76 KUNIKIYO, 77 KUNIMARO, 78 KUNIMARU, 79 KUNIMASA, 80 KUNIMASU, 81 KUNIMITSU, 82 (Kunimori) HARUMASA KOCHOYEN, 83 KUNINAO, 84 (Kunisada) TOYOKUNI II. (Kunisada, changed to), 85 (Kunisada) TOYOKUNI (Kachoro), 86 KUNISADA, 87 KUNISADA II. (Baichoro), 88 KUNISATO (Ryusen), 89 KUNITERU (Issensai), 90 KUNITOMI (Kwasentei), 91 KUNIT-SUNA (Ichiransai), 92 KUNITSURU (Utagawa), 93 KUNIYASU, 94 KUNI-YOSHI (Ichiyusai), 95 KYOSAI, 96 MASANOBU (Okumura), 97 MORONOBU (Hishikawa), 98 MUNEHIRO, 99 NIHO, 100 NOBUHARU.

.5S.

101 RvtjseN, 102 SADAFUSA (Gokitei), 103 SADAHARU (Hasegawa), 104 SADA-HIDE (Gountei), 105 SADAHIRO, 106 SADAKAGE (Gokotei), 107 SADAMASU (Gochotei), 108 SADANOBU (Hasegawa), 109 SADASHIGE (Utagawa), no SADATORA (Gofutei), in SADAYOSHI, 112 SADAYUKI, 113 SENCHS (Seitotei), ii4SENCH6(Tei IISSHIBAKUNI, n6SHigEFUSA(Shigeharu's pupil), 117 SHIGEHARU (Ryusai), 118 SHIREHARU (Gyokuryutei), 119, SHIGEMASA (Kitao), 120 SHIGENOBU (Nishimura), 121 SHIGENOBU (Ichiyusai), 122 SHIKQ, 123 SHINSAI, 124 SHIZAN, 125 SHUNCHO.

126 SHUNKI, 127 SHUNKO, 128 SHUNKYO (Katsu), 129 SHUNMAN, 130 SHUNSEI, 131 SHUNSEN, 132 SHUNSHI (Seiyosai), 133 SHUNSHO, 134 SHUNSHO (the same artist, 135 SHUNSHO (pupil of Shunkosai), 136 SHUNSUI (Tamagawa), 137 SHUNTEI, 138 SHUNTEI (Ryo), 139 SHUNYEI, 140 SHUNYO, 141 SHUNZAN, 142 TAMEKUNI (Jiryosai), 143 TERUSHIGE (Katsukawa), 144 TOMINOBU (Kwasentei), 145 TOMIYUKI, 146 TONAN, 147 TOSHIHIDE (by special order), 148 TOSHIKATA 149 TOSHINOBU (Okumuru), 150 TOSHINOBU (by special order).

17ft 151 TOSHU, 152 TOYOHURA (Utagawa), 153 TOYOHIDE (Kitagawa), 154 TOYO-

HIRO, 155 TOYOHISA, 156 TOYOKUNI (I.), 157 TOYOKUNI (I.), 158 TOYOKUNI (Gosotei), 159 TOYOMASA (Ichikawa), 160 TOYONOBU, 161 TOYOSHIGE (Toyokuni's son), 162 TSUKIMARO (Bokutei), 163 UMEKUNI (Juk-yodo), 164 UTAMARO, 165 UTASHIGE, 166 YEIRI (Rekisentei), 167 YEISHI, 168 YEISHO, 169 YEIZAN, KIKUGAWA, 170 YENCHO, 171 YOSHICHIKA, 172 YOSHIHARU, 173 YOSHIFUJI (Ichiosai), 174 YOSHIKADS, 175 YOSHI-

KATA.

176 YOSHIKATSU, 177 YOSHIKAZU, 178 YOSHIKUNI (Jukodo), I7Q YosHIMORI, ISO YOSHIMUNE, l8l YOSHISHIGE, 182 YOSHITAKI, 183 YosHITORA (Kinchoro), 184 YOSHITOSHI, 185 YOSHITOYO, 186 YOSHITSUGU (Sada-yoshi's pupil), 187 YOSHITSUNA, 188 YOSHITSURU, 189 YOSHITSUYA (Ichiyeisai),

190 YOSHIYUKI, 191 Gwa â painted, 192 Fude â painted with brush, 193 Dxu â composed, 194 Utsusu â copied, 195 By special order.

Some of these names will be repeated in the long list mentioned above. The last three names bring us to the close of the nineteenth century. Kiosai, the Mark Twain of the brush, died in 1889; Zeshin in 1891; and Yosai in 1878. Zeshin poked fun at the classical side of the Kano school, treating the gods with scant ceremony. Yosai confined his attention to figure painting. The modern section at the Exhibition introduced painting in oil, and the pictures I saw differed but little from our own. The catalogue might be that of an English gallery, except for the names of the artists. " Oil-painting An Ever-crystal Stream by Morinosuke Yama-moto; Oil-painting Chrysanthemums by Toraji Ishikawa; and Oil-painting Morning Scene at a Railway Station by Morinosuke Yamamoto," are indications of modern thought in Nippon. We can both appreciate those indications and regret them so far as they leave the old inspirations. Rather are we not beginning to understand the soul of the East through the art of Old Japan, as the Japanese are likewise learning something of the soul of the West. A complete rapprochement is not yet!

A LIST OF THE CHIEF ARTISTS WHO DESIGNED COLOUR-PRINTS

With approximate dates of their work where actual dates of birth and death are not known

BAIREI (Kono).:. worked c. 1875-1895

BANKI. "V;. c. 1800

BUMPO (Shunsei). worked c. 1800-1830

BUNCHO (Ippitsusai). V '. worked c. 1764-1796

BUNCHO (Tani). Â. c. 1763-1841

CHIHARU (Takashima). 1776-1859

CHIKANOBU.,. â â Â- 186 Â

CHINNEN (Onishi). worked c. 1820-1840

CHOKI (Yeishosai). . worked c. 1773-1805

FUMINOBU. c. 1853

FUMIYOSHI. C. 1853

FUSATANE. Â. C. 1853

GAKUTEI (Yashima). worked 1800-1840 GEKKO. c. 1896

HANZAN (Matsugawa). worked c. 1835-1851

HARUNOBU (Suzuki). HARUSHIGE (Suzuki). HARUTSUGU. HIDEMARO (Kitagawa). HIROSHIGE (Ichiryusai) HIROSHIGE II. (see Shigenobu). HISANOBU (Hyakusai) HOKKEI (Todoya). HOKUBA (Teisai). HOKUGA (Hotei) HOKU-JIU (Shotei). HOKUSAI (Katsuchika) HOKUYEI (Shunkosai)-.,". ISSAI (Kat-suchika). ITCHO (Hanabusa). KAIGETSUDO (Yasumoto). KANRIN (Katsuren Okada) KEINEN (Imao) KEISAI (pupil of HOKKEI). KIGAKU.

KlkUMARO.

KIYOCHIKA (Kobayashi). KIYOHIRO (Torii) KIYOMASU (Torii). KIYOMINE (Torii) KIYOMITSU (Torii). KIYONAGA (Torii). KIYONOBU (Torii). KIYOSHIGE (Torii). KIYOTADA (Torii) KIYOTOMO (Torii). KIYOTSUNE (Torii). KOCHO.

KORIN (Ogata). KORIUSAI (Isoda) KOTEI. KUNICHIKA (Ichiyosai) KUNIMARU (Utagawa) KUNINAGA (Icbiunsai) KUNINAO (Utagawa)

KUNINOBU (Pupil Of TOYONOBU)

KUNISADA (Utagawa) KUNITSUGU (Kozo). KUNIYASU (Ipposai). KUNIYOSHI (Utagawa) KWAZAN (Watanabe) worked worked worked worked worked worked worked 1703-1770 1747-1818 c. 1770 c. 1804-1817 1796-1858 1782-1832 c. 1800 c. 1800-1840 1770-1844 c. 1850 c. 1820-1830 1760-1849 c. 1830-1850 c. 1850-1865 1651-1724 c. 1700 c. 1832 c. 1892 c. 1830 c. 1850 c. 1789-1829 c. 1880 1708-1766 1679-1762 1786-1868 1735-1785 1752-1814 1755 or 1756 c. 1716-1735 c. 1714-1739 c. 1725 1664-worked worked c. 1830-1864 1660-1716 1720-6. 1782 c. 1890 worked c. 1830-1865 1786-1817 c. 1810 c. 1825 c. 1775 1785-1864 c. 1840 1799-1830 1797-1861 c.

KYOSAI (Shofu). 1831-1889

MASANOBU (Okumura). worked c. 1685-1764 MASANOBU (Kitao). 1761-1816

MASAYOSHI (Kitao). 1761-1824

MASUNOBU (Tanaka). worked c. 1754-1771

MATORA (Oishi). worked c. 1820-1833

MITSUNOBU (Hasegawa). worked c. 1724-1790 MORIKUNI (Tachibana). 1670-1748

MORONOBU (Hishikawa). 1648-1715

NAGAHIDE,. c. 1840

NANGAKU,?. e. 1853

NANREI. c. 1853

OKYO (Maruyama). 1733-1805

RINSAI. c. 1853

RINSHIN. c. 1853

RlnTEI. C. 1853

RISSAI. c. 1854

RlsSEN.Â â,. C. 1848

SADAFUSA (Gokitei). c. 1825 SADAHIDE (Utagawa). worked c. 1820-1864

SADAKAGE (Gokotei) c. 1835

SADANOBU (Hasegawa) c. 1840

SADATORA (Gofutei). c. 1825 SEITAI (Watanabe). c. 1890

SEKIYEN (Toriyama). worked c. 1773-1784

SEKKYO (Sawa). c. 1790

SEXTAN (Hasegawa). worked c. 1790-1839

SHARAKU (Toshiusai). worked c. 1775-1810

SHIGEHARU. c. 1853

SHIGEMARU. c. 1852

SHIGEMASA (Kitao). 1738-1819

SHIGENAGA (Nishimura). 1697-1756

SHIGENOBU (Nishimura)-,,. worked 1700-1740 SHIGENOBU (Tsunegawa). â â c. 1725

SHIGENOBU (Yanagawa). v. 1782-1832

SHIKIMARO (Tokeirin) Â ". worked c. 1790-1805 SHINSAI (Ryuryukio). worked c. 1803-1845 SHOSENSAI. c. 1850 SHUCHO (Tamagawa). worked c. 1790-1800 SHUMBOKU (Ooka). 'Â,".,. 1676-1760

SHUNCHO (Katsugawa). worked c. 1770-1790 SHUN jo (Katsugawa). worked c. 1780-1790 SHUNKO (Katsugawa). worked c. 1765-1790 SHUNKO (distinguished as SHUNBENI). c. 1850 SHUNKYO (Katsugawa). Â. " â Â. c. 1810 SHUNKYOKU (Katsugawa). c-

SHUNMAN (Kitao) SHUNSEN (Kashosai). SHUNSEN (Katsugawa) SHUNSHO (Katsugawa) SHUNTEI (Katsugawa) SHUNYEI (Katsugawa) SHUNZAN (Katsugawa) SOBAI

SOKKEN (Yamaguchi) SOSEN (Mori).

SOSHISEKI SUGAKUDO

SUKENOBU (Nishikawa)

TAIGAKU.

TAITO (Katsuchika).

TAKEKIYO

TAKISHIBA

TERUNOBU (Katsnmura)

TOICHI.

TORIN (Tsutsumi)

TOSHINOBU (Okumura)

TOYOHARU (Utagawa)

TOYOHIRO (Utagawa)

TOYOKUNI (Utagawa)

TOYOKUNI (Gosotei).

TOYOMARU

TOYOMASA (Ishikawa) TOYONOBU (Ishikawa) UTAMARO (Kitagawa) YASUMICHI YEIICHI (Seisai) YEIJU (Chokosai) YEIRI (Yeishi's pupil) YEIRI (Rekisenti) YEISEN (Keisai) YEISHI (Chobunsai). YEISHIN.

YEISHO (Chokosai). YEISUI.

YEIZAN (Kikugawa). YOSAI (Kikuchi) YOSHIHARU (Ichimesai)

YOSHIKAZU YOSHITOMI

YOSHITORA (Ichimosai) YOSHITOSHI (Taiso).

worked c. worked c. worked c.

worked c. c.

worked c. â '. c.

c. worked c.

c. worked c.

worked c.

c. worked c.

worked c.

worked c.

worked c.

1785-1815 1790-1829 1724-1792 1769-1820 1769-1819 1776-1800 1677-1751 1816-1853 1716-1736 1780-1820 1720-1763 1733-1814 1773-1828 1769-1825 1774-

1835 1770-1780 1710-1785 1754-1806 1780-1810 1789-1848 1780-1805 1800-1829 1787-1878 1855 1860-1892

THE life of a nation depends upon its virtue, its relation to its highest standards of conduct, regardless of all except the purity of those standards, by which thoughts and actions are examined and regulated. Whether we understand religion as a divine system of faith and worship to which its followers are bound, or as a line of conduct founded upon the life and teachings of some great prophet whose disciples imitate both, or as a revelation from what we call nature, or as a mere means of discipline, we arrive at a conclusion justified by history, that such religion in its purity is both an inspiration to the individual and a safeguard of the national life. In its purity is the crucial test, the rock upon which happiness and security are both founded and built.

These thoughts are suggested by the study of the history of Nippon, which I am treating here, mainly in relation to its progress towards Western civilisation. We can never trace the origin of the old nations, we can only surmise, for legends and myths embodying the supernatural cloud and hide the facts. In this sense it is not intended to dwell upon those far-off days; in a few words it will suffice to begin with Jimmu Tenno, the founder of the present dynasty, who reigned about 665 B. C., with the Empress Jingo, who conquered Korea in A. D. 201, with the introduction of Korean civilisa-t ion eighty years later, and to come to the advent of Buddhism- bout A. D. 550, which was followed by its acceptance by the Emperor in A. D. 624.

the old Shintoism, " the Way of the Gods," regarded the dead as spiritually living; the new philosophic Buddhism, the " Way of the Buddha," considered the living as spiritually dead. Hence the two systems progressed side by side. The first established the divine right of kings from the very beginning, and was the source of an intense patriotism, regarding the Emperor as its emblem, its soul, its glory. The second was atheistic in its essence, though it degenerated into idolatry, in which Buddha was adored as the ideal of intelligence, goodness, and beauty, worthy of the imitation of mankind. The art of Japan, inspired by Buddhism, prospered under its protection; many of the great masters were priests who lived in monasteries.

The military power had been deputed by the Emperor to the Shogun as commander-in-chief as early as the sixth century. In time it became the custom to grant the office to one of two rival clans, the Taira and the Minamoto. In 1192 Yoritomo was Shogun. He usurped the temporal power, confiding the spiritual to the Emperor, or, as he is sometimes called, the Mikado, who constantly resided at Kyoto through all the troubles that came. But the term Mikado is used to signify the person of the Emperor, not his government. The sovereign of Japan is the Emperor; the gate of the Imperial Palace, mikado, exalted gate, is a figurative term which indicated his spiritual office. Following the isolation and seclusion of the religious head of the nation, whose powers were limited and submerged during this period of the Shogunate, came sanguinary struggles for supreme power amongst the feudal princes. These lasted for four centuries, the Minamoto clan gradually gaming ascendancy; but before lyeyasu victorious laid the foundation of the hereditary line of the Tokugawa Shoguns by his victories over the princes of the south, another influence appeared, the first coming of the European, the herald of Western civilisation.

Marco Polo spent many years travelling in the East from 1272 to 1295, and visited Japan amongst other countries. On his return to Venice, his native place, he fought against Genoa and was taken prisoner. Whilst in prison he dictated his " Maravigliose Cose," an account of his adventures, which was published in 1559, just a year before Mendez Pinto, a Portuguese adventurer, finally left Japan to return to his own country, a first visit in 1537 being followed by other trading vessels, by the establishment of settlements, by the introduction of the arquebuse and the method of making gunpowder, and by the arrival of Jesuit missionaries. The government of the Tokugawa lyeyasu was firmly established in 1600, but ten years before that the Portuguese and their missionaries were expelled from Japan, and this expulsion was followed by a cruel persecution of the native Christian converts which lasted till 1642. The Portuguese, during a century's trading, appear to have affected the art of that country but little. With the Dutch, who were suffered, under severe restrictions, to remain in their settlements, the exportation of " Old Japan " porcelain to all parts of Europe, from 1600 onwards, was so great that large vases, entirely out of place in the decoration of the native home, were specially made for export in the style known as " Old Imari," which had a peculiar decoration of red, green, blue, and gold, in shaped panels, with diapers and landscapes, upon a ground of peonies or chrysanthemums. Later examples show Dutch ships and men in European costume, and similar ships may be found in some paintings and colour-prints. With the exception of the Dutch and Chinese, right on till 1853, all foreigners were rigidly debarred from the country. In that year other forces from the outside world came into play, and the government was compelled to revise its position, which, inside, was endangered by the jealousies, intrigues, and quarrels of the princes and Daimios.

From the United States, the American Commodore Perry led an expedition, which was courteously received, but not encouraged, so it stayed only a few days in the July of that year, yet the result was satisfactory, as a commercial treaty between the two nations was signed in the March of the next year, 1854. In October a similar treaty was concluded with Great Britain, which was followed in 1855 by another with Russia, These treaties were made by the Shogun or Taiko, whose other name from 1854 was the Tycoon, and this assumption of supreme power led to grave consequences some years later. The combined effect of these treaties and the influence of the outside world was to open two ports to European commerce. They were Nagasaki and Hakodadi.

On December 12, 1860, Sir Hope Grant, the Commander of the Forces in the Chinese war of 1860, when the Peiho Forts were captured and Pekin looted, visited Japan on what he termed " a pleasure trip," and his impressions gathered during a fortnight's residence there are worth quoting, but space only permits a few words: " A short time before our arrival, three Russians and a Frenchman had been assassinated, and the crime was imputed to the Daimios," who " entertain a great hatred towards all foreigners, and especially towards the Englishâ and with good reason. They are aware that we have taken possession of the whole of India; and they have seen China, one of the largest empires in the world, completely broken up by us." " Each Daimio's retainers consider it to be their duty to carry out their chief's behest, even though death or torture is certain to be the consequence." "The houses are built of wood, except the foundations of those belonging to the Daimios. Very destructive typhoons and earthquakes are of constant occurrence, and a short time ago (Dec. 1854) nearly the whole of Yedo was, in consequence, shaken to the ground."

Two years after this, Mr. Richardson was murdered and his companions cruelly treated by the followers of one of the Daimios, who were involved in the struggle between the Emperor and the followers of the Tycoon or Shogun, which came to a crisis in May 1868, when the latter defeated the former after having first suffered defeat. The Shogun Yoshinobu resigned his office before this struggle began. In July of the same year the Emperor was successful in quelling the Rebellion, his power was established in Church and State, the Shogunate of the Tokugawa family was abolished, and the land, freed from the oppression of the Daimios, who relinquished their feudal rights, flourished under its reformed government, whilst its people, with new strength and spirit, marched onwards along a new road to Western civilisation. Looking backwards we can hardly realise that in 1860 the Japanese began " to wear European clothes."

The continuation of the history is from a " Short Description of the Exhibits at the Japan-British Exhibition' issued with the compliments of the Committee governing the Department of the Imperial Army:

"The adoption of European methods in military drill by the Samurai of Tokyo was followed by various provinces supplanting bows and arrows in favour of firearms. During the Restoration War, 1867-8, peace was secured mainly by the Western mode of fighting, which was followed on the rehabilitation of the reigning sovereign by the establishment of a War Department controlling the Army and Navy. The defence of Kyoto, the then Imperial capital, was assigned to recruits of various Daimio troops, but some provinces adopted the English or Dutch systems, others the French, which last system was modified and adopted as the Army system in 1870. An arsenal was then inaugurated, and simultaneously a law of recruits was ordained, and a select body was thus organised at headquarters, by calling up five qualified persons, irrespective of social status, per a certain estate (e. g. ' man-goku ') from each province, in which sixty regulars were also enlisted, besides commissioned officers. The new military ordinance settled various groups of the force, such as battalions or companies, according to local conditions; the men comprising the standing army were then gradually assigned to a number of services, horse and foot, artillerymen and engineers.

"The Imperial Guard, composed of infantry, yeomen, and artillery, were for the first time in 1871 selected from the troops of the three provinces of Satsuma, Choshu, and Tosa. Two garrisons of the Eastern and Western military provinces were expanded into four, situate respectively at Tokyo, Osaka, Kumamoto, and Sendai, the voluntary standing army which formerly belonged to provinces being now assigned to garrisons. At Tokyo ten battalions were stationed, at Osaka five, Kumamoto two, and Sendai one. The absolute control of the soldiery, by this process, once again came to the person of the August Sovereign.

"The Departments of the Army and of the Navy were both established in 1872. In addition to the Military Academy and Preparatory School previously formed, an institute for training principally non-commissioned officers entitled ' Kyododan' had been inaugurated. About that time a number of French officers headed by Lieutenant-

Colonel S. Marquerie of the General Staff were invited to Japan in order to take up the training of officers, commissioned and noncommissioned, and the evolution of the services was now followed by great strides being made at the arsenals in the production of ordnance and small-arms, as well as of subsidiary stores. By thus supplying the requirements of the regulars and of the reserves with home manufactures, Japan had no longer to depend entirely upon the importation of war stores. In the latter part of the year 1872 an Act of Conscription came into force based on a combination of the ancient and national customs and of the Western models. Every male subject of the Empire now had to undergo military service for seven yearsâ namely: in the regulars for three years, and in the reserves and the landwehr two years each. The Samurai with his hereditary fighting privileges no longer exists.

"In the following year (1873) two garrisons (at Nagoya and Hiroshima) were added to the existing four, these six districts being each divided into two sub-districts provided with stations and detachments. The newly enrolled units were completed in the requirements for various grades (except the gendarmes, who were created in 1881) and their strength was fixed on a peace footing at 31,680 men, as well as in the time of war, when they aggregated 46,350 men. In addition, there was the Imperial Guard intact, consisting of four battalions of infantry, a cavalry squadron, and an artillery battalion. The soldiery, besides the Imperial Guard, were then formed into fourteen regiments of infantry, the subdivision of which was forty-two battalions, three cavalry squadrons, eighteen sub-companies with guns, ten sub-corn- panics of engineers, six sub-companies of transport troops, and nine companies of coast-defence artillery. When the conscripts were thoroughly trained those voluntarily enlisted were gradually discharged. The Imperial Guards were first presented with their colours when their battalions were consolidated into two regiments in 1874. All the garrisons were afterwards presented with their regimental colours by the Emperor.

"In the ensuing year, 1875, the Army was again reorganised, especially as to the Imperial Guard, to which an engineering company and a transport company were added. Hokkaido, the northern island, began to be protected by a newly organised troop residing there with agricultural pursuits, most of whom were recruited from the adjacent prefectures. The conscription was unpopular in those days, but eventually a good discipline prevailed. In the ordnance and small-arms a vast improvement was achieved. The rifles of the Gewehr pattern gave way to the Enfield type at the garrisons of Tokyo, Osaka, and Kumamoto, whilst the rest were armed with either the Snider or the Allimi. During the insurrection of the South, 1877, the ammunition for these rifles as well as for those of the Zundal type were manufactured and sent into the field.

"The military affairs of the Empire were placed in order during the years 1878 and 1879 by the Department of the Army, the General Staff, and the Inspector-General, each responsible direct to the Emperor. While the Department undertook the military administration, the national defence and strategy were entrusted to the General Staff, the Inspector-General reviewing the whole Army and going into its accounts. Under the Inspector-General, at headquarters in Tokyo, three divisional chiefs were appointed in the eastern, the middle, and the western sections; each governed two military districts, from which could be formed a corps d'armee to promptly meet any emergency. The terms of the reserves and the landwehr had been again extended to three and four years respectively, thus making a ten-year service for a conscript. Consequently, about one-half of the drilled men had remained in the service, by which extension no voluntary recruits were necessary even in a bellicose operation. Exemptions from the conscription have been rather easily obtained under the new regulations. The invention of the Murata rifle by a Japanese officer of that name resulted in the equipment for the first time of the soldiery with a uniform pattern of rifles, the employment of other types disappearing.

"The Emperor issued his Imperial Injunctions to his Army and Navy in 1882, recalling their prime object and urging them to personally cultivate the five cardinal principles of Loyalty, Courtesy, Valour, Veracity and Modesty. A subsequent rescript for the expansion of his forces was due to observation of the status of the world. Accordingly the plans for the national defence were greatly altered; in addition to the Imperial Guard twelve brigades of infantry, six regiments each of cavalry and artillery, and six regiments each of engineers and transport were now formed. Towards the end of the year 1882 a regular training of staff officers of the Army was inaugurated at a college under the direct supervision of the Chief of the General Staff. Early in 1883 the rules governing the Military Academy were reconstructed, and German was added to the curriculum. A staff officer of the Prussian Army in the person of Major Meckel was invited to be an adviser to the General Staff; through this officer's services there have been remarkable strides made in the tactical trainings. Thenceforth Prussian models were freely adopted by the Japanese authorities in their ordinances, and an extension of the conscript service to a term of twelve years had resultedâ namely, three years in the regular service, four in the reserve, and five in the landwehr. Through the enactment of the new conscription law, an exemption could no longer be procured save on account of physical incapability. In a decade afterwards, i. e. in 1894, the required number of Army Divisions would be formed.

"A reform of the administrative bureaux was decreed in December 1885; universal education spread, commerce and industries improved. The Army's development was also one of the signs of the times. The military engineering depart- ment was well occupied in the following year, fortifying various points. The coasts were strongly defended. The standards admitting the cadets to the Military Academy were altered in 1887, when the present qualifications of a candidate for a commission were framed. The Corps d'Armee system superseded the garrisons in 1888. The staffs of the Army and Navy had been severally administered under the supervision of the ' Sangun," an office which was abolished in the following year. A severe enforcement of conscription ensued, and various regulations pertaining to the plans to meet an emergency, for military education, inspection, and supplies were issued. The improved Murata rifle of the 1885 pattern had now developed into a repeating type, and in the height of manufacturing these small-arms at the arsenals, in 1894, Japan was forced into war with China.

"After the restoration of peace in 1895 it was decided, in consequence of the general situation, to strengthen the armaments. In the third year afterwards the units of the Army were increased to thirteen divisions, including the Imperial Guard; thus were created six new divisions, the Seventh to the Twelfth, besides a new establishment of two brigades each of cavalry and artillery. In order that uniformity might be maintained in the plans of defence within various jurisdictions, and for co-operative strategy of various divisions and for their discipline, three ' Totoku ' or Generals-commanding were created, each directing four divisions, and having their headquarters in Tokyo. They were under the direct orders of the Emperor, and by his order inspected a division or the manoeuvres of combined divisions. During the six years, 1898-1904, the Gensuifu, an assembly of the highest military advisers, composed of Field-Marshals and Admirals of the Fleet, a General-Superintendent of Military Training, and a Board of Military Councillors, came into existence in the place of the Inspector-General and the 'Totoku." Generals Kuroki, Oku, Prince Fushimi, Nogi, Kawamura, Nishi, and Hasegawa were among the Board, with Admirals Inouye, Prince Arisugawa, Yamamoto, and Togo.

"The training of non-commissioned officers was henceforth entrusted to each individual regiment, thus abolishing an institution called ' Kyododan." The repeating rifles of the Murata pattern were supplanted by the much improved 1897 type. Quick-firing field and mountain guns of the 1898 type, designed by General Arisaka, were adopted, replacing the former 7 centimetre bronze guns. A certain revision of the ordinance respecting the Imperial Camp in time of war gave to the Chief of the Staff of the Army and the Head of the Naval Board of Command power over their respective staff officers in the preparation of strategical plans.

"The efficient state of the Imperial Army was visible in the operations of 1904-5. Complying with the requirements of the then war footing, the service period of a conscript had to extend to a term of seventeen years and four months â namely, three years' service with the colours, four years and four months in the reserve, and ten years in the landwehr. During the progress of the war, and following the restoration of peace, a projected expansion of the Army aiming at efficiency was accomplished. The thirteen divisions then existing were raised to nineteen divisions, supplemented by four cavalry brigades, two artillery brigades, a field-artillery brigade and a brigade of communication troops. Two brigades of heavy artillery were organised in place of the coast-defence troops. The rifle of the 1897 pattern had to be remodelled to a certain degree. As to the mountain guns and field guns, a system of checking recoil was adopted. Various equipments have thus been added to the whole army since the events of 1904-1905, and further improvements are constantly being made in order that the Services may remain always abreast of the times."

I have much pleasure in tendering my best thanks to the Committee, and do not think such history is misplaced in a book dealing with the Arts of Japan, because they to a great extent depend upon the governing classes, upon peace or war, and upon the luxury rather than the necessity of the people. Thus, in art metal-work, the armour worn by a General or Prince furnished wide scope for the artist; the State Armour, the Body Armour, and the Lower Body Armour were all elaborate, so were the Arms and their accessories. Steel helmets were used in place of hide and leather from A. D. 1543, and leather " Iyo " armour, so called from the province in which it originated about 1464, was displaced by wonderful suits of armour for horses as well as men. Over fifty great classes of articles constituted an outfit for an army, and in each of these the units were exceedingly numerous, as I have shown in the sword and its belongings. The siege and fall of the Castle of Osaka, 1614-15, which resulted in yeyasu's victory over the Toyotomis, was not alone the beginning of the Tokugawa Shogunate, which lasted for fifteen generations, but re-established peace so that the Arts flourished greatly, as they had done under the Ashikaga Shoguns from 1392 onwards for two hundred and fifty years. Peace and progress have followed the war with Russia in our own days. And in looking back upon Old Japan and its miracles of Art, we may have some regrets because they are passed and gone, but not for ever. There is still hope for a Renaissance. Meanwhile we agree with the following opinion:

"Though America first broke down the barriers, it was Great Britain, more than any other nation, that in the end helped and encouraged the regeneration of Japan. The intimate relations between the two countries began at a time when Japan seemed still struggling with adversity. The community of interest, which was presently to ripen into a iirm alliance, found expression at a period when Japan's prowess was unrevealed and her prosperous future unforeseen. We are, however, far too prone in England nowadays to allow our minds to revert to the glittering spectacle of Japan militant and victorious. We fail fully to realise that, though the national genius of Japan has found successful expression in war, it is chiefly and honourably desirous of winning world-wide recognition in the domain of peace."

The modern Art of Japan in the Exposition at the White City in 1910 was full of promise. In the paintings, especially those without traces of Western influence, no story of decadence is told, in the lacquer and the carvings in ivory, in the cloisonne ware "and pottery, and in the designs for textile fabrics, there are evidences of re-animation, and thereat we rejoice and hope. And, for a few last words on the history which we are beginning to study with awakened attention, we may note that in the news of July 25, 1910, amongst the metropolitan items was the following: " Prince Tokugawa, the President of the Japanese House of Peers, last night entertained at dinner, at the Hyde Park Hotel, a large number of Japanese gentlemen."

Still later, to bring history as close as can be in this book, I note the annexation of Korea by Japan at the end of August in the same year. The text of the treaty included the following striking clauses:

"Article I.â-The Emperor of Korea makes complete and permanent cession to the Emperor of Japan of all rights of sovereignty over the whole of Korea.

"Article 3.â The Emperor of Japan will accord to the Emperor, ex-Emperor, and Crown Prince of Korea, their consorts and heirs, appropriate titles, dignity, and honour, and sufficient annual grants for the maintenance thereof.

"Article 6.â The Government of Japan will assume the entire government and administration of Korea, and will undertake to afford full protection to the persons and property of Koreans obeying the laws there in force, and will promote the welfare of such.

"Article 7.â The Government of Japan will so far as circumstances permit employ in the public service of Japan those Koreans who accept the new regime loyally and are duly qualified for such service."

It was stated that the Emperor Yi-Syek and ex-Emperor Yi Heni willingly gave their assent to the annexation, and the only hesitation shown was when the titles of the former emperor were discussed. The Japanese proposed the title of Grand Duke, but the Emperor insisted upon being styled " whang " or king. To this the Japanese finally consented.

The later Exhibitions of Modern Art of Japan include one at Earl's Court in 1911, in which were some wonderful specimens, not only reproductions of ancient examples, but recent work of considerable merit. The minute cloisonne enamel designs with cloisons in gold were as striking as those in which cloisons were employed to build up the designs and removed in the finishing, leaving a surface entirely covered with enamel, giving effects altogether admirable.

FINIS.

T " HERE has been no special demand for Japanese art for some-â â long time, so that the Hamilton Palace Sale still furnishes an approximate guide to values. The Happer Sale of colour-prints is of more recent interest, and the priced catalogue, though only noting items of Â 10 or more, will be of much value for reference.

SALE-PRICES OF

OLD JAPAN LACQUER

AT THE HAMILTON PALACE SALE, JUNE AND JULY 1882

A circular box and cover, of red Soochow lacquer, carved all over with flowers and ornaments, the top encrusted with pierced and carved jade ornaments, Â 155. 6d.

A large black and gold card-case, with fish and male figures in red and gold, Â 3 135. 6d.

An oblong box and cover, with foliage and flowers in a landscape in relief, and encrusted with flowers and ornaments in silver-gilt and coloured stones, Â 141 155.

A black and gold nest of three boxes, and cover, with chrysanthemums and foliage, Â 10 los.

Another, with two boxes and cover, with foliage in gold, Â i i os. 6d.

An oblong stand, of black and gold lacquer, with a river scene, buildings, boats, and figures, 15 155.

A black and gold medicine-case, in four compartments, with a river scene in gold, Â 2 2s.

Another, in five divisions, with a river scene, boat, and flowers in relief, Â 4 45.

A nest of five trays, of black and gold lacquer, containing three small ivory boxes, with figures and flowers in mother-o'-pearl and other materialsâ in black and gold cover, Â 55.

An octagonal tray, with figures and foliage in gold on black ground, Â 6 i6s. 6d

A pair of black lacquer cups and saucers, with buildings and foliage in gold, Â 3 135. 6d. An oblong box and cover, with tray inside, with utensils and other ornaments in colours and gold, 38 is. A black and gold box and cover, with landscape on the lid, containing four smaller boxes of gold lacquer, Â 55. A pair of square ditto, with foliage in gold, and four small boxes inside, Â 7 75. A medicine-box, in five divisions, with monkeys on horseback, 4445.

A pair of fan-shaped boxes, of red and gold lacquer, with landscapes, trees, and buildings, each containing two small boxes, Â 28 75. A small shrine, of black lacquer, containing three figures minutely carved in rice grains, 5 155. 6d. An oblong gold snuff-box, the top formed of a plaque of fine old japan lacquer, with a male figure in relief in gold colour on black ground, Â 60 i8s. A small shell-shaped gold lac box and cover, with a landscape, Â 12 I2S.

A medicine-box, with five divisions, and an owl, a spider, and foliage in relief, Â 4 45. An oblong tray, of black lacquer, with foliage in red and gold,

A small black and gold cabinet, with folding doors, containing numerous drawers, trays, and boxes, 37 165,

A shaped oval black box, the sides decorated with landscapes in gold, a group of flowers in mother-o'-pearl and gold lac on the lid, tray inside, Â is i8s.

A fine oblong black and gold box and cover, with landscapes, figures, and buildings in gold, inscribed inside "Maria Van Dieman "â glass shade and stand, 315.

A very fine oblong chest, of black lacquer, with raised landscapes in gold, and studded with animals, birds, and other objects in silver and gold, and with a large medallion, similar inside the lid. Formerly the property of Napoleon 1. Â 73.

An hexagonal tray, of gold lacquer, with a river scene, mountains, and buildings in trellis border; and a gourd-shaped box of red and gold lacquer, Â 6 6s.

An octagonal nest of boxes, formed of thin pieces of bamboo lacquered with gold, Â 2 12s. 6d.

A fan-shaped box and cover, of black and gold lacquer, with bamboos and pine-trees, 13 2S. 6d. Another, with birds and flowers in colours, and tray inside, Â 445. An oblong black box and cover, with gold ornament on the lid and link border, Â 4 145. 6d. A small nest of three boxes, powdered black and gold lacquer, with diamond-shaped ornaments, Â 2 2s. An oblong black and gold box and cover, with a vase and foliage and border of ornaments in gold on the lid, and landscape inside, Â 68 55. An oblong stand, on feet of gold lacquer, with a river scene, birds, and buildings, 15 45. 6d. A square box, of black lacquer powdered with gold, with a group of three cranes, and fir-tree in gold, Â 13 25. 6d. An oblong tray, powdered black and gold, with chrysanthemums on the border; and a red and gold letter-case, with cords, Â i 5. An oblong stand, on scroll feet, engraved with foliage and insects in colours on trellis ground, 36 155. A pair of hexagonal gold trays, with a river scene, mountains, boats, and trees, Â 4 145. 6d.

A pair of small oblong boxes, black and gold, with chrysanthemums on trellis ground, Â 4 45. A pair of quatrefoil black and gold boxes, with river scenes and buildings, and boxes insideâ on high stands of the same, Â 30 9. A round box, with dragons and clouds in gold on the lid, enclosing four smaller boxes and covers, Â 36 155.

A small oblong gold tray, with chrysanthemums, Â 6 i6s. 6d. A square-shaped tray, of powdered gold lac, with bamboos in gold, Â 9 195. 6d.

A gold lac box and cover, formed as a house, Â 11 us. A pair of large circular trays, black ground, with birds, foliage, and flowers in gold, Â 42. An oblong box, of black and gold lacquer, with figures in a landscape, chased gold mount, Â 71 8s. A very small gold lac medicine-box, in four divisions; and a small diamond-shaped black and gold box, Â i us. 6d. A pair of small gold lac boxes and covers, formed as geese in different attitudes, 44 25.

A shaped oval box, of gold lac, with a large and small male figure in low relief on the lid, 13 135. A circular box and cover, of gold lac, with chrysanthemums and foliage in low relief, enclosing four small fan-shaped boxes and covers, 50 8s. A pair of small nests of three boxes, with river scenes, buildings, and trees in gold, enclosed in case of the same design, 29 8s. A pair of oblong trays, with shaped ends, with landscapes and buildings in gold, Â 6 i6s. 6d. A shaped oval tray, with a river scene, buildings, and an angler in gold, and an oblong black and gold stand on feet, 3 135. 6d. A pair of small black and gold basins, red inside; a pair of small oval-shaped trays, with landscapes; and a square tray, on stand, 5 155. 6d. An oblong black and gold tray, with plants in two medallions, Â i us. 6d. A round box and cover, with chrysanthemums on gold ground, Â S 55. A large oblong tray, with flowers and foliage in gold, on powdered gold ground, Â 17 17 s. A long oblong box, with utensils, trefoil, and other ornaments in relief, on powdered gold ground, Â 21 ics. 6d. A beautiful cabinet, of gold lacquer, with flowers and foliage in relief, in mother-o '-pearl and silver, drawers inside, 267 155. A double-shaped box, of gold lacquer, with horses in a land- scape, Â 86 2s. An oblong gold tray, on feet, with foliage in relief on engraved concentric ground, 30 95. A large black and gold cabinet, with folding doors, landscapes, figures, and buildings in gold â on carved ebony stand,

An old japan lacquer coffer, with a bullock carrying a vase of flowers, and vases of flowers in gold and colours, with gilt metal mounts â on black and gold stand â 3 ft. i in. by i ft. 4 in., i ft. 7 in. high, 315.

A square cabinet, of old japan lacquer, with folding doors, enclosing drawers, landscapes, foliage, and birds in gold on black ground, and with engraved metal-gilt mounts, Â 66 35.

The companion cabinet, Â 95 us.

A canteen, of old japan powdered gold lacquer, containing a nest of five boxes, two trays, and a box with a large grotesque male figure, decorated with circular ornaments, bamboos, and foliage, and contained in open case, with silver handle, on metal-gilt foot, Â 39 i8s.

A rosewater-ewer and dish, of old black and gold japan lacquer, with figures and landscapes, 15 155.

The companion ewer and dish, 13 135.

A pair of hanging vase-shaped jardinieres, of black and gold japan lacquer, Â 2 125. 6d.

A small cabinet, of black and gold japan lacquer, with drawerâ ii in. by 6 in., 10 in. high, Â 9 195. 6d.

An oblong box, of old japan lacquer, with a cart and plants in gold, mounted with metal giltâ 16 in. by 13 in., 13 135.

A pair of vases, covers, and stands, with buildings, birds, and plants in gold on black ground, mounted with twisted snakes of ormolu, Â 210.

A black and gold japan lacquer nest of five boxes, 9- in. high, Â 7 17 s. 6d.

A deep black tray, with a tree in gold; and one, on feet, Â 22 is.

A very fine oblong coffer, of old japan lacquer, with a large landscape, buildings, trees, and a river, with a bridge and figures in the foreground, in border of birds and scrolls, animals and birds in gold and silver in relief, similar landscapes on the front and ends and inside the lid, black and gold trellis-border, with circular ornaments, inlaid with mother-o'-pearl, chased metal-gilt mountsâ on carved and gilt wood standâ

4 ft. 6 in. by 2 ft. 3 in. From the Collections of the Cardinal Mazarin, the Due de Bouillon, and Fonthill.

Â 682 105.

A bamboo match-pot, carved with figures and trees, Â 2 2s. A square nest of three boxes, of black and gold japan lacquer, Â 12 I2S.

An octagonal tray, with handle of black and gold lacquer, inlaid with mother-o'-pearl; a pair of square trays, black and gold; and an oblong stand, 3 135. 6d.

square tray, of gold lacquer, with plants in gold in circles, Â 2 2s. Two round boxes, of the same, with round medallions, 3 135. 6d. scalloped tray, with black and gold, and gold trellis border; and a circular black and gold tray, with a landscape, Â 2 2s. A pair of boxes, with a dragon, utensils, and characters in black and gold, Â i 55.

A pair of panels, with figures and landscapes in coloured mother- o'-pearl, Â i us. 6d. A nest of three boxes and stand, with figures in gold on black ground, Â i 185. A pair of square lacquer bottles, with foliage, in borders inlaid with mother-o'-pearl, Â 7 75. A figure of the Japanese idol Amida, on gilt stand and wood plinth, glass shade. From Fonthill. 131 55. A pair of large seated male figures, of black and gold lacquer, with movable heads, and carrying branches decorated with utensils, foliage, and circular ornaments in gold, the faces and hands gilt, Â 60 i8s. An oval-shaped lacquer box, with tray inside, with landscapes in red and gold in low relief on black ground; and a black and gold lacquer box and cover, 3 35. A pair of oblong metal plaques, with views of the Palais Corsini, and Palais Caprarole, Rome, in gold on black ground of old lacquer, Â 26 55.

A writing-desk, with a fir-tree in gold, Â g 95. A box and cover and an oblong tray, with flowers in gold, Â 9 95. A black and gold cabinet, formed as a pagoda, Â 4 145. 6d.

OLD JAPAN POTTERY AND PORCELAIN

Fifteen plates, with vases of flowers in the centre, Â 20 95. 6d.

Five ditto, with baskets of flowers; and ten, with vases of flowers, Â 16 55. 6d.

Eleven ditto, with three vases of flowers in the centre, 13 135.

Ten ditto, with pomegranates on the border, and deep-blue compartments, 15 155.

Sixteen ditto, with bamboos and flowers, Â 17 6s. 6d.

Twenty-four ditto, with lotos-flower compartments and pomegranates in the centre, 30 95.

Twenty-five ditto, Â 32 os. 6d.

Sixteen ditto, with flowers, a circular medallion in the centre, Â 17 6s. 6d.

Eleven ditto, with a vase of flowers and scroll in the centre; and six with vases on a table, Â 18 iss.

Thirteen ditto, with landscapes in square medallions, birds, and ornaments, Â is 18.

Eleven ditto, with a vase of flowers in the centre, 15 45. 6d.

A pair of brown-ware tea-pots and covers, formed as groups of bamboos, 7 in. high, Â 20 95. 6d.

A pair of Kaga-ware bowls and covers, with figures and ornaments in red and white inside, the outside in imitation of black and gold lacquer, 9 in. high, Â 8 8s.

A pair of Kaga-ware basins, with flowers and ornaments in red and blue on trellis ground, and enamelled inside, on chased ormolu altar-shaped stands, 6Â in. high, 58 i6s.

A bowl and cover, with red, blue, and gold ornaments, mounted with silver-gilt, 4 in. diam., Â 13 135.

A basin, pale-brown outside, enamelled with lotos plants, mounted with silver gilt, 5 in. diam., Â 22 is.

A bowl and cover, with fish and aquatic plants in colours, mounted with handles, borders, and feet of chased and engraved silver-gilt, 6 in. high, Â 48 6s.

A pair of octagonal dishes, with vases of flowers and foliage in red, blue, and gold, eight circular pierced medallions on the border, 8Â in. diam., Â 15 155.

An eggshell bowl and cover, with hawks and foliage in gold on white ground, mounted with borders, feet and top of silver-gilt, 4Â in. high, Â 33 12s.

A pair of vases and covers, with flowers and birds in compartments in red, blue, and gold, and perforated medallions on the shoulders and covers, 18 in. high, 120 155.

A pair of very large vases and covers, with buildings and landscapes on white ground, and borders of trellis and semicircular ornaments, 36 in. high, 225 155.

A pair of oviform vases and covers, with buildings and trees in two medallions, and flowers and foliage in red, blue, and white, and trellis-pattern bands of paler blue and gold, 27 in. high, Â 315.

A pair of jars and covers, with flowers and foliage in red, blue, and gold, and borders of smaller flowers, the covers surmounted by gilt groups of kylins, 2 ft. n in. high, 336.

A pair of octagonal vases and covers, with foliage and flowers in red, blue, and gold, and kylins in medallions on the shoulders, the covers surmounted by figures of kylins, 19 in. high, Â 168.

MASANOBU (Okumura)

A humorous Tan-ye showing Daikoku, the god of wealth, as a child being carried to the temple to be re-named. He is borne on the shoulders of Yebisu, god of daily food, followed by Fukurokujiu, who holds an umbrella over his august head, while Hotei offers gifts, and Benten follows carrying his pipe case and mamori fuda or child's charm bag; very large size, upright; signed OKUMURA MASANOBU, c. 1700,

Three-sheet Beni-ye set of lovers, umbrella-sharing in spring under a plum-tree, summer under a willow, and winter under a maple; Hosso-ye form, printed in rose-pink and olive-green; signed HOGETSUDO OKUMURA MASANOBU, c. 1715.

Â lo 105.

A grand Urushi-ye print, coloured by hand, an actor as a woman with a flower basket on wheels; Hosso-ye form; signed OKUMURA MASANOBU, c. 1720, 17 IDS.

SHIGENAGA (Nishimura)

Love's calendar. A man and girl standing in front of a screen painted with bamboo, against which a broom is laid. He leans on her shoulder looking over an open scroll with particulars as to the luck of the months of the year; Hosso-ye form, printed in rose-pink and green; signed SENKWADO NISHIMURA SHIGENAGA, and dated 1747, Â 11.

Hachirakaki, large size, Tan-ye. An actor standing, full-length, holding a love letter; signed SENKWADO NISHIMURA SHIGENAGA, c. 1730, Â 37.

SHIGENOBU (Tsunegawa)

A woman standing under a cherry-tree to which a screen for a garden party has been tied, looking at an open paper; Hosso-ye form, Urushi-ye, coloured by hand, and sprinkled with gold; signed TSUNEGAWA SHIGENOBU, c. 1725, Â 15.

KIYOMASU (Torii)

An undivided triptych, Hosso-ye form. San to Bijin, "Beauties of the three Capitals," full-length figures of three courtesans each with her kamuro in front of the yoshiwara cagesâ Takao of Miura-ya, Yedo; Handayu of Ichi-mon-ji-ya, Kyoto; and Yugiri of Ibaraki-ya, Osaka; printed in beni and green; signed TORII KIYOMASU, c. 1746, 25 los.

TOYONOBU (Ishikawa)

Hachirakaki of large size. A courtesan reading a letter, standing, full-length, accompanied by her kamuro, holding a small table and a sake kettle; Tan-ye, coloured by hand; signed TANSENDO ISHIKAWA SHLUHA TOYONOBU, c. 1750, Â 41.

An undivided triptych, Hosso-ye form. Title: " Koyomi Samboku tsui " (Maple viewing triptych); in each section two lovers standing under maple trees, and above them small views in clouds, of peasants harvesting rice, cutting, tying in sheaves, and knocking out the grain; printed in beni and green; signed ISHIKAWA TOYONOBU, c. 1750, Â 20 i os.

A woman slightly draped standing beside the shutters of a room in front of the bed curtain; Hachirakaki form, printed in three colours; signed TANSHINDO ISHIKAWA SHIU-HA; sealed TOYONOBU, c. 1765, Â 16.

HARUNOBU (Suzuki)

An actor in the role of Banto Hirosaburo Shinsui, a ronin, full-length; an early Hachirakaki, in three colours and one superposed; signed SUZUKI HARUNOBU, c. 1760, 13.

Two girls, on a balcony, one carrying a samisen and a book, the other lifting a curtain to enter a room. The colouring is very rich, for they stand on a floor of opaque cream, against an orange balustrade, and the curtain a slatey blue. The younger girl's dress is red with slatey-blue pattern, and purple and white obi, while the other has opaque cream kimono with purple obi and under parts; large size, almost square, poem in clouds, with deep and decisive gauffrage; signed HARUNOBU. One of a set â ' Fuzoku Shiki Kasen " (Social Customs of the Four Seasons), 1770. This is for the flower month, April. Â 25 ics.

A young man disguised as a komuro, with basket head-dress and bamboo clarionet, secretly visiting two young girls whose heads appear behind a barred window. An exquisite piece of soft colouring; the opaque cream of the man's robe, gauffred to give the effect of crepe, with rich black girdle and under side of the robe, make a startling figure on the sunlit grass of yellowish-green, with a slatey-blue stream, large size, almost square; poem in clouds; signed SUZUKI HARUNOBU. One of the same set as the foregoing, and for the same flower month, April. There being thus an intercalary month in this year, the set must have been 13, and the date can be fixed at 1770. Â 25.

Taking a young girl to a temple for the Meyamairi ceremony of naming, the party have just arrived within the red lacquered columns of the Torii at the gate. This is one of the most superb examples of the complete mastery of a full palette of colours of this ever-varying artist in the height of his power and popularity. The various shades of colour baffle description, and the tone of the background is a mystery of colour that no lens could pick up, while the gauffrage gives to the folds of the garments a rounded reality quite wonderful; large size, almost square; poem in clouds; signed SUZUKI HARUNOBU. One of the same set as the foregoing for the Kagura month, 1770. Â 50.

Night scene: a young man standing on a fence, breaking off a branch of plum blossom for his lady love who is leaning on a garden lantern. This is one of the most extraordinary prints the artist ever produced, the whole background, except the stream, being black. Moonlight is no doubt intended, the stream catching the full rays, which shine also upon the youthful figures, but without shadows, according to the convention of the period. The robes are olive-green with purple stripes, showing red in the under parts; the fence red, and the lantern, a neutral stone tint; large size, almost square; poem in clouds; signed HARUNOBU. One of the same set as the foregoing; this is the second month, 1770. Â 40.

A lady and two children playing at a Daimyo's procession, one of the children holding aloft a mop, and the other riding a hobby-horse; interior scene, with a large leafy branch straying across a railed opening in the background; large size, almost square, with many colours, and high gauffrage in faultless condition; signed HARUNOBU; best period, c. 1766-70, Â 26.

Two young girls standing by the garden gate, one holding by a string a small dog, a stream in the centre, and thatched houses and landscape in the distance. The garden fence is in the deep brick red which Harunobu often employed, against which the soft violet and grey of the girl's robes, and the solid black of her shikake stand in quiet relief, with only a slight gauffrage; large size, almost square, in fine condition; signed SUZUKI HARUNOBU; best period, c. 1766-70, Â 13 i os.

A young girl within an upper chamber looking across the balcony at a distant autumn landscape of hills peering through mist, with a maple tree under the balcony; large size, almost square, in many tones, and in almost pristine condition, gauffrage giving slight relief; signed HARUNOBU; best period, c. 1766-70, Â 24.

A lady with an umbrella under a blossoming fruit-tree, watching a little boy on a hobby-horse, with a wooden covered way as part of the background. The lady's dress, with its quiet stripes and purple obi, is in strong contrast with the 1 bright-coloured child's clothes, and the gauffrage throws up the folds into graceful curls; large size, almost square without any text, and in perfect condition; signed SUSUKI HARUNBOU; best period, c. 1766-70, Â 20.

Two girls reclining on a low bench covered with a rose-pink cloth, beside a stream under the full moon; one holds a fan and looks up at the moon, the other contemplates the rising smoke from a small brasier; the canopy of clouds contains a poem; large size, almost square, in exquisite condition; signed SUZUKI HARUNOBU; best period, c. 1766-70, Â 24 i os.

A Samurai and a young girl in the upper room of a tea-house overlooking the Sumidagawa with its river commerce, the delicate blue and grey striped robes of the girl, and the solid black jacket over a wine-coloured clinging robe of the man, in delicate contrast to the apple-green cloth covering the low benches; red lanterns showing strongly against a black sky behind the houses on the far side of the river; large size, nearly square, in absolutely perfect state; signed HARUNOBU; best period, c. 1766-70, Â 25. V â

HARUTSUGU

Hachirakaki. A girl and her lover, standing on the engawa of a house, attracted by the sounds of music above, are looking upward to where, in an upper chamber, a girl is playing the samisen, her shadow being reflected on the shoji, while a man leans against the partly opened window; printed in six colours; signed HARUTSUGU, c. 1770, Â 15 IDS.

KORIUSAI (Isoda)

Hachirakaki. A girl standing by the seashore with two buckets before her, looking up into a pine tree where a No dancer's hat and robe are hanging. This is probably an allusion to the hagoromo or feather robe worn in the No play of that name, wherein an angel alighting on the shore of Japan put off her feather robe, and hung it on a pine tree while she danced in joyous ecstasy, till, frightened by a fisherman, she fled to heaven, leaving her robe behind. Signed KORIUSAI, Â 10.

A woman, with slight drapery hanging over one shoulder, disrobing for her bath, and looking down at her own form; through the window-bars of the apartment a cherry tree is seen in blossom. In the poem, the revelation of form is compared to the sight of Fuji, beautifully white, when the robe of mist, loosened at the waist, disappears. Beautifully bold free lines, and subdued colour scheme; Hachirakaki form, paper slightly toned; signed KORIU, c. 1770, Â 16 155.

A girl standing in front of a garden fence with flowers straying over it, by the angle of a verandah, pulling at a monkey who has drawn her kimono aside, revealing her limbs. The soft grey-blue of her robe is decorated with butterflies, her obi being of sage-green and white crepe. A fine impression, in grand condition; Hachirakaki form; signed KORIUSAI, c. 1775, Â 20 105.

Scene from the Chiushingura, with female characters, Uranosuke reading a letter on the verandah of the tea-house Ichiriki, while the spy Kudayu is concealed below, and a woman with a mirror is up in the balcony reading the reflected writing; grand full composition, admirably balanced, and in fine condition; Hachirakaki form; signed KORIU, c. 1775,

KIYONAGA (Torii)

Hachirakaki. A Yoshiwara beauty with her kamuro, standing under the eaves of a house decorated with the shime kazari of fern leaves, paper gohei, etc., for the New Year; overhead a crescent moon shines upon a clump of bamboos, which are printed from colour-blocks without any key-block. The girl's kimono is yellow, with a loose over-robe of red, and purple obi. Signed KIYONAGA, Â 20 los.

Four prints from a set of eight â " Shiki Hakkei " (Four Seasons, eight Views). No. I is Spring, two Yoshiwara girls returning home accompanied by a boy with a branch of peach blossom; No. 2. Summer, at sunset, a woman seated by a stone lantern under a pine tree loosening her robes, and another standing talking to her; No. 3. Autumn, on a breezy day, a young ferryman bringing his boat to some steps to take two ladies across the stream; No. 4 is also Autumn, two girls talking at the angle of a house overlooking a garden, one stooping to dip some water out of a stone cistern. All are large size, nearly square form, in fine condition; signed KIYONAGA, c. 1785, Â 18.

SHUNSHO (Katsugawa)

An actor in female character, standing before her toilet case, holding a mirror; Hosso-ye form; signed SHUNSHO, c. 1770, Â 10 IDS.

SHARAKU (Toshiusai)

The man with a pipe. A half-length portrait of an actor in the character of Banzuiin Chobei, the head of the Otokodate, who befriended Gompachi and finally buried him; full- sized print in colours on a silver ground; signed TOSHIUSAI SHARAKU, c. 1795, Â 34.

The man with a fan. A half-length portrait of an actor as an old man holding a closed fan in his right hand; full-sized print in colours on a silver ground; signed TOSHIUSAI SHARAKU, c. 1795, Â 20.

A full-length portrait of an actor as Kono Moronao, Lord of Musashi, in the play Chiushingura, standing under a branch of plum blossom, in a splendid black outer robe with white design; large Hosso-ye form; in grand condition; signed SHARAKU, c. 1785, 13.

UTAMARO (Kitagawa)

A grand full-sized diptych. A group of noble young ladies and children having a day's outing in the country, attended by their tutor and governess, who are carried in kogos. The scene is under the pine trees on the seashore, looking out towards a white Fuji rising beyond the Izu peninsula. This is a most splendid composition, printed in six colours, a very fine impression, with gauffrage, and in faultless condition, c. 1788, Â 14.

TOYOHIRO (Utagawa)

Yebisu the God of Daily Food, sharing an umbrella with a girl in a snow-storm; small size, almost square; signed TOYOHIRO. One of a set of the seven Gods of Fortune, c. 1790.

Â l 12S.

TOYOKUNI (Utagawa)

Ladies' occupations in winter. Triptych; an indoor scene with shoji open, looking on to a garden covered with snow. In the centre a lady is cutting down some branches of a dwarfed budding tree for interior decoration, while some other ladies and children have been making a large snow-ball. Full-size, upright; each signed TOYOKUNI, c. 1800, Â 10 155.

View of the Ryogoku Bridge and the Sumida River from the Yedo Shore. Pentaptych. In the foreground a number of gaily dressed women and others of humbler rank are parading in front of the booths that line the river bank; the great bridge is seen at an angle extending over the three centre sheets, and the river traffic on the far side flanked by tall trees completes the wonderful panorama of Yedo life. Full-size, upright; each sheet signed TOYOKUNI, c. 1805, Â 22.

HOKUSAI (Katsuchika)

An original drawing in water-colours, Yama Uba, the " old woman of the mountain," foster-mother of Kintoki, seated in a reclining posture; on paper, oblong, unsigned, Â 16.

Original drawing in colours. A boy faggot-gatherer crouched up asleep under the trunk of an old pine tree, his basket of sticks standing behind him; on paper, unsigned, Â 10.

Original drawing in colours. A peasant in rain-hat and straw cloak, with mochi pounder over his shoulder, rubbing over the side of a mochi mortar with a wisp of straw; on paper, unsigned, Â 10.

HOKUSAI

Complete set of the thirty-six views of Fujiyama, with the ten Supplementary Views, making forty-six in all; original impressions and issued between the years 1823 and 1829; all signed. Sold separately. The best prices follow:

Sen pu Kai sei. A beautiful day and south wind on the slopes of Fuji, the lower part covered with trees, the upper part red, and the summit and crevices filled with snow; great masses of straight white clouds in the sky. No. 8, 15 IDS. Yama shita Shiro ame. Lightning at the base of the mountain; daybreak is illumining the snow-clad mountain's peak, the lower part being in darkness save for the flash; the clouds are curling white clusters. No. 9, 17. LJshibori in the province of Hitati. Fuji seen across a misty bed of water-reeds to the right, and a great junk moored in the foreground, partly hidden in a blue overhanging cloud. No. 12, Â 10.

3uwa Lake, in the province of Shinano, with the shades of evening falling. In the foreground a thatched cottage under two tall pines leaning to right and left. No. 13, Â 11 los. Senju. View of Fuji from Senju, looking across the town of flowers (Yoshiwara). In the foreground a procession of men carrying muskets in red cases. No. 37, Â 10. Toto Sumidagawa Gotenyama no Fuji. Fuji seen from Goten- yama, across the Sumida river. Clusters of people ascending the hills for a picnic at the cherry-blossom time, and a view of the adored mountain. No. 40, Â 10. Kanazawa oki nami ura. " The great wave at Kanazawa "; an exceptionally brilliant impression; framed, 23 IDS.

MATAHEI SCHOOL

A man carrying a hawk; one of the very early coloured drawings known as Otsu-ye, i. e. Otsu pictures, which were the precursors of the Ukiyo-ye colour-prints. Such examples are now of the greatest rarity, and in the condition of this specimen are scarcely known; c. 1675, Â 10.

MASANOBU (Okumura)

An actor in the role of Sanokawa Ichimatsu, carrying an umbrella under a maple tree; one of a set of three Aigasa san boku tsui, "Umbrella-sharing set of three "; printed in rose-pink and chrome, the beni applied from colour-blocks without any key-block of black outlines; Hosso-ye form; signed HOGETSUDO OKAMURA MASANOBU, Â 22 los.

Two sheets of a triptych, Beni-ye; on one a young girl attending to the coiffure of the Saint Daruma, and on the other a girl on a ladder supported against the head of Fukurokujiu, invoking the assistance of the Lover Stars for her older sister standing behind the ladder; Hosso-ye form; one signed HOGETSUDO OKUMURA BUNKAKU, the other OKUMURA MASANOBU, c. 1730, Â 11.

TOYONOBU (Ishikawa)

Hachirakaki. A woman disrobing for the bath; printed in three coloursâ lilac, red, and green; signed ISHIKAWA TOYONOBU, c. 1760; in very good condition, Â 42.

Lovers under an Aigasa, " the umbrella of loving accord "; one of a triptych Aigasa Samboku tsui, "Umbrella sharing "; printed in beni and pale green; Hosso-ye form; signed ISHIKAWA TOYONOBU, c. 1750, Â 12.

A girl leaping from the parapet of Kiyomidzu temple to get an answer to her prayer; illustration to a poem; Hachirakaki form in two coloursâ pink and a slatey blue; signed TAN-

SHINDO ISHIKAWA Sniu-HA; sealed TOYONOBU, c. 1755, Â lo IOS.

An Awabi diver standing by the edge of the sea wringing her skirt; full-length figure almost nude; Hachirakaki form; printed in two colours â pink and a slatey blue; signed TANSHINDO ISHIKAWA SHIU-HA; sealed TOYONOBU, c. 1755,

KIYOHIRO (Torii)

Hachirakaki. A girl holding her lover on her back so that he may reach up to a flowering cherry tree to attach poems to the branches; printed in three colours: signed TORII KIYOHIRO, c. 1758, Â 12 los.

A woman semi-draped coming from her bed-chamber with a letter in her mouth; early two-colour print in rose-pink and green; Hosso-ye form; signed TORII KIYONOBU, c. 1745, Â 16.

KIYOMITSU (Torii)

Full-length figure of a woman in a rain-hat out walking; Hachirakaki form; printed in two colours â red and green; signed TORII KIYOMITSU, c. 1760, Â 12 los.

A Yoshiwara beauty standing beside her tobako-bon smoking and watching the rings float away in the air; a very graceful composition in Hachirakaki form; printed in three colours â rose-pink, green, and grey; signed TORII KIYOMITSU, c. 1765, Â 13 los.

A woman in winter garb, hooded, hurrying along and casting a glance behind her; Hachirakaki form; printed in three colours â fawn, grey, and very pale pink; signed TORII KIYOMITSU, c. 1770, Â 16 los.

HARUNOBU (Suzuki)

Hachirakaki. A girl in a storm, with Futen the Wind-god above her, holding a scroll, and driving dark clouds and tempest downwards, blowing her garments open, and scattering her sheets of toilet paper; her kimono is striped yellow; obi black with grey design; on the sign-board at the top are weather notes, commencing with the 2oth and 22nd days, when there will be great anxiety for the rice crops; the letter in the hands of the god is his answer; signed HARUNOBU, Â 56.

A woman completing her toilette, standing watching a cat who is playing with the skirt of her kimono, with background of shutters, and glimpse into another room; Hachirakaki form in five colours; signed HARUNOBU, c. 1762, Â 15 IDS.

An Oiran seated in a cage writing a letter, while two men view her through the bars; beautiful soft coloured composition in five tones; Hachirakaki form; signed HARUNOBU, c. 1762, Â 14 IQS.

A snow scene outside a garden gate and fence, coloured in orange-red, overhung by a clump of bamboo; a young samurai is parting with the object of his affection; large size, almost square, printed in six colours, with very sharp gauffrage, throwing the snow into relief; signed SUZUKI HARUNOBU; no text; c. 1766-70, Â 25.

A young lady in a red and blue striped kimono, followed by her maid in violet kimono and chrome obi, carrying an insect cage, walking by the seashore; the sea is coloured a delicate straw colour, and the ground is grey; large size, almost square, no text; signed SUZUKI HARUNOBU, c. 1766-70, Â 24.

A rainy dayâ street scene; a young lady attended by her maid, who holds an umbrella over her, passing a little girl who is just opening her umbrella, and exchanging comments; beside them two dogs under the shelter of a house in the background; very full colouring in varied tones, some gained by the superposition of colours; large size, nearly square, a magnificent impression, and in faultless state; signed SUZUKI HARUNOBU, c. 1766-70, Â 25.

Scene on a country road beside a river, with a high fence enclosing a clump of bamboos; at the corner of the fence two girls are stopping, one standing listening to the Spring song of the birds, the other stooping to pick some wayside flowers just springing into life; a lovely print in only six colours, but instinct with beauty, the exquisite poise of the girl standing before the deep-red fence, heightened by the gauffrage; large size, nearly square, in faultless state; signed HARUNOBU, c. 1766-70, Â 23.

By the seashore at low tide; a samurai and a young girl collecting marine objects, the man stooping pointing to a shell he has just found, the girl standing with one hand on her chin and the other holding up the edge of her long sleeve, with a junk beached just in the rear; exquisitely beautiful composition and colour scheme, mostly in quiet tones, and the folds of the robes sharpened by gauffrage; large size, nearly square, in perfect state; signed SUSUKI HARUNOBU, c. 1766-70, Â 25.

A girl standing in a boat poling it up a stream, by a jutting bank where water-reeds grow; in the boat Daruma with a red hood looks into the water and sees himself mirrored. This is a well-known and much admired work, and this copy is a very fine impression, the orange of the boat but very slightly decomposed. No text in the clouds; large size, nearly square; signed SUSUKI HARUNOBU, c. 1766-70,

A girl kneeling, assisting her mistress to robe on the day of the Tanabata festival, i. e. The Meeting of the Lover Stars. The shoji of the upper room are partly open, showing beyond the balcony some house roofs, a great shinto lantern, and some branches of bamboo loaded with lucky symbols; the lady's robe, of pale striped blue, is a daring contrast with the apple-green ground of the floor, yet is very pleasing. Large size, nearly square, in superb state; signed SUSUKI HARUNOBU, c. 1766-70, Â 19.

KORIUSAI (Isoda)

Two lovers standing under a blooming plum-tree, to which they have tied poems, the girl lighting her pipe from her companion's; a simple and graceful composition, printed in four colours; Hachirakaki form; signed KORIUSAI, c. 1770, Â 15.

A nude woman with a child in her arms stepping out of a bathtub on to a box placed beside it, behind her the clothes-rack on which her garments are hung; a composition to which, besides his signature, the artist has placed his seal SHOBEI, in pink with white raised characters; Hachirakaki form; signed KORIUSAI, c. 1775, Â 21 IDS.

Nature's mirror; a youth carrying a hooded girl on his back has paused on the brink of a stream where he can get a reflection of his love's face. In Japan the superstition that foxes assume the forms of beautiful girls to lure their victims to destruction is very strong, and as water reflects the truth, he has taken this method as a test, but the girl comes out triumphantly in the ordeal. A superb print, but the colours somewhat faded; Hachirakaki form; signed KORIUSAI, but part of the signature trimmed off, c. 1775, Â 10.

KIYONAGA (Torii)

Hachirakaki. A mother seated under a willow-tree, with bosom bared, and another woman holding a baby boy who is struggling to get to his mother; a very choice composition, and very curious but harmonious colour scheme, especially in the robes of the seated woman; signed KIYONAGA, Â 14.

SHUNSHO (Katsugawa)

Two women in a field under a willow, one down at a wash-tub, the other stretching and drying cloth tied to a roller fixed to a tree, with background of a fence; printed in six colours, and full of the Harunobu influence, even to the apple-green ground, and full gauffrage; large size, almost square; signed KATSUGAWA SHUNSHO, c. 1776, Â 18.

One of a series of Rokkasen, girls as types of " The Six Poets," representing Ono no Komachi plucking a branch of sakura, the large flowering cherry, while a female attendant stands by holding another branch; printed in six colours, with gauffrage, and strongly reminiscent of Harunobu in the pale lavender sky and deep-red tree trunk; large size, almost square; signed SHUNSHO, and sealed with the jar-shaped seal, c. 1776, Â 20.

Illustration of a poem by Kisen Hoshi, one of the Rokkasen or '– Six Great Poets "; a man and a young girl preparing for the tea ceremony; large size, nearly square, in beautiful condition; signed SHUNSHO, c. 1776, Â 10.

SHIGEMASA (Kitao)

The dropped love-letter; a woman with an umbrella standing under a willow beside a stream, while adjusting a hair-pin, has, in her trepidation, dropped a love-letter which has stirred her heart, as the breeze is rustling the willow; Hachirakaki form, in three colours, in beautiful condition; signed KITAO SHIGEMASA, Â 12.

MASANOBU (Kitao)

Yoshiwara Shin Bijin Awase Jihitsu Kagami, "A Mirror of the Beauties of the New Yoshiwara and their handwriting "; first edition, Yedo, 1782, i vol.; 14 full-sized pages of illustrations in colours, making 7 double-page pictures, and 2 pp. of text at each end; signed KITAO SHINSAI MASANOBU,

TOYOKUNI (Utagawa)

Hachirakaki of special size. An actor seated in his dressing-room beside his make-up box, having a cup of sake, being visited by one of the fashionable ladies of the day;

printed in four colours, the obi of the lady being in figured silver; signed TOYOKUNI, c. 1804, Â 15.

Hachirakaki of special size. A man and woman standing in front of a bamboo grille with a football above their heads; printed in four colours; signed TOYOKUNI, c. 1804, Â 10.

Hachirakaki of special size. A woman, loosely robed after her bath, seated in a dressing-room, and a man pushing aside the reed blind, looking in on her; printed in six colours; not signed, c. 1804, Â 11.

Hachirakaki of special size. A woman standing on the edge of a landing-stage at night, holding a lantern, which throws a light upwards, and an actor seated in a boat moored to the stage; printed in six colours; signed TOYOKUNI, c. 1804, jjÂ.

Hachirakaki of special size. An actor, as a samurai, seated before a mirror at his make-up, and a lady fully dressed for outdoors, standing behind him, waiting for him to write on her fan; printed in six colours and mica; signed TOYOKUNI, c. 1804, Â 16 los.

Hachirakaki of special size. An actor in his dressing-room, with his tobako-bon before him, holding a fan and smoking a pipe; behind him a decorated shoji, which has been pulled open, and a bevy of girls are looking in at him; printed in five colours; signed TOYOKUNI, c. 1804, Â 18 IDS.

KUNISADA (Utagawa)

View of Futami ga ura, Ise. " The Husband and Wife Rocks " lashed together with a straw rope as a charm for the New

Year festival of sun worship; on the horizon the sun is just beginning to slant its broad rays over the darkened sky and sea; full size, oblong; signed KACHORO KUNISADA, c. 1830, Â 15 105.

HOKUSAI

Two large sheets of flowers: one very fine, peonies and a butterfly; the other, somewhat discoloured, iris blooms and leaves; both oblong; signed ZEN HOKUSAI I-ITZU, c. 1820, Â 19 105.

Two large sheets of flowers: one very fine, convolvuli; the other, fairly good, peonies and butterflies; both oblong, but only one signed ZEN HOKUSAI I-ITZU, c. 1820, Â 19.

Hokusai's complete set of " The Famous Bridges." Original edition, entitled " Shokoku Meikio Kiran " (Views of the Bridges of various Provinces), published 1827-30, n sheets. The order given corresponds with that of De Goncourt. Sold separately at prices below Â 10, except those described.

Kameido Tenjin Taiko bashi. "The Drum Bridge at the Temple of Tenjin, Kameido," Yedo. A semi-circular wooden structure beside a trellis of pine trees. No. 7,

Settsu, Temma bashi. " Temma Bridge (at Osaka), Province of Settsu." Evening scene, on the occasion of the Festival of Lanterns. No. 9, Â 12 los.

FUSATANE (Tsshosai)

Diptych. A girl letting a crane out of a basket on the seashore. The favourite sport of Yoritomo was flying these birds with labels on their legs requesting those who caught them to report where they were found, and then fly them again. Full size, upright; signed FUSITANE, c. 1850, Â 10 105.

Omi Hakkei, "Eight Views of Lake Biwa," complete set, on four sheets; full size, oblong; signed FUSATANE, c. 1850, Â 10.

KIYOSHIGE (Torii)

Hachirakaki. The actor Danjiuro as Kiichi Hogen, the military adviser and strategist of the Taira, holding one of his tora no maki, or books on the art of war; signed TORII KIYO-SHIGE, c. 1725, Â 38.

Hachirakaki. An actor as Kakogawa Honzo in the Chiushin-gura, standing, full-length, holding the basket hat and bamboo clarionet of a Komuso; very large size; signed TORII KIYOSHIGE, c. 1725, Â 40.

HARUNOBU (Suzuki)

A girl dancing the Nunozarashi, with long streamers of white linen waved in serpentine movement in the air, her pink dress decorated in the upper part with chess-men, and the lower part in purple stripes; colours mellowed by exposure; Hosso-ye form; signed SUZUKI HARUNOBU, c. 1758, Â 14 IDS.

Two girls fishing in a stream where iris and other plants are bloomingâ one girl in the shallows with a net, the other holding a small globe supported by a string and a bit of stick, with fish in it; the bank is yellow, indicating full sunlight; the stream one of those curious neutral tones that are indescribable; the dresses, red, purple, and green; the print is unsigned, but the absence of signature in no way causes a doubt as to the identity of the artist; no imitator could produce a work of such beauty and fail to add the name of the man he was imitating; large size, nearly square, without text; best period, c. 1766-70, 30.

The girls' festival in March. Two girls under a blossoming peach-tree in an open field, one stooping to pick wild flowers, which the other is admiring, standing upright, hat in hand; a beautiful impression in six soft colours, without any background or text, the peach blossom and the folds in the robes slightly in relief by gauffrage; large size, almost square, in fine condition; signed SUZUKI HARUNOBU; best period, c. 1766-70, Â 22.

Picking young pines for the New Year festival. Two girls in an open grassy glade beneath an old pine tree, one stooping picking the young growth, the other standing looking on; the stooping girl wears an orange kimono, decorated with white plum blossom, and the other a wine-coloured robe with autumn-coloured maple leaves, the under-skirts of each being white; large size, nearly square, fine condition; signed SUSUKI HARUNOBU; best period, c. 1766-70, Â 21.

A young samurai presenting his lady love with a nightingale in a cage; interior scene, with open shoji in an arch showing a blossoming plum-tree outside; a poetical combination very dear to Japanese artists; large size, almost square, without any text or cloud drapery; signed SUSUKI HARU-NOBU; best period, c. 1766-70, Â 21.

The sick rooster. A girl standing at the angle of a house in a garden holding a rooster in her arms, and another girl on the verandah holding a small cup of warm sake for the bird to drink; a glimpse into the interior shows a dadoed wall in which an opaque white is used and a relief design impressed thereon; large size, nearly square, without any text, in perfect condition; signed SUZUKI HARUNOBU; best period, c. 1766-70, Â 26.

A lady and a domestic passing along in front of a partly open house with a vermilion-floored verandah, and a straggling branch of peach bloom across the reed blind; against the vermilion, the robes of the figures appear quiet gradations of soft material in motion; large size, nearly square, without text, and in grand condition; not signed; best period, c. 1766-70, Â 12.

Picking young pines for the New Year decorations. A young girl and her mother by a hill-sideâ the girl stooping, pointing to the fresh shoots, and the mother standing, pushing back her hood and looking on; the colours of this print, naturally subdued, have been mellowed by exposure, but it is a good impression; large size, almost square; signed SUZUKI HARUNOBU, c. 1760, Â 19.

Two girls on a balcony overlooking the Sumidagawa at sunset, with Fuji in the distance, and part of the Riyogoku bridge on the rightâ one standing, the other reclining against the balustrade; a fine impression, but the colours mellowed by exposure; large size, nearly square; signed SUZUKI HARUNOBU; best period, c. 1766, Â 24.

A scene from the Ise Monogatari; two girls lost in the open country by night are being searched for by men with torches; an early print with soft colouring, but somewhat stained by exposure; large size, nearly square, no text, and no signature, c. 1760, Â 23 los.

Hachirakaki. A burlesque of the scene in the Chiushingura, where Uranosuke reads the letter at the tea-house Ichiriki; a girl takes the hero's place, a black dog that of the spy Kudaya, and the Saint Daruma looks out from a kakemono to read the letter the girl is holding, instead of Okaru; the background wall is finely embossed, and also the girl's robes; the colours are brick-red, orange, lilac-green, and pink; signed SUZUKI HARUNOBU, Â 25.

KORIUSAI (Isoda)

Lovers seated over a hibachi, the girl fanning the charcoal; outside the rain is pelting down, and the willow branches swaying in the wind; large size, almost square; signed

KORIUSAI, c. 1773, Â 10. Two pheasants by a clump of bamboos, and a full moon rising behind clouds; large size, nearly square; signed KORIU, c. 1774, Â 15 los. A girl standing behind a youth kneeling playing a tsuzumi, a line of hills in the background; and a girl giving a juggling performance; both small size, nearly square; signed

KORIUSAI, c. 1774, Â 10.

KIYOTSUNE (Torii)

Hachirakaki. Early morning, with a man sleeping under a mosquito net, and a girl just awakened, pushing her head out to have a quiet smoke; these are seen through the open shutters of a room, while, outside, another girl with a dressing-gown is raising the wick of a lamp that has gone dim. An illustration of the poem above, which means: The morn has come too soon; The early bell is a knell to all the pleasures of the night. A very beautiful composition, printed in four colours; signed KIYOTSUNE, c. 1775,

KIYONAGA (Torii) . Mill-sized sheet, upright, one of a triptych. Four ladies visiting a temple; two are standing under a torii at the foot of stone steps, and two others are on a stone bridge under an old tree; behind them on a high bank are men, women, and children passing to and fro; fine colour scheme of pink, purple, orange, and solid black; in splendid condition; signed KIYONAGA; best period, c. 1785-90, Â 14.

Two full-sized sheets, upright, from a triptych. Five women passing along under a trellis of wistaria, with long racemes of flowers, beside a lake, the one leading just about to ascend a high curved bridge; full landscape background in Kiyon-aga's best sunshine style, and the whole picture a wealth of colour harmoniously displayed, and in grand state; signed KIYONAGA; best period, c. 1785-90, Â 20.

Full-length figure of a lady with an umbrella under a willow-tree; printed in four colours, a good impression; Hachira-kaki form, paper a little browned; signed KIY-ONAGA, c. 1782, Â 18.

MASANOBU (Kitao)

Hachirakaki. Two ladies, full-length figures, standing side by side; signed KITAO MASANOBU, Â 52.

UTAMARO (Kitagawa)

A Tokugawa princess visiting a lady of high rank. In the centre, the princess is alighting from a goshoguruma, drawn up under a flowering cherry-tree, helped by a lady-in-waiting, while another kneels holding a Court fan significant of her rank; on the right, a noble lady is seated behind a reed blind, with two of her ladies-in-waiting ready to conduct the illustrious visitor; on the left, three of the princess's maids are bringing forward the presents; full-size, printed in five colours; each sheet signed UTAMARO, c. 1790, Â 10 10.

Hachirakaki of special size. A woman standing looking down at her little boy, who has placed his head under her diaphanous robe through which his face is seen, while the nurse holds him by the girdle; an exquisite bit of printing in six colours, the soft under-tunic which encloses the woman's bosom is silvered; signed UTAMARO, c. 1804, Â 46.

A woman on a verandah stooping over a stone cistern, and lifting out a block of ice in which the dipper is frozen, and a woman standing behind her; a very beautiful Hachirakaki of small but wide form, printed in five colours; signed UTAMARO, c. 1804, Â 24.

Raihin Dzui, "Exotic Birds," Yedo, 1793, 2 vols. complete, first edition; vol. I. contains 12 double-page illustrations in colours, and gauffrage; vol. II. consists of text only, an explanation of the birds and plants illustrated; edited by Seki Eibun; the first bird plate signed UTAMARO, and at the end of the second vol. the signature KITAGAWA UTAMARO â with an altered later print of the first bird plate, in which the name of UTAMARO has been cut away from the block, and that of KEISAI inserted, above the seal of MASAYOSHI, and with translations of the Chinese and Japanese prefaces into English, Â 26.

SIX GREAT ARTISTS

Otoko Toka, the name of a dance for the i4th day of the ist month; or Otoko Fumi no Uta, "Poems written by Men," 1 really poems for the New Year, i vol., first edition, Yedo, 1798, Â 10.

CHOKI (Yeishosai) the late artist name of SHIKO (Momokawa).

Triptych. Scene in the garden of the tea-house Naniwa-ya, outside the grounds of the Asakusa Temple; a party of ladies with a gentleman, who have been pleased with the productions of the publisher, Tsutaya Juzabro, have paid a visit to the temple to see his grave, and are taking refreshment in the gardens of the tea-house; on the shaft of the lantern is inscribed: â ' Dedicated to Asakusa Temple of Kwannon with prayers for felicity "; full size, upright; each sheet signed CHOKI, c. 1797, Â 23 IDS.

Hachirakaki. Full-length portrait of a lady standing, holding a fan which is decorated with Sharaku's celebrated print, "The man with a pipe," an actor in the character of Ban-zuiin Chobei; a rather remarkable tribute of the appreciation of Choki for Sharaku's work; printed in four colours; signed CHOKI, c. 1797, Â 54.

SHUNCHO (Katsugawa)

A wet day. Triptych. Scene on a stone-walled bank overlooking a river, with scenery and buildings on the other side; the rain is pouring down, and four young people are standing under a tree on the right, three girls are in the centre hurrying along, one holding an umbrella over another; and on the left two ladies and a boy have just crossed a bridge; large size, upright; each signed SHUNCHO, and sealed CHURIN, c. 1785, Â 29.

In the bath-room. Hachirakaki. Two women, one half-clad, standing in front of the grille, and the other nude, stooping, drawing a cloth out of a pail of water; very full size, printed in three colours, sealed CHURIN, c. 1785, Â 14 los.

The early morning. Hachirakaki. A female domestic has just pushed back the shutters, and js standing on the edge of the engawa, beside a flowering shrub in a pot, getting a breath of the sweet morning air; on the cross-beam above her head is pasted a paper charm, o-mamori, given at one of the temples for the protection of the house; full size, printed in three colours; signed SHUNCHO, c. 1785, Â 11.

SHUNMAN (Kubo)

Scene in a tea-house overlooking the Sumida river. Diptych. On the right a lady and gentleman are playing forfeits, while others are preparing the refreshments, and making ready the samisen; on the left a man leans against the square pillar, while a lady is standing behind two others getting tea; full size, upright; one sheet signed KUBO SHUNMAN, and the other SHUNMAN, c. 1795, Â 32.

YEISHI (Chobunsai)

The Eight Beauties of Matsuba-ya. Triptych. Four full-length figures of Tai yu, or high-class courtesans on each of two of the sheets, and on the third, four female domestics, and four kamuro leading the procession; full size, upright; each signed YEISHI, c. 1 800, Â 29.

The Good and Evil Influences. Triptych. Scene in the Yoshi-wara, the women receiving and entertaining guests, while mingling among the company are a number of tiny figures, some clothed, others nude to the waist, with bald heads and characters for faces, some urging the company on to excesses, and others endeavouring to restrain; full size, upright; each signed YEISHI, c. 1800, Â 1 los.

The Ship of Good Fortune. Triptych. A long boat with prow in shape of a ho-ho bird, and at the stern pine and bamboo, with nine gaily dressed women aboardâ six seated and three standing; full size, upright; each signed YEISHI, c. 1800, Â 21.

Prince Genji at a garden party. Triptych, showing the prince seated on the right attended by three ladies, a lady approaching carrying an ornament, three playing the dosho, tsuzumi, and a large gong, surrounded by the Shinto fire emblem, and two more in the rear. One of a series of triptychs: Furiu Yatsushi Genji, â " A Fashionable (or Modern) presentation of Genji "; full size, upright; each signed YEISHI, c. 1790, Â 34.

HOKUSAI

Kanatehon Chiushingura. Complete set of eleven scenes; full size, oblong; c. 1825; on six sheets, 18.

"Shika Sha-shin-kyo " (The Imagery of the Poets). Complete set of ten, revealing the Great Master's grandeur of design and power of colouring at the height of his fame. A whole chapter (XXXVI.) is devoted by De Goncourt to this set, in which he gives the date of issue as 1830. Â 340.

An album of original drawings in black and white, containing 44 figure subjects, mostly women, Â 25.

Hokusai Mangwa, "Drawing." Complete set of 15 vols., the first 12 published during the years 1812-34, vol. XIII. in 1849, vol Â XIV. in 1875, and vol- XV. in 1879; the last three after the artist's death. Vol. XV. is a printer's proof copy. With translation of preface. Â 21.

YEIZAN (Kikugawa)

Eosei Kantan no Yumi. Triptych. A Japanised version of the story of Chao Lu Sheng at Kantan, where, while his millet was being cooked, he fell asleep and dreamed he had become Minister of State to the Chinese Emperor. Here the pleasure of his dream consists in the good time he is having with the demi-monde of the northern quarter; full size, upright, early work; signed KIKUGAWA YEIZAN, c. 1800, Â 14.

A Tokugawa princess alighting from her goshoguruma, drawn up under a flowering cherry-tree, to receive a lady who kneels before her, while at her rear her ladies-in-waiting bring out a present; triptych, full size, upright; each sheet signed KIKUGAWA YEIZAN, c. 1800, Â 12 IDS.

Furiu Saku Asobi san Bijin, "Three Graceful Beauties and sake drinking sport." Triptych. Three women seated and kneeling, playing at forfeits in front of shutters, on which the geisha and hokan (buffoons) are silhouetted; full size, upright; each signed YEIZAN, c. 1812, 15.

YEISEN (Keisai) Kakemono-ye. Moonlight scene of a bridge across a river, flanked by high trees and tall mountains in the background; in the centre valley there are some fine effects of trees in mist; mainly printed in blue and a deep red; signed

KEISAI, sealed YEISEN, c. 1832, Â 84. The great carp. Kakemono-ye. A carp making its way up a waterfall, the Japanese emblem of perseverance; signed

KEISAI, sealed YEISEN, Â 25.

HIROSHIGE (Ichiryusai)

The Kiso Mountains under snow. Triptych; signed HIROSHIGE, dated 8th month, 1854; framed, Â 22. The Rapids of Awa no Naruto. Triptych; signed HIROSHIGE, dated 4th month, 1854; framed, Â 11. View of Kanazawa, in Musashi, by moonlight. Triptych; signed

HIROSHIGE, dated th month, 1854; framed, Â 13.

KUNIYOSHI (Utagawa)

Set of original drawings for the key-blocks of colour-prints; in black and white, never used. Ka Meisho hon Chiushingura, the eleven scenes of the Drama of the 47

Ronin; full size, oblong; signed ICHIYUSAI KUNIYOSHI; mounted on six sheets, Â 11.

Original drawing. The celebrated swordsmith Sanjo Kokagi Munechika forging a blade in the grounds of the Temple of Inari, assisted by a fox spirit in the form of a woman; full size, upright, black and white, tinted; signed ICHIYUSAI KUNIYOSHI, Â 10.

The ghosts of the Taira. Triptych. When Yoshitsune fled from the wrath of his half-brother Yoritomo, with Benkei and a few companions, he took boat and sailed across the straits of Shimonoseki, where a great storm arose, and the ghosts of the Taira, slain at Dan no Ura, assailed the vessel, led by their Admiral Tomomori, when Benkei defied them, and, having prayed to the gods, the storm abated and the wraiths disappeared; full size, upright; each sheet signed

ICHIYUSAI KUNIYOSHI, C. 1830, Â lo IOS.

Memorial portrait of Ichiyusai Kuniyoshi, by his pupil, Ikkeisai Yoshi-iku, with poems by literary men, and the following particulars. He was called Magosaburo (Cho-oro). Real name, Magosaburo Igusa. Posthumous name, Shinshuin Hosan Kokuho Shinshi. Died Bunkwa, year of the cock ((1861), 3rd month, 5th day; and was buried at Daisen Temple, Hachikenji machi, Asakusa. Full size, upright. The artist is represented seated with pencil and paper in hand, and ink slab before him. Â 10 los.

SHUNKYOKU (Katsugawa)

A tea-house waitress, standing, full length, by the engawa of a tea-house by the grounds of the Asakusa Temple, holding a cup on a red lacquered tray; Hachirakaki form, printed in five colours; signed KATSUGAWA SHUNKYOKU, c. 1754, 31.

HARUNOBU (Suzuki)

A girl kneeling on a verandah completing her toilet before a mirror, and holding up another to catch a view of the back wave of hair; the shutters of the house behind her partly conceal a youth who is looking round the corner and tickling her foot with a stick; the scene is in the early morning of summer, and her light garments reveal her bosom, while their transparency also shows the shape of her arms and curve of her back; the floors and rock fountain are olive-green, verandah orange, sliding shutter yellowish-brown, the girl's kimono a slatey blue, while the cat has its details embossed; large size, almost square, no text; signed HARUNOBU, c. 1776-70, Â 33.

girl seated playing the tsuzumi in front of a recess with a kakemono of Hotei against the wall; through the open shutters, a stone fountain and a patch of iris. A good impression, with designs on robes and on wall raised by gauffrage, but colours faded and stained by exposure; large size, nearly square, without text; signed SUZUKE HARUNOBU, c. 1766-70, Â 29 105.

A refreshment stall beside a torii at the entrance to a temple, and a girl hurrying forward with a tray of fruit, the wind parting her garments and revealing her limbs; all in quiet subdued tones; large size, almost square, no text; signed SUZUKI HARUNOBU, c. 1760, Â 16.

An archer about to go out for practice with his bow, being dissuaded by two young girls seated beside a screen, who playfully hold on to his bow-string to retain his company. The ground of this fine print is of a peculiar bluish grey tone, which has become decomposed, the other colours remaining in beautiful condition; large size, almost square, no text and no signature, c. 1766-70, Â 16.

A snow scene, with two lovers under an aigasa, " the umbrella of loving accord"; a striking contrast here presented between the solid black coat of the young samurai and the pale pink of the lady's costume, with its brocade pattern raised by gauffrage. This is considered one of Harunobu's finest productions, and is a fine impression, but has unfortunately been considerably discoloured by exposure; large size, nearly square, without text; signed SUZUKI HARUNOBU, c. 1766-70, Â 10 los.

A snow scene; exterior of a house with woman engaged in pruning dwarfed trees in pots on a low stand, the snow lying in thick light masses on the branches, and on the tree beside the house. Here, although the colour of the paper has been browned by exposure, the colours of the print have remained almost intact, and the effect is very pleasing; large size, nearly square, without text or signature, c. 1766-70, Â 18.

A boy and girl looking into a well, both standing, the boy's arm placed affectionately round the girl's neck, while he drops a stone in to see if he shall get his desire; above the well the Pawlonnia Imperialis spreads its branches and flowers, the emblem of rectitude; fine composition, the colours somewhat mellowed by time; large size, nearly square, without text; signed HARUNOBU, c. 1766-70, Â 22.

A windy day in a sun-lit field, where two ladies are striving to keep their hats on, and their garments under restraint, the willow branches lashing overhead, and tall grasses bending as they pass; colours, naturally subdued, have slightly faded, but the effect is good; large size, nearly square, without text; signed SUZUKI HARUNOBU, c. 1766-70, Â 51.

A girl stepping off a high bank on to the prow of a boat driven end on against the shore, and her companions seated under an awning; a nice quiet composition in soft fawn and grey tones, with a faded pink; large size, nearly square, without text; signed HARUNOBU, c. 1760, Â 16.

An Oharami wood-seller resting by the roadside, seated on a tree-trunk, wiping her bosom with a handkerchief, and her little boy, who is about to throw a stone at a cicada which has settled on the trunk of an old fir-tree; in a panel at the upper corner, a peasant's hat and rain cloak; a beautiful print in spotless condition; large size, nearly square, without text or signature, c. 1766-70, Â 24.

Hachirakaki. Two girls, one seated and one standing, by the red lacquered column of a temple torii; the seated figure in olive-green kimono is reading one of the kibiyoshi (" yellow books," or novelettes) by Kitao (Shigemasa); her companion has brick-red sleeves, olive-green striped obi, and blue skirt; the background is one of those soft indescribable washes so frequently used by this artist; signed HARUNOBU, 78.

A tall graceful woman standing beside the Tama river looking at the reflection of the full moon on its waters; Hachirakaki form in five soft tones; signed HARUNOBU; one of a set of " Six Tamagawa "; c. 1765, Â 30.

KUNINOBU

Hachirakakı. A young samurai and a girl in winter clothing, with uchikise on their heads, passing along under a sprouting willow, the man carrying an odawara lantern; robes in buff and chrome, obi in drab and red; signed Kunindsu, c. 1775. Â 52.

KORIUSAI (Isoda)

Aiter the bath. A semi-nude girl seated against the railed window fanning herself; a black and white dog in the foreground. Fine sharp impression, but colours mellowed by exposure; Hachirakaki; signed KORIUSAI, c. 1778, Â 20.

A lucky omen. A tall figure of a woman, with robes decorated with the fruits of the egg-plant, and, above her, Fuji surrounded by clouds, lucky things to dream of; magnificent impression of a late work; Hachirakaki form; signed BUKO YAGENBORI INSHI KORIUSAI; " Yedo. The retired man Koriusai 1 c. 1781, Â 21 los.

KIYONAGA (Torii)

A windy day. A girl with a jet black hood and garments tossed about, struggling along against the wind, which is whipping-up the long wistaria flowers overhead; a beautiful print in four colours, and in splendid condition; Hachirakaki form; signed KIYONAGA, c. 1782, Â 39.

Scene in a joro-ya. In the foreground a girl is just about to turn the corner of a screen, which divides the picture, so that a view of another apartment is shown, where a girl is seated beside a man asleep, with a draught screen behind them; a wonderfully good composition in this Hachirakaki form, in four colours; signed KIYONAGA, c. 1782, Â 10 los.

Komurasake and Gompachi. The girl is standing in a bathhouse of the Yoshiwara, wearing only a loose robe, talking to Shirai Gompachi through the grille of bamboo rods; a well-planned Hachirakaki in three colours; signed KIYONAGA, c. 1780,;Â io.

MASANOBU (Kitao)

Hachirakaki. A lady disrobing for the bath; a fine study of drapery slipping off fair shoulders, and having a curious form of gauffrage in the under-robe, which is made to look like red crepe; not signed, but unmistakably the work of Masanobu, Â 40.

MASAYOSHI (Kitao Keisai)

Riyakugwashiki, "Methods of Cursive Design." A complete set of 6 vols. tinted. Vol. I. mainly Figures, 1795; vol. II. Birds and Insects, with translation of the preface, 1797; vol. III. Human Figures, 1799; vol. IV. Landscapes, 1800; vol. V. Fishes, 1802; vol. VI. Herbs and Flowers, 1813. Â 20 IDS.

UTAMARO (Kitagawa)

Large head portrait of a woman of the Tama-ya, as the poetess Komachi, holding a brush to her lips and a roll of paper in her hand. One of the first series of courtesans in large bust form, entitled Seiro Nana Komachi, "Seven Komachi (poetesses) of the Tea-houses "; full size, upright; signed SHOMEI UTAMARO, c. 1790, Â 13 IDS.

Gompachi and Komurasaki; half-length of the lady in the foreground, and the man standing behind her; Hachirakaki form, in four colours; signed UTAMARO, c. 1790, Â 12 los.

A mother asleep leaning on a box while her baby boy is upsetting the fish pond, and dragging a plant out of a pot; and another of a mother and child, with a lady friend; both from the series, Furiu Ko-takara Awase, "A comparison of dear and beautiful children "; full size, upright; both signed UTAMARO, Â 14.

SHUNCHO (Katsugawa)

Spring in the rice-fields. Diptych. On the right, a female domestic stopping to tie her mistress's sandal, with a man behind carrying flowers, etc.; on the left, three ladies coming towards the others, two of them holding hands; landscape in the background; full size, upright; both signed SHUNCHO, sealed CHURIN, c. 1785, Â 22 los.

YEIRI (Rekisenti)

Triptych. A noble lady standing under an old pine tree by the seashore, reading a letter, one of her attendants holding a large red umbrella over her, others behind her, and in front on the left an attendant holding a box in which a man has brought the missive; full size, upright; each sheet signed REKISENTI YEIRI, c. 1800, 25.

HOKUSAI

Twenty-five out of the known twenty-seven sheets of The Hundred Poets, entitled " Hiakunin isshu Ubagawa Yetoki" (The Hundred Poems explained by the Nurse). Original issue, published in 1839; all in fine condition. The order given is taat of De Goncourt. The prices of Â 10 and more follow:

Poem by Harumichi no Tsuraki. Scene of two sawyers at work cutting a huge log, very similar to those in the thirty-six views of Fuji, and a woman and child crossing a stream tinted by autumn maple leaves, which a man is dragging out. No. 32, Â 12 55.

Poem by Bunya no Asayasu. Women in a boat on a lake where waterlilies grow, gathering the leaves and flowers; the " unstrung jewels everywhere scattered." No. 37, 10 ics.

Poem by Sanji Hitoshi. A daimyo accompanied by his sword-bearer and a retainer, passing into the vapours of the dying day, lying over a plain of young bamboo, muses as to his hard lot in losing his love. No. 39, Â 10 los.

Poem by Fujiwara no Yoshitaka. A great bath-house overlooking a lake where water-birds are diving, clouds of steam rising from the bath, and bathers on the balcony, resting or completing their toilette, while one man muses that once life was not dear, but now for her sake he would that it should endure. No. 50, Â 10.

Poem by Fujiwara Michinobu. A great flat plain with winding roads seen from a hill-side, the trees on the horizon silhouetted against the early morning light. The coolies have risen to commence their toil, and already are rushing along carrying their heavy loads, with the feeling that, though night will come again to give them rest, yet they hate the morning's light. No. 52, Â 10.

YEISEN (Keisai)

Three blue prints of courtesansâ two from the series Hokoku Hakkei, "Eight Views of the North Country," i. e. Yoshiwara, and one very fine of a woman by an arched window; full size, upright; each signed KEISAI YEISEN, Â 11.

Two blue prints with the under-parts of the garments showing red, from a series Riuki Ai Shitate, "Fashionable Blue Costumes "; each is a figure of a woman out walking in front of a fence, with trees in the background; full size, upright; each signed KEISAI YEISEN, and numbered 4 and 5 respectively, Â i i.

KAIGETSUDO (Yasutomo)

A courtesan of the Genroku period, full-length figure; not signed, c. 1700; kakemono, Â 10 105.

Printed by Hasell, Watson â Viney, Ld., Lonion and Aylesbury, England-

LaVergne, TN USA
13 October 2010
200668LV00007B/123/P
9 781151 733009